ALSO BY SARAH SMARSH

Heartland
She Come By It Natural

BONE OF THE BONE

Essays on America

by a Daughter of the Working Class

2013–2024

SARAH SMARSH

SCRIBNER

New York   London   Toronto   Sydney   New Delhi

SCRIBNER
An Imprint of Simon & Schuster, LLC
1230 Avenue of the Americas
New York, NY 10020

First Scribner hardcover edition September 2024

SCRIBNER and design are trademarks of Simon & Schuster, LLC.

Simon & Schuster: Celebrating 100 Years of Publishing in 2024

For information about special discounts for bulk purchases,
please contact Simon & Schuster Special Sales at 1-866-506-1949 or
business@simonandschuster.com.

For more information about the author or to book her for an event,
visit www.sarahsmarsh.com.

Interior design by Alexis Minieri

Manufactured in the United States of America

3   5   7   9   10   8   6   4   2

Library of Congress Cataloging-in-Publication Data has been applied for.

ISBN 978-1-6680-5560-1
ISBN 978-1-6680-5561-8 (ebook)

For the unseen

CONTENTS

BONE OF THE BONE

INTRODUCTION

My early career as a journalist coincided with the collapse of the newspaper industry. A generation prior, I might have spent years filing stories for the same newsroom. Instead, following my graduation with degrees in journalism and English in 2002, out of economic necessity my writing took many forms: daily news stories for struggling midsize papers, culture pieces for alternative weeklies in major cities, travel features for global airline magazines, even grant proposals for statewide social service agencies.

Meanwhile, through my twenties I tended my yearning to go deep and long with narrative; many nights, I worked on a book about my rural, working-poor family. (Other nights, to make ends meet, I poured whiskey at a biker bar on Interstate 70.)

Along the way, I earned an MFA in nonfiction writing from Columbia University, taught journalism as an adjunct at a small private university, and became a tenured professor of nonfiction writing at a midsize public university. My writing labors turned academic; amid teaching undergraduates, I revamped the English department's journal, wrote research papers, organized author lectures, sat on writing-conference panels. Even then, to augment my modest salary, I remained an ink-stained hustler. During one summer break, I researched and wrote two pop-history books for a small publisher in order to pay for my own wedding.

While it required dexterity to do so, I was fortunate to make—or half make—a living as a writer through that perilous new digital moment when print journalism became "content," TV news became "infotainment," local newspapers and even major magazines folded, and media in general became more urban, more coastal, more class-privileged. One former colleague after another was laid off by some news organization and found work in public relations—in many cases, creating the spin we were trained to outsmart in pursuit of facts. A decade into my career, among my graduating class from a venerable journalism school, I was one of the last reporters standing.

Simultaneous with this historic, consequential reshaping of an industry, a more personal tension pressed against my journalistic calling: where I came from.

My first news story distributed by the Associated Press, in 2001, when I was a college senior, had documented classist frameworks for determining student financial need at the US Department of Education. Ever since, my work had exposed various sorts of marginalization. I never set out with such a mission. Rather, as a woman out of rural poverty, my own marginalization—not just in our society but in the newsrooms covering it—trained my eye on injustice.

As political and cultural fractures deepened during the Obama era, I saw that the increasingly corporatized, digitized, and monopolized news industry didn't just have blind spots.

Rather, it viewed places like my home at the center of the country through a telescope from a faraway dimension and, worse, pronounced its misunderstandings with palpable smugness.

Many fine, underpaid journalists preserved local reporting in such places wherever possible. These were no "media elites," to be sure. Yet, even they were from a different world, a place where parents had college degrees, kids went to summer camp, clothes came brand-new from the mall, and no one had ever eaten turtle caught from a cattle watering hole—conditions my own family regarded as "rich."

By the 2012 presidential election, when I was in my early thirties, I had left academia. I had left a marriage too. I had left, as I reference in more than one of these collected essays, assorted manner of bullshit. A cleared vessel, I could feel my voice throbbing in my throat, aching to scream what few, if any, in mainstream news media could see or name: the multipronged classism of these United States and related stereotypes about rural America.

I felt that I could be of best service to my profession not only by reporting objective information about those matters but by contextualizing them with subjective personal truth. That effort should not be the detached analysis of the op-ed pages, I thought, but a direct witnessing.

Such a turn involved several obstacles.

To begin with, entering the story is generally frowned upon by reporters of a certain era, those who taught me that "I" is an embarrassing pox upon the dissemination of facts. (That shame is applied selectively; those same reporters tend to venerate the White, male, upper-middle-class gonzo "journalists" of the mid–twentieth century who not only employed the first person but wholly fictionalized their accounts whenever it suited them.) For years I had successfully compartmentalized my journalistic work and a years-long memoir project, allowing the first person into the latter but never the former. While I remain a purist about conveying facts—in my work, no direct quote shall be altered, no detail shall be conjured, and even in memoir the fallibility of memory shall be acknowledged—I had come to believe that personal perspective might deepen the resonance of those facts without blurring their edges.

This interior triumph, overriding a learned distaste for my own voice, had difficult timing. My country was not ready to hear what I had to say. Or, rather, the gatekeepers of an increasingly exclusive industry were not ready to let me be heard. For several years, even as I landed a couple major digital bylines for *Harper's* reporting on a state constitutional crisis over school funding in Kansas, my essays on class were turned down repeatedly by newspapers and magazines. The first such essay of mine to go viral, a 2014 examination of access to dentistry as class signifier, was rejected by multiple US outlets before finally being published by the digital magazine *Aeon*, based in London—a place that, while no less rife with class problems, differs from mine for having discussed those problems for centuries.

Then there was the matter of needing to eat. The first essay in this collection, a 2013 piece for the *Huffington Post*—notoriously built on the labor of unpaid writers seeking a "platform"—received zero compensation, though I was no fledgling journalist; I was thirty-three and had been a professional writer for more than a decade. Two years later, for a *New Yorker* digital piece about laws that unfairly punish the poor, also included here, I received—for at least forty cumulative hours of research, writing, and responding to the meticulous editing and fact-checking that makes the *New Yorker* a standard-bearer worldwide—$250. Within hours of its publication, my excellent editor there, whom I trust was working with a scant budget of someone else's design, emailed to say the piece was the second most popular read at the *New Yorker* website.

Being underpaid by the world's eminent newspapers and magazines for illuminating socioeconomic struggle would become the central paradox of my work as an essayist—an insult that validates the points I make in their pages about undervalued labor and the chattering classes who can afford to write for peanuts since their wealth is assured by other means.

Due to the biases of such publications, preserving the dignity of the people I document often has required running defense against edits, headlines, or accompanying photographs and illustrations that conveyed the very stereotypes against which I wrote. If I filed a two-thousand-word, thoroughly researched piece on, say, the large, diverse minority of liberals and progressives in "red states," without my vigilance it would be packaged with a headline such as "A Different Perspective from Trump Country" and a photo of round White men wearing red "Make America Great Again" hats. In the fast media landscape, these trimmings affect a reader's posture before she ever reads my words. I have been largely successful in my requests that editors and art departments eschew these clichés, but such requests by a freelance writer are generally considered audacious.

I summon that audacity on behalf of the poor and the working class not because they are a sentimentalized ideal from my past—some salt of the earth I reflect on from an apartment building with a doorman—but because they are the complicated, human core of my present. They are my neighbors in rural Kansas. They are my blood. They are the foundation of who I am and the reason my voice exists. Their relentless portrayal as scapegoats for a nation's ills evoked in me a relentless rebuttal—which, across publications, required repetition of specific points that I hope you'll forgive in this collected format.

I have written about them in specific, individual terms only when I had their blessing to do so. While I will not claim that it has always been easy for the people described in these essays to see their private traumas and shames offered up to the masses as evidence of socioeconomic injustice, I have never sought a blessing that wasn't given.

The sharing of intimate information—in my case, not just the details of my life but my voice—isn't easy for me either. It might surprise readers to learn that I am one of the most private people I know; my memoir books and essays are by no means a litany of the worst or most shocking things I've experienced but rather have been selectively rendered to illuminate our shared public concerns. My impulse toward withdrawal and self-protection in today's garishly confessional world is often painfully at odds with my obvious calling to be heard. The essays in this book differ in form and theme; they range from political commentary to media critique, from reportage to memoir, from policy analysis to cultural criticism. They frequently address gender and the environment, with class as the ever-present underpinning, whether implicit or explicit. While they vary in these ways, not one was published without my becoming nauseous at the thought of it being read.

Despite these barriers, the essays in this collection (and many more, left out) entered the world. Because they did, I met some people who changed my life.

I met the literary agent who represents me, the editor who shepherds the books I write, the publishing house that pays me very well for those books, even major celebrities who publicly endorsed my work. But I met someone else who, in some ways, changed my life even more.

I met you.

Many thousands of you, relieved to read about the aspect of American identity for so long ignored that you struggled to articulate it about your own lives.

You are poor. You have never contacted a writer before. You joined the military to pay for college, or you were homeless for twenty years. You can't get Medicaid to cover the treatment you need because you smoke. At a free dental clinic, they pulled out all your teeth. You knew I was the real deal because I wrote about the good times poor folks enjoy. You would rather be a toothless old witch laughing with her friends at Dollar General than the queen of England, because you couldn't live with yourself hoarding so much material wealth.

Or you used to be poor, and now you aren't. You are from a working-class family in Pennsylvania and attended an elite university, or you grew up in the South Bronx and now afford things your family of origin can't. You feel emboldened to call out class condescension. You are from Somalia and now study at a state university in North Dakota. You are wondering, how do I navigate the feeling of isolation both where I began and where I've landed? You are from the Appalachian Mountains and feel like an alien at the office. You are twenty-three and feel like you've lived decades longer, or you are sixty-two and will never forget how your father brought home roadkill and fried the meat. You were raised on tribal lands, which is a rural experience. You loved reading about the three-wheeler, which reminded you of your grandparents' house, where you spent a lot of time for complicated reasons. You feel like you aren't as good as other people, even though intellectually you know that's not right. Your White mom met your dad, a recent Vietnamese immigrant, while working at a drill bit manufacturing company. A guy from the city bought your mom's farmhouse, and later you discovered a blog post he wrote about the "redneck refuge" she left behind. You are from Louisiana and believe my White grandmother and your Black mother might be the same woman. You are a Bay Area director crying on your way to work. You are no longer humiliated by someone else's descriptions of your background. You define yourself.

Or you never were poor. You are a physician who treats elderly immigrants in Massachusetts, a relatively generous state, and even there your patients struggle to access care. You are a dairy farmer in upstate New York, getting by but angry about corporate greed. You are a young television writer who will be following my work. You are a Swedish woman who wants me to know that, despite the social safety nets, class is a problem in your country too. You are a White man who volunteers on the board of a health clinic and admires the clinic's toughest staff worker, who used to be in a gang in California. You will remember what I wrote and meet people where they are without pity or condescension.

This dialogue we have found over the years is the honor of my life. I hope you will share with others what you have shared with me. If you do, we will transcend the failing of newspapers and the rise of social media, which eventually will fail too. So long as we keep talking—bearing witness to our own truths while staying humble to what other eyes have seen and open to the facts that would disrupt our assumptions—we will uncover the single, unchanging reality that we are all writing, reading, posting, sharing, and speaking toward: our connection to one another.

Sometimes, "I" is just another word for "we" or "you." The White, rural, working-poor people about whom I most often write—they are your people too.

August 31, 2023

HOW I MOVED TWENTY-ONE TIMES
BEFORE COLLEGE

Parcel, 2013

1. **Decision.** Maybe it was made of necessity—a rent payment couldn't be made, a job beckoned on the other side of town, a cruel or wishy-washy or absent husband made a place unbearable. *This place doesn't have a good vibe* was reason enough, because the reasons didn't matter so much. Reasons were intangible or, at best, details. Action was real life.

2. **Notification.** Tell the boss, call the utility companies. One last outing at the bar with friends from work, maybe. Family members might receive a casual announcement, at the last minute. Mom told me about her first divorce while we were folding towels on top of the dryer, and neither of us cried. I tried to hide my excitement as I asked to call my only friend on our rural party line to break the news. My dad embraced a drunken depression, as any rational person might, but Mom had about her a thrill, a cat's quickened scratching at the door upon sensing that it soon would

open. While Dad silently moped off to construction sites and wheat fields, she filled out change-of-address forms and made to-do lists in gorgeous cursive on dollar-store legal pads. (Also an option: Leave now, report later.)

3. **Sorting.** We did the grunt work ourselves, of course. I had no idea a professional moving industry existed. We gathered cardboard boxes from grocery stores, avoiding those that had stored produce, as they smelled rotten and had big, square holes in the bottoms. But before we could stuff them with shirts and papers and pictures from drawers, plates and vases from cabinets, wrenches and canned food from basements, we made two piles: things we'd keep, and things for the garage sale to be hosted by whichever family member lived on the highest-traffic street of Wichita at the moment. I spread my toys across my bedroom floor and discerned what I really needed. I implored my four-year-old brother to consider that he never played with that G.I. Joe anyway. Mom was in the living room getting down to business. Hand-sewn Halloween costumes of Dorothy, the Scarecrow, an Indian girl? Halloween is over. Almost-new lamp? Reminds me of the ex-husband who bought it. Coffee table? Piece of junk from someone else's garage sale anyhow. Into the sale pile.

Sarah, have you seen my lighter?

4. **Sale.** The night before our sales, which we called garage sales even when they took place on driveways or front yards, I made signs with cardboard and black, inch-thick markers that squeaked as I colored in the arrows that would point bargain hunters our way. I made the signs because everyone knew I could draw a straight line. Mom, a saleswoman,

knew the best price to write on adhesive tags, and Grandma Betty was a formidable opponent in haggling matches. Aunt Pud was good at spotting thieves, and her boyish daughter Shelly could carry a solid oak headboard on one arm. We all had our specializations.

On the eve of a sale, after sorting and pricing and spreading items onto long card tables to be kept in the closed garage until early morning, we rigged the homemade sale signs to impromptu stakes, taking care that arrows on opposite sides of the sign pointed in the same direction. We loaded the signs into a pickup bed and lurched around the neighborhood of the moment, the driver idling the engine as the rest of us jumped from pickup to curb, laughing in the darkness as we pounded the stakes into hard earth with hammers. At least one sign would give us trouble, refusing to pierce the ground deeply enough to be stable; at sunrise, when someone went to get a fast-food breakfast and a newspaper—to check on the classified ad we took out (HUGE SALE)—the stubborn sign would have fallen. But we counted ourselves lucky if it hadn't rained overnight and made a soggy mess of the cardboard.

If the newspaper ad said the sale started at 8 a.m. on Thursday, the female bargain warriors arrived before seven, their hair wet in the early summer sun, faces makeup-free, agendas fierce.

Do you have any lamps, what do you want for the mirror, and would you take a quarter for these tennis shoes because they're pretty dirty.

Male patrons often were war veterans who wanted to chat about the old days; they sought tools and antique toys, maybe some dated electronics.

Over two or three days our inventory shrank, and the

purchase list we kept on a legal pad grew longer. The list included three or four columns to track separately each seller's profits, since the whole family joined in the sale, even if only one person was moving. I sat with a calculator at a card table and made change from a brown metal cash box, as I did every Fourth of July when we sold firecrackers under a tent in a field.

Sarah, have you seen the marker? Where are the scissors? Mark down the underwear table to a nickel apiece. Hey, check out the van—plenty of room for them to take our junk.

Everyone was sweating. The sales usually ended Saturday afternoon.

5. **Donation.** After the exhausting, three-day sale, we threw what remained into plastic trash bags and drove it to a thrift store. But before that, a friend of the family would decide to take the floral comforter that hadn't sold.

C'mon, let me pay you something for it.

Aw hell, just take it.

6. **Packing.** I put Matt's tiny clothes and my slightly less tiny clothes in boxes. My hands were black with newspaper ink from wrapping whiskey tumblers with Mom in the dining room. Bedding, curtains, pillows, and stuffed animals went into trash bags because they couldn't break and would squish into tight spaces in pickup beds. Last to go were bathroom items, magnets on the fridge, mustard in the fridge.

7. **Departure.** We loaded a pickup and a trailer hitched behind it. Heavy stuff went in first, or steering would be a real bitch.

Then the mailbox was in the rearview mirror, and the cats were in the cab of the truck, clinging to the vinyl seats.

Sarah, run in and tell them five dollars unleaded and a pack of Marlboro Light 100s.

8. **Transit.** During the drive—thirty minutes, maybe—from old place to new place: the lightness.

9. **Arrival.** We pulled into our new driveway. We unpacked cheap decorations, decided what shelf the extra sheets would go on, cleaned the bathroom the last resident left filthy with thick hairs and rusty razors.

What day does trash go out? Did you get the toilet to stop running? Jiggle the handle? Where is the light switch? This bedroom seems to stay cooler. Sarah, write "roach trap" on the grocery list. I found the fan. You see an outlet?

HIGHWAY CONSTRUCTION MAY UNEARTH
HUMAN REMAINS

The Huffington Post, 2013

In a recent *New Yorker* story called "Rush," a South Indian man says of his region's growing East Coast Road, "Civilization only kills. I was much happier before we became civilized." His wife, similarly devastated by their teenage son's death in an automobile collision but recalling nights in a thatched hut surrounded by howling jackals, has a more nuanced take—the highway should be safer, its drivers better trained.

I'll be the last to romanticize the rustic and the first to appreciate a paved road. Highway 54 in southern Kansas, visible on the flat horizon from my upstairs farmhouse bedroom, eased a portion of the hour-long bus ride to and from my crucial public education. (In a handful of years, I experienced three school-bus flips and crashes on muddy, snow-packed, or deer-frequented dirt roads.)

After school I often drove one of our Honda three-wheelers, first to the cattle pasture with feed buckets and then miles away to the closest county bridge over 54; I'd park the ATV, climb onto the concrete safety barrier, and dangle my legs. When eighteen-wheelers zoomed toward me at eighty miles per hour, I'd pump an arm in the air and clutch the railing as they *whooshed* beneath my feet, their friendly honks echoing from beneath the bridge, my hair lifting toward the sky on swift gusts.

It was a rush, as was the day I drove that same highway toward the University of Kansas in Lawrence, the hilly, treed town I have at times called home in the northeast corner of the state.

There, in coming weeks, construction of the South Lawrence Trafficway—six miles of broad highway meant to circumvent the college town—is set to violate a swath of the Wakarusa Wetlands, 640 acres of hydric soil rich with biodiversity and cultural significance. Following decades of legal battles, the $150 million project finally would join existing stretches of Kansas Highway 10 to east and west of Lawrence. The southern loop would provide a handy bypass for semitruck drivers and other commuters between Kansas City and Topeka (most efficiently linked at present by more northern points along Interstate 70).

Environmentalists, biologists, Indigenous tribes, and others have been fighting for an alternate route since the 1980s; some of them occupied the area, recently sliced by a wide, mowed path marked for digging, for three days this month.

As Akash Kapur's *New Yorker* story demonstrates, progress is in the eye of the beholder. In many American cities, strategically charted twentieth-century highways represented "urban renewal" for white-collar commuters but meant, in James Baldwin's words, "Negro removal" for established Black neighborhoods suddenly isolated from goods and services. To small towns, meanwhile, highways have been what railroads were during the nineteenth century: economic life or death.

The folk singer Tift Merritt describes the latter conundrum in a song perhaps inspired by Bynum, North Carolina, the former cotton-mill town where she got her start as a young performer. As Merritt sings about a new highway laid through the next town over, "Some nights, I'm glad it passed us by / Some nights, I sit and watch my hometown die."

The South Lawrence Trafficway means destruction not for neighborhoods or industries but for one of three sensitive wetland ecosystems in Kansas. Points on quantitative ecological losses and conservation merits are best left to scientists and groups such as the Sierra Club, which called the would-be highway one of the fifty most environmentally offensive projects in the country. But many Kansans have become experiential experts on the Wakarusa Wetlands area—by leaving our computers and cars and entering it.

We've witnessed its snakes, herons, and turtles, touched its grasses in their tall autumn season, and worn its spring mud on our feet. We've watched its flowers open toward the sun, its foxes and owls move in and out of sight with the moon.

We are qualified to speak of its value and its life-forms, who suffer greater dearth of habitat than do we of asphalt thoroughfare. Where will they go? It's a question imperialists and capitalists historically ask as afterthought and answer in whatever manner suits their purposes—as Indigenous tribes, African Americans, agricultural communities, the inner-city poor, and others know all too well.

The threatened wetlands border Haskell Indian Nations University, a four-year institution that opened under very different purposes in 1884 as the United States Indian Industrial Training School, a federal outpost for cultural genocide. The swampy area at the southern edge of the existing Haskell campus is held in memory and ceremony as a place to which terrorized children escaped to speak forbidden tongues, practice forbidden customs, remember themselves, and find family members. Haskell students died from disease, abuse, or suicide; a small campus cemetery contains more than a hundred of their bodies, but many were thrown, tribal elders say, into the wetlands.

State consultants, after reviewing such reports by trafficway objectors, said insufficient evidence existed for halting the project. In 2012, a federal appeals court made way for construction to begin.*

Officials have promised the highway won't dig into deep soil and that tribal representatives may attend excavations. If construction workers hit human remains, officials have said, they will stop, notify police, call the state archaeologist.

As for environmental considerations, about $23 million of total funds have been earmarked for tending surrounding areas and constructing new wetlands and an education center. Since 1968, nearby Baker University has owned most of the wetlands area and used it for field research and education programs, while much smaller sections belong to Haskell, the University of Kansas, and the Kansas Department of Wildlife and Parks.

No habitat goes unchanged, and our species is a flicker in infinite transitions of place. But we choose what role we play in that unfolding, and our choices reveal what we value, what our highways mean to us.

An improved life?

For whom?

In the case of the South Lawrence Trafficway, many commuters may enjoy an even faster transit. Wealthy developers and

---

* The South Lawrence Trafficway opened in 2016 and is now part of a major transportation corridor in northeast Kansas. Its impact on the surrounding wetlands remains a point of research and concern.

corporations will garner much of the projected $3.7 billion in commercial impact. An ecosystem will suffer, increasingly so as the highway gives rise to surrounding development. And, should construction machinery strike human remains, children's bones will be disturbed by civilization for the second time.

DEAR DAUGHTER, YOUR MOM

The Morning News, 2014

Your mom walks into Hooters. She's wearing the famous spandex uniform. She's eighteen. In her wallet is a Mensa membership card, which she knows is distasteful and wouldn't show a soul but carries to remind herself that she knows a thing or two—a point that's easy to forget and harder to share in necks of certain woods. When she's a little older she'll consider the ironic elements of the costume: the tank top's wide-eyed owl, symbol of wisdom she's possessed since birth, stretched across round breasts she herself sometimes admires; the nylon shorts' neon hue, "safety orange" as the hunting garb she sometimes wore around the family farm to keep from getting shot. But right now she's thinking about her body. Does it look good?

"What do you think, Billy?" the skinny manager, Bones, says to the squat, wolfish assistant manager. They're both looking at her crotch. (The two men are also roommates, and Bones just handily won a debate about pubic hairs on bars of soap. Billy, who may have been inspired by dialogue on *Friends*: "Soap cleans itself." Bones: "You're an idiot, Billy.")

"Turn around," Billy tells your mom. Her heart races as she pivots awkwardly on her white high-tops. "Shorts are too big," he says.

"What?" she says, playing dumb. She's five foot three. She knew the smallest available uniform size would be required to achieve protocol, but she gave it a shot—not because she wouldn't be seen in shorts shorter than her ass but because she's genuinely worried about how her ass looks.

"They're too big. You need the smallest size," Billy says, rubbing his hand along his short black beard.

"I don't think so," your mom says, her voice firm. Her hair is blond, as in any good joke. "These are fine," she says.

"Maybe she's right," Bones says, looking your mom in the eye.

But Billy orders her to put on smaller shorts. She smiles on her way to the back room so as to not seem difficult or defeated. Your mom is here to make however much money a Hooters Girl might make without flirting or tolerating abuse. She's tired and unimpressed and knows that plenty of jobs are worse than this one.

Your mom's previous summer job involved weighing wheat trucks, wearing a hard hat, and hauling feed sacks into the volatile mill of a rural grain elevator just after an elevator down the road exploded, killing seven people. When she was a child, her carpenter dad took a second job transporting industrial chemicals and, after fumes leaked into the cab of the truck, foamed at the mouth in an emergency room. Her uncle died when his tractor slid off a muddy bridge and pinned him to a creek bed. Her great-grandma was raped while closing a small Wichita hamburger stand. Her grandma chased and counseled felons as a cop and probation officer (but was shot at home by an ex-husband with her own gun). Your mom's mom spent many summers under a hot tent (with your tiny mom), in a field whose stubble was sometimes on fire, unloading and peddling Chinese fireworks that are now illegal. There were many other dangerous jobs, homes, and men. Taking all this into account, your mom—the accidental daughter of a very smart and rightfully angry teenager—decided early to do things differently than everyone around her. That meant she would not drink, smoke, have sex, or get any grade but an A until she had a job and a home where she was safe.

Your mom got a full ride to the biggest university in Kansas, the only school to which she applied. The guidance counselor at her three-hundred-student, rural high school—which had no Advanced Placement program and sketched out for her a loose individualized education plan with a teacher for gifted students who served multiple underfunded school districts—had forgotten to tell her she should take the SAT, which many top universities required of applicants. (She did take the Preliminary SAT one morning, somehow, but was exhausted from waiting tables at Pizza Hut the previous night and, thinking it an inconsequential practice exam, answered questions with uncharacteristic carelessness. Weeks later, the counselor approached her in the hallway. "You only missed National Merit by a few points," he said. "What's National Merit?" she asked.) She experienced her enrollment at the University of Kansas as a supreme success, though, attributed in part to not drinking or smoking but, above all, to not letting a single penis anywhere near her vagina.

A few days after she turned eighteen, before the Hooters gig, your mom loaded the back seat of her car, which she bought with money earned at the grain elevator and at a Best Western reservations call center in Wichita, with her books, swing CDs, corduroy, and journals. She drove alone three hours from the dirt road to the county blacktop to the interstate to her new town, following directions she'd carefully highlighted in mailed packets back in her bedroom. (This was, at least among a certain class, just before the digital age.) When she found her dorm room, her three roommates were there with their parents, who wrote them checks when they left.

Your mom took many jobs that freshman year. She worked the front desk at her dorm, taking messages and sorting care packages from mothers into appropriate mail bins. She tutored mostly Black junior high students in Kansas City and Topeka. She organized and led a mostly White environmental cleanup crew at Lake Erie over spring break. She worked on the stage crew for a major performing arts center and wrote popular columns for the college paper. She often was recognized on campus, though, as "the *Loveline* girl," a moniker that arose when Adam Carolla pointed her out as "a piece of candy you can't unwrap" before thousands at the events venue where she worked, and as a featured guest in a black cowboy hat at a party launching the first-ever "Women of KU" calendar, though later she declined to be featured in said calendar. Your mom always acted composed and self-assured, but it was a harrowing task, discerning among the vocations inherited from her family, suggested by the world, and authentic to herself.

Your mom double-majored in journalism and creative writing. (She was among the first in her family to finish high school, so she received little reliable advice on such matters. She'd intended to be a paleontologist, but after she'd said as much for years, when she was ten or so your well-meaning grandpa asked what a paylia-whatever was, shook his head, and told her that a girl could be a teacher or a nurse.) She got straight

As. She got a little drunk but not too drunk. She barely let a single penis anywhere near her vagina.

After her front desk gig and dorm government involvement, the housing department offered your mom a coveted resident assistant position. She declined because the placement was for the all-girls dorm where most Greek pledges lived until moving into their respective sorority houses as upperclassmen. Making her home in such an environment, where girls indirectly abused one another, she imagined, would sap what not even Lilith Fair could restore. But her current approach to self-sustenance, working several minimum-wage jobs while taking eighteen credit hours of honors courses per semester, wasn't sustainable either. She was eighteen and tired. Sometimes she had to steal food. (There no doubt were less-draconian options—slow down, take fewer classes, work even longer hours—that she either rejected or couldn't see.) She needed fast money, both in yield per hour and in the immediate form of cash. She heard a high school friend had worked at Hooters. She'd been hearing about her own breasts the last few years. So that summer after freshman year, while living in Wichita, she put on the orange shorts and the tank top with the owl. She turned nineteen that August and, when sophomore year started, moved three hours up the highway again and changed restaurant locations to a Hooters in an affluent Kansas City suburb—moving up.

Most of her fellow Hooters Girls enjoyed their roles, it seemed; they accepted invitations to caddy for NBA players at golf tournaments or attend parties after last call or hold car washes in the parking lot to attract customers from the highway. Your mom, though, drew a durable line between herself and her job and stuck to the necessities: put on the uniform, show up, take orders, set beer and chicken wings on tables, collect payment. She smiled; she worked quickly and efficiently. She relished slow shifts that allowed for existential conversations with chain-smoking cooks or for learning about the children and modeling dreams and military husbands of her fellow waitresses, who were startled by her interest and obliged with photos and stories.

She took any chance to sell merchandise rather than serve beer. Merch girls were slightly detached from broader operations; they wore all-black getups that set them apart on the floor and, without the kitchen-staff middlemen required for food sales, enjoyed considerable opportunity to rob the place blind. On nights peddling merch, your mom, the quiet Hooters Girl in black, dispensed golf balls, key chains, and T-shirts bearing the corporate slogan's unnecessary comma and apparently unintentional redundancy of meaning, and she neglected to report about a quarter of the proceeds.

Your mom didn't hesitate to steal a little from Hooters. She knew the people who ran the joint stole a little from it too. And she didn't worry about getting caught. In junior high she'd walked out of drugstores with entire sets of Topps baseball cards under her jacket; she enjoyed the cards for a while and then sold them (except the Kevin Seitzer rookie card, with which she couldn't bear to part) to buy Christmas presents for her family. Back then, at night she cried and prayed fervently to the Holy Trinity for forgiveness. By college she was less convinced about where the guilt lay. She didn't hesitate to steal a little.

She did, however, hesitate every time she drove to work, first in Wichita and then in the wealthy Kansas City suburb. The entire Hooters corporation, whose inner workings she saw laid bare, was in her eyes a cynical affront to many things, perhaps most of all the souls of men. But any judgments she passed on Hooters and its trappings were, of course, judgments on herself; an indignant, self-righteous Hooters Girl is still a Hooters Girl, and the meaning of her title is up to her. For plenty of her coworkers, it seemed, the title meant fun, attention, happiness, power, which she never begrudged. But for your mom, right or wrong, it meant sacrifice and discomfort. She clenched when she cautiously mentioned her job to her fifteen-year-old brother, once a child she'd cared for in many ways, who openly cherished her as a hero. He wept. "Don't *lower* yourself," he said, snot running out of his nose.

After almost a year of feeling uncomfortable at Hooters, keeping her job a secret from most and agonizing over its implications, your mom remembered the question she began asking when she was little, before her ovaries dispensed their eggs. When she met a crossroads in her strategic pursuit of a life that nurtured rather than poisoned, she'd ask herself, *What would I want for my daughter?* As in, what would she advise you to do? When your mom imagined you, even during her own childhood, translucent neck hairs stood up in wonder. The love was beyond categorization and made clear the right course of action. If you felt naked yet unseen, coveted yet unappreciated in some uniform, what would she want for you?

She quit Hooters.

What would I want for my daughter?

The answer was always correct and its implementation reliably unpleasant. Human intimacy, so she suffered hugs until she became enthusiastic with affection. Honesty, so she said what she meant. Love, so she showed hers.

She claimed she wanted all those things for herself, but that didn't always get the job done. So your mom treated herself as sacred because you so obviously would be, and because she had enough sense to know that if one person is sacred, she must be too.

This way of being raised some eyebrows. Your mom absolutely cared what people thought of her and daily sought courage to bypass that concern when it countered your (her) highest good. In terror and discomfort, she broke much more important commitments than a job at Hooters, because even pretty-okay-but-not-quite-right wouldn't be good enough for you. Once, in a single year, your mom experienced two major injuries and, seeing how her husband didn't take care of her, ended a fifteen-year relationship; had her personal life introduced as a discussion topic among professional colleagues and, discerning a broad institutional context of gender disparity, resigned five months after gaining tenure; found out your grandma had advanced breast cancer and, realizing that we'll all die, sold most of her belongings, put her house on the market, and drove west to connect with the mom who'd been too young to raise her.

What would I want for my daughter?

The idea of you delivered her; she became the girl she loved. Spirit-child midwife, thank you. If one day you are manifest in this heavy, confusing form and face a tough decision, you might ask two questions:

What would I do for the most precious thing on earth?

What would I do for myself?

You will know your own integrity when the answers are the same.

FREEDOM MANDATE

Guernica, 2014

Students have fifteen seconds to make a decision: Will they discuss a handout on the US Constitution in pairs or in small groups? The fifth graders huddle, whisper over desks in a Kansas classroom painted to look like a jungle.

"Sparkle when you're done," says teacher Pat Zimmerman. It's September 2013, and she has just started her twentieth year at Perry-Lecompton Unified School District 343, a small network of brick rectangles between ethanol-bound corn and the forested dam of man-made Perry Lake. These unfussy classroom buildings sit in the rural, northern fringes of the I-70 corridor between Topeka and Kansas City. As the twenty White students conclude private deliberations, they do jazz hands and make soft noises to "sparkle." Half the class wants to work in pairs, half wants groups.

"*Oh*, we have a split vote," Zimmerman says, affecting fascination for the teachable moment. "That happens sometimes in committee." At this hitch in democratic process, Zimmerman sends female students to the front of the classroom to pick boy partners. The girls line up before a sleek, digital whiteboard and old-fashioned cubbies, above which flash drives marked with student initials dangle from hooks. They giggle, point, cup hands on ears, and hint at their crushes.

"Ladies, come on!" says Zimmerman, who wears thick, straight black bangs and a utilitarian ensemble of white shirt, blue skirt, and comfortable sandals. "We're strong women here. Make decisions."

Soon co-ed pairs sit on beanbags, reading and discussing a *Scholastic News* cover story on the First Amendment called "The Right Stuff." In addition to definitions for "censored" and "party" and a web address for petitioning the government, the spread features images of the 1963 March on Washington, a smiling Anderson Cooper, and a tween with green hair flashing a peace sign.

The classroom activity is Zimmerman's response to Celebrate Freedom Week, an unorthodox new curricular mandate by the Kansas legislature—traditionally charged with funding, not shaping, public education—that all students, kindergarten through eighth grade, receive instruction on this country's founding documents during the week of Constitution Day, September 17. Last year, Kansas became the fifth state, after Texas, Arkansas, Florida, and Oklahoma, to pass legislation embracing the initiative, pioneered in 2001 in Texas by Republican representative Rick Green. While specifications differ by state, its purpose, according to Kansas House Bill 2261, is "to educate students about the sacrifices made for freedom in the founding of this country and the values on which this country was founded."

When students return to their desks, a boy with a notebook of careful Snoopy sketches offers me a seat at "the beach," bright

Adirondack chairs beside a small aquarium and palm-tree wall-paper. Just to the left, an impressive mural of parrots, monkeys, and foliage—painted by Zimmerman herself—surrounds the teacher's desk. The ceiling, from which green plants dangle, showcases animal paintings done as student research projects. Zimmerman, who once got in trouble with the fire marshal for adorning the walls with actual palm fronds, has learned to make the space indelibly hers while following the rules—physically approximating the intersection of academic freedom and institutional standards that every teacher must navigate in classroom content.

"What does the First Amendment protect?" Zimmerman asks, ready to list hallmark freedoms in alternating red and blue.

The first shout: "Religion!"

With her digital stylus, Zimmerman writes "freedom of religion" on the glowing board, which is synced to her laptop.

"In some countries, the government says, 'You must all be—*Catholic*,'" she hypothesizes for discussion. "Who's Catholic?" A few hands go up. "You'd be fine with that, wouldn't ya? If you do *not* go to a Catholic church, do you want to be forced to go to a Catholic church?"

The tepid consensus: no.

"What if the government came in and said, 'Okay, all of you have to be *Buddhist*.'"

"No one knows what that means," one girl submits.

Emboldened, a boy weighs in: "I don't know what Catholic *or* Buddhist is."

Zimmerman is unfazed.

"Or—'If you are *Christian*, you will go to *jail*!'" she tries. This elicits the grumbles that signal insult and thereby com-prehension.

Past the window on this sunny afternoon, the American flag

slumps at half-staff, marking the Washington Navy Yard shooting two days prior. Like tropical beaches, the nation's capital is a long way from Perry-Lecompton public schools, but its reach is evident here. In 2011, Zimmerman and fellow teachers started phasing in the Common Core State Standards Initiative, the contentious curriculum pushed by the Obama administration and adopted by all but five states. Though derided by opponents on both sides of the aisle and now facing a swell of repeals, Common Core is more flexible than the standardized-testing measures of the Bush era, according to Zimmerman, as it favors integrating multiple subjects into themed units. Common Core, set to hit full steam in most states by 2016, uses math and reading as springboards to other topics, a strategy Zimmerman already employs heavily in social studies. (During the upcoming American Colonies unit, students will study simple machines like windmills in science, sample meat puddings in health, and learn building measurements in math.)

The only National Board–certified teacher at her school, Zimmerman makes no bones about her professional excellence, the magnificence of her creative space ("Are all the classrooms this cool? No."), or her suspicion of didactic texts. Like most Kansas school districts, hers affords great liberty in instructional approaches and text selection, and thereby Zimmerman's plucky individualism shines.

"We have a basic outline curriculum, and then how you get there is up to you," she says. That state curriculum tasks fifth-grade teachers like Zimmerman with covering colonial and early Revolutionary War history; civics follows in eighth grade, with additional American history by way of language-arts reading materials during junior and senior year. The Kansas State Board of Education oversees these broad standards and their implementation, while state legislators allocate funding and enact professional contracts. But deciding precisely what to teach, and when to teach it, largely has been left to those trained in such matters for more than 150 years.

Enter Celebrate Freedom Week, by which state representatives effectively tell teachers what to do. Touted as a means for addressing Americans' infamous civic ignorance, the Kansas incarnation of the law calls for lessons "concerning the original intent, meaning and importance" of the Declaration of Independence and US Constitution "in their historical contexts." In particular, the bill's authors state, "The religious references in the writings of the founding fathers shall not be censored when presented as part of such instruction."

If this esoteric stipulation was an evangelical wink—some legal wiggle room for religious proselytizing while teaching the very subject that addresses separation of church and state—the Kansas State Department of Education seemingly winked back with its list of recommended resources for school districts developing Celebrate Freedom Week curricula. Cited sources include secular nonprofits, apolitical state organizations, and major academic publishers, but also, among others, the American Heritage Education Foundation (AHEF), whose teaching materials include *The Miracle of America: The Influence of the Bible on the Founding History and Principles of the United States of America for a People of Every Belief*. According to the AHEF website, this compendium "shows how the Bible and Judeo-Christian thought are arguably the nation's most significant foundational root and its enduring source of strength." Exemplifying the contemporary allegiance between free marketeers and the religious right, for whom one shared goal is the privatization of schools, AHEF was cofounded by Richard Gonzalez, the now-deceased top economic adviser to Exxon ancestor Humble Oil and Refining.

Meanwhile, Celebrate Freedom Week progenitor Green now operates Patriot Academy, a traveling political training camp at which current and former elected officials teach young people how to campaign and about systems of government "from a Biblical worldview." Green himself hasn't held elected office since 2002, when he lost a reelection bid after using his statehouse office for a health-supplement infomercial and advocating for a financial fraud convict who lent money to his father's company.

Zimmerman, unmoved by any new effort to disrupt a secular education, is less concerned with Celebrate Freedom Week's mission than with its practical application. The date-specific edict, she says, disrupts the careful order of classroom operations; she typically lays colonial-era groundwork during the fall to help ready students for a spring-semester democracy unit she designed (it features a mock tax system wherein locker contents are property and hallways are highways).

"You get stuff handed to you that says you have to do this on this day or this week. It's a matter of figuring out, how can I take that pause from what we're doing and connect it some way and move on?" Zimmerman says. "You tie yourself in knots if you get mad or frustrated with it." She understands pinning Celebrate Freedom Week to Constitution Day, also known as Citizenship Day, which since 2005 has carried a federal mandate that public schools somehow address the Constitution—commonly done with school-wide activities or extracurricular projects. "But," she adds about the classroom itself, "I don't know anybody that teaches the Constitution at the beginning of the year."

With help from students, Zimmerman continues outlining the First Amendment, listing each hallmark freedom on the board and voicing real-world applications: a local immigrant family that recently fled religious persecution in Russia; the mortal peril of journalists in modern-day China; one student's grandfather sitting on the local school board.

"Our founding fathers took care of a lot of things in one amendment," she says. Several impressed students look around with wide eyes and slack jaws. A boy in glasses raises his hand and says, with the unemotional wonder of a biologist counting monarch butterflies on their migration this month through Kansas, "It's so much freedom."

For years, members of the religious right have redrawn science standards to make way for natural creationism in biology class. Now, with the passage of Celebrate Freedom Week, they make way for historical creationism in social studies. A civics teacher selectively emphasizing, say, Christian threads of American history isn't perfectly parallel to a science teacher presenting "intelligent design" as alternative to evolution. History, though we hope it is rooted in fact, is the province of interpretation; biology is data-reliant and less vulnerable to human beliefs. But the trouble with Celebrate Freedom Week's religious accent isn't open acknowledgment of the theological influence on America's framing. It's the agenda of those behind the legislation to erode the separation of church and state.

The law is more severe in Oklahoma, where third through twelfth graders must use "Creator" language in reciting the Declaration of Independence, barring excusal via parental request. Florida's and Texas's laws contain similar requirements. Oklahoma social studies coordinator Kelly Curtright told the *Kansas City Star* last year that Celebrate Freedom Week had not, in fact, "opened a Pandora's box" of classroom evangelizing there. But Celebrate Freedom Week risks invitation not only to religious bias but to curricular interference by lawmakers who know far more about politics than pedagogics.

One of the Kansas bill's most vocal objectors was Mainstream Coalition, a nonpartisan, Kansas-based watchdog over separation of church and state. During House floor testimony in February 2013, Micheline Burger, Mainstream Coalition's former president, raised hell for two hours over the bill's religious origins, its unsupported implication that Kansas public schools have failed to teach students about government history, and its conceit that one token week might address issues of social studies proficiency anyway.

"If the point of the bill is simply to emphasize teaching about the Constitution, the Declaration of Independence, and our form of government, then it is totally unnecessary; Kansas law already requires other bodies, not the Legislature, to make provision for the curriculum in the public schools. If these bodies, including the Kansas State Board of Education, are not doing their jobs, then let's deal with that. But I have heard nothing to this effect," Burger wrote in an account of her testimony at the website of Jill Docking, a Democrat and former chair of the state Board of Regents now running for lieutenant governor with gubernatorial candidate Paul Davis. "If, on the other hand, the objective of the bill is to promote religion in the public schools, then we have a very serious problem."

Like the war protestor accused of hating America or the scientist accused of hating God, Burger found herself in the position of defending her own allegiance—in this case to American-history education—to ideological wolves in sheep's clothing. "It is hard to explain to people what is wrong with legislation titled in such a positive way; to oppose it would seem to declare war on motherhood, apple pie, and the American way," Burger wrote.

To some, though, the title is the first sign of mischief. Like a father with a camera telling his kids to smile like they mean it, the law says that you *will* celebrate how free you are. In naming Celebrate Freedom Week, Green may have successfully employed the linguistic strategies of those people who brought us "pro-life" and "freedom haters," but his political portfolio is hardly coded. He facilitates firearms training with his so-called Constitutional Defense class, whose promotional web copy promises, "Even if you know nothing about the Constitution and you have no experience with a handgun, your Constitutional knowledge and your passion for American Exceptionalism, as well as your handgun skills, marksmanship and safety awareness will all dramatically improve." He performs across the country with self-described "God's comic" Brad Stine in a bookable Comedy and the Constitution Tour. On Sunday mornings after shows he is available to speak at church services. A status update on his Facebook page warned that food-stamp recipients could become dependent like wild animals fed by tourists in national parks.

Since 2001, the year Green introduced the Teach Freedom Act in Texas, he has been a public representative for WallBuilders, a revisionist-history organization founded by fellow Texan David Barton, with whom he cohosts a syndicated radio show. Barton, author of *The Founders' Bible*, which casts the US as a Christian nation and the Constitution as derivative of Christian doctrine, recently blamed natural disasters on America's "wicked" policies and was urged by Glenn Beck to run for the Texas Senate in 2014. Kansas governor Sam Brownback is an open admirer of Barton, who endorsed his 2008 presidential run. Brownback has said Barton's research "provides the philosophical underpinning for a lot of the Republican effort in the country today—bringing God back into the public square." Barton's research, however, is less lauded in other corners; his

2012 book *The Jefferson Lies*, which proclaims that Thomas Jefferson was no secularist, was pulled by publisher Thomas Nelson for containing, well, lies.

Barton and Green both are active in the ProFamily Legislative Network (PFLN), an offshoot of the WallBuilders group devoted to fighting, at the policy level, issues it terms "homosexual indoctrination" and "fetal pain," as well as to promoting school vouchers, homeschooling, and charter schools. It was at PFLN's annual conference that Kansas representative Kelly Meigs was inspired to champion the Celebrate Freedom Week legislation. She joined Green and Barton on their radio show in July 2013 just after the Kansas law, cosponsored by twenty-nine fellow Republicans, passed handily. She thanked Green for his help and lamented opposition from those who thought "we were mandating the teaching of certain things in the schools." They had it backward, she said.

"When I was debating it on the floor, that's what I was trying to get across to people—that this was *freedom*. This wasn't a mandate," said Meigs, who in two terms has helped pass laws requiring photo identification for voters and illegalizing late-term abortions except in case of risk to the patient's life. But for Meigs, a graduate of Springfield's Evangel University, speaking on the talk show of two avowed crusaders for merging church and state, "freedom" may well mean the "freedom to infuse teachings with Christian views."

Rob Boston, who for over twenty-five years has reported on inappropriate religious presence in schools for Americans United for Separation of Church and State, sees a longtime campaign to miseducate Americans about their own rights. "It's to social studies and history what creationism is to biology," Boston tells me by phone from his Washington office. "It's an attempt to rewrite the accepted history and substitute a religious-right version of events that really doesn't have any support in the academy. But that doesn't mean it doesn't have political support."

Barton is notorious for finding such support. He lifts convenient quotes from America's founding documents to create what Boston calls a "cut-and-paste revisionist history," and politicians such as Green bring him through statehouse doors as an adviser. Barton, who has no training as a historian, has helped shape history curricula in California and Texas and has lobbied to remove the phrase "separation of church and state" from education standards, arguing that it doesn't appear verbatim in the Constitution. In 2012, Mike Huckabee, the former Arkansas governor and presidential candidate, joked that all Americans should be forced at gunpoint to listen to Barton's teachings.

"The creationists in biology are really good at isolating a specific piece of information, presenting it out of context. Real scientists come along and demolish them every time, but of course in politics facts can only take you so far," Boston says. "Barton and Green's shtick is very similar. It's not about history. It's not about civics. It's about ideology."

Boston says the law reliably prevails against such ideologies in public education. But foes of church-state separation often succeed insidiously. A 2007 national survey of more than 900 biology teachers, part of a major study by political scientists, suggested that 13 percent taught creationism or intelligent design, and more than half avoided taking a direct stance on the topic of evolution. Boston says Green, Barton, and their supporters want to create a similar dynamic, wherein "some teachers will be afraid to teach the real story of the development of the United States and its system of government."

In early 2013, a variety of Kansas education bills already had created a climate of concern about the government's power and intentions. Jana Shaver, chairwoman of the State Board of

Education, wrote a letter to legislators asking that they not over-step their authority. "We respect the Legislature's constitutional responsibility to provide for the suitable finance of education for Kansas students," Shaver wrote—a nod to then-pending litigation against the state for underfunding schools (later, the state Supreme Court would set national precedent by ruling in favor of schools). "We ask that our legislators likewise respect the State Board's constitutional responsibility for the general supervision of schools, which includes accrediting schools, pro-viding for academic standards and the licensure of teachers."

As the bill came down the pike, Micheline Burger tried to convince legislators that Celebrate Freedom Week was not only unnecessary but also poorly conceived. "I was told that the US Constitution is based on the Bible and contains passages from the King James Bible, that the majority should prevail in what religion is promoted in the schools, and that the *Drudge Report* is a reliable source of factual information. . . . I was told, in no uncertain terms, that there is no such thing as separation of church and state," Burger wrote in her online account of debate on the House floor. "It is ironic that members of the Education Committee expressed such strong concern about the lack of [student] understanding of the three branches of government, because it appears that some of their colleagues could use a refresher course in this area themselves."

Legislators who need civics education passing laws about civics education: it's the kind of irony that threatens democracy. To be sure, Celebrate Freedom Week and the forces behind it pull at the seams of public education. But when considering the experience of the student and her direct learning, all education is local. As Kansas Department of Education science consul-tant Matt Krehbiel told a Lawrence newspaper in 2012, while leading the restoration of rigorous teaching standards several years after the state board made world headlines by approving a creationism-friendly definition of science, "... The standards themselves won't make that difference. It's the teachers in the classroom that make the difference."

It's Celebrate Freedom Week 2013 and, in a cinder-block-walled classroom at South Middle School in the hilly town of Lawrence, between Topeka and Kansas City, Tom Barker is celebrating his freedom to teach Latin American studies.

At the beginning of last period, he tells fidgety seventh graders to text message from personal gadgets the two major languages of Latin America. (Their answers, appearing in real time on a computer projector screen, in order of popularity: "Spanish," "German," "waffles.") After this warm-up, students collect textbooks from a wall of particle-board cabinets and break into groups.

The classroom features a nineteenth-century Lawrence map, a contemporary world map, two globes, and a tiny plastic wisp of an American flag. Students recently enjoyed a flag-designing exercise, during which many focused on sports teams; one colored-pencil creation, referring to University of Kansas head basketball coach Bill Self, rings with unintentional profundity in a classroom where adolescents learn about the tensions between individual freedoms and state protections: "In Self we trust." Tomorrow is, after all, Constitution Day, when Barker will add a handout on the Bill of Rights to his existing lesson plan—artfully complying with Celebrate Freedom Week while focusing on other priorities in the complicated landscape of standards, tests, and the individual student needs he navigates daily. It may have the capacity to wreak havoc in the wrong hands, but in practice the curricular mandate reveals an earnest army of teachers doing good work.

This expert handling of a potential problem brings to light the lesser-told true story of American public education: it works. Diane Ravitch, the former assistant secretary of education and No Child Left Behind proponent who now rails against the charter-school movement and standardized testing, said as much to NPR's Steve Inskeep last year. "Let me tell you what I think everyone needs to know," Ravitch said, citing record graduation rates and test scores across demographics. "American public education is a huge success." She pointed to lacking resources rather than inherent dysfunction as the source of documented strife.

Policymakers may tinker on behalf of special interests, with consequences echoing throughout budgets and curricula. But if the ultimate goal for schools is student learning, the person who wields the most influence is the one standing at the front of the classroom. Anyone who loved astronomy in the sixth grade, when the science teacher poked constellations into a flashlight-lit bedsheet, but lost interest the following year, when the teacher read about planets from a creased textbook and then napped at his desk, knows this. Teachers are the most powerful people in public education.

Barker, a first-year teacher finishing his PhD in social studies education at KU, delivers world studies to about one hundred seventh graders at South, where demographics closely align with state averages. About half of the students qualify for free or reduced-cost lunches; about a third are racial minorities. He admits, after following the legislation through local news outlets and awaiting direction from administrators during the busy beginning of the school year, he gave the state order little attention until I looked him up. ("When you emailed me, I was like, 'Well, crap, do I need to take this seriously or what?' Because I was just going to ignore it.") The large Lawrence district struggled to coordinate elementary- and middle-school efforts for Celebrate Freedom Week by prescribed September dates. Eventually the state board clarified that a line in the bill allowed schools to observe it during the week of their choosing; the district chose to wait until the week of Veterans Day in November.

The clumsy dance of bureaucracy in public education is one that Barker, a ruddy, thirty-something California native trained to be a teacher of teachers, pokes fun at from the middle of the floor. "*Mission statements*," Barker says, in a tone suggesting he has seen administrators' mouths write checks their asses could not cash. "We do this to make it look like we're doing something. 'Oh, we *have* to have a mission statement.' You'll see some that say, like, 'Have students who are globally mindful and prepared for a global economy.' What does that mean? It sounds good on paper, but how do I *do* that?"

To find out how others are doing it, Barker surveyed more than four hundred Kansas social studies teachers as part of a thirty-five-state study of twelve thousand instructors—the largest of its kind in three decades. The resulting research published in the 2013 academic text *The Status of Social Studies: Views from the Field* provides a snapshot of how teachers frame history and discuss religion. The results suggest few differences in self-reported content priorities among teachers in states as disparate in character as Oregon, Kansas, and Virginia.

Indeed, while the five states with Freedom Week legislation share a certain blush, to conclude that so-called red states are necessarily more fertile for religious-right hijinks in public education would be an oversimplification. The 2004 Dover, Pennsylvania, evolution dustup, in which the school district added a plug for intelligent design to its biology curriculum, happened in a Republican-majority county of a then Democratic state; in

2006, parents sued the local school district in blue California over a course promoting creationism.

Even more local than the district is the classroom. The broader landscape is "definitely gonna influence *curriculum*," Barker says. "But if you want to know what kids are being shown, look to the philosophy of the teacher." He points to a bookshelf containing one of his chosen classroom texts for teaching US history, a comic book based on Howard Zinn's *A People's History of the United States*—the stuff of scandal in some conservative corners of social studies, perhaps. While Barker admits his own slant, he says he stops short of preaching it. After watching videos of differing perspectives on the Keystone pipeline, which began moving Canadian oil through Kansas in 2011, students expressed ethical confusion and wanted to know what Barker believed. He wouldn't share. "That's not my job."

Overall, Barker is unimpressed by the new law's implications. "We need to revive civics ed," he says. "But I don't think just me teaching about civics and responsibility and giving my kids tests is necessarily going to change or fix that."

American civics has been a running joke for decades—from its frequent depiction as the most insufferable class period (think droning teacher voice in *The Wonder Years*) to embarrassing national-assessment scores (according to a 2010 report by the US Department of Education, more than a third of high school seniors couldn't demonstrate basic civics knowledge such as constitutional principles, and only 7 percent of eighth graders showed complete understanding of checks and balances among the three branches of government) to history-themed installments of *The Tonight Show*'s old "Jaywalking" segment

(Leno: "Who sewed the first American flag?" Dude on street: "Who *sold* it?").

In the last few years, though, a host of factions have called for the reconstruction of civics education. In 2009, former Supreme Court justice Sandra Day O'Connor, who describes the current state of civics ed as a "crisis," founded iCivics, an online platform offering cutting-edge classroom resources. In 2012, the Obama administration released a report calling for "Reinvigorating and Reimagining" civics education. To ensure that Common Core's basic-skills focus isn't a coffin nail for its field, in 2013 the National Council for the Social Studies released a recommended classroom-standards framework, the result of a multiyear, twenty-one-state collaboration that included Kansas educators. Groups such as the Center for Civic Education, the Campaign for the Civic Mission of Schools, and even an organization founded by actor Richard Dreyfuss lobby for democratic literacy. Meanwhile, by tapping legislative power, extreme agendas like Green's and Barton's melt into the curricular alloy that teaches young people what it means to be an American.

Perhaps no Kansas school district more acutely faces the task of citizen-rearing than Garden City, a meatpacking hub of about thirty thousand in Finney County, western Kansas. At most of the district's sixteen public schools, at least half the students are Hispanic—in some cases, close to 90 percent, with comparable poverty rates. Finney County is one of five in the state with minority-majorities.

Garden City school administrator Martha Darter appears unaware of Celebrate Freedom Week's religious undercurrents, but she hints at the redundancy of its purported mission in a school district that has been assimilating children of immigrant Mexican, Somali, and Burmese factory workers for decades. "We've always done Constitution Day," says Darter, who describes a commitment to let students share customs, languages, and experiences from mother countries even as they study America and sing patriotic songs in English. "We've had such a diverse population for so many years. But we are living in America."

According to the National Assessment of Educational Progress, poor, minority, and immigrant students score lower in civics than their peers. The social repercussions of this disparity are far-reaching. Harvard University education professor Meira Levinson observes a "civic empowerment gap" in which disenfranchised groups vote and participate less and have a poorer sense of their own political efficacy than the rich. The most destitute members of the "99 percent" may have been too busy, sick, or exhausted to join the Occupy Wall Street movement, and too illiterate or media-averse to follow it. Ignorance of rights and powers most harms those in the severest need of revolution. At this demoralized American moment, at stake in the fight for civics education is the only public institution through which Americans gain understanding of their own inalienable powers.

On Kansas Day 2014 in Kansas City, Kansas, in a trailer whipped by polar wind, most of the seventh graders speak with Mexican-American accents; though it's a frigid day in late January, many wear short-sleeved shirts.

"It's Kansas's anniversary," announces Central Middle School teacher Marsha Sudduth, who has a short mop of thick, white hair and speaks with a powerful Oklahoma drawl. Students wear the unisex school uniform of white, collared shirts and black pants—instituted to curb violence by the gangs who marked the outside of this trailer with graffiti. Ninety-six percent of Central students live in low-income households, more than doubling the school eligibility requirement for federal Title 1 funding. Beyond the schoolyard are railroad tracks, factories, bars, peeling houses with concave roofs; in here, laminated descriptions of the Bill of Rights, Native American dream catchers, timelines for abolition and the civil rights movement, images of wheat stalks.

On this date in 1861, Kansas joined the Union by way of the Wyandotte Constitution, pivotal for the nation in declaring Kansas a free state. The document was drafted in this northeastern outpost along the Missouri River called Wyandotte County, now among the poorest in the state. But today's lesson isn't about history. Students unfold paper atlases while Sudduth fires up an old analog projector and readies films of typed and handwritten instructions for plotting a road trip among state landmarks.

"I'm gonna take you on an imaginary field trip," she says. "Here's the magic dust I'm throwing on you. I'm going to go out and rent all the dream cars that everyone wanted."

"Not on a teacher's salary," a girl says.

"You got me," Sudduth says. "What is your dream car? What's the car you wanna drive?"

Camaro, Ferrari, Hummer.

A boy leans back and says, "A pink Lambo, so I could ride like dis."

For the sake of easy figuring in this exercise inspired by standardized testing's emphasis on math and reading, everyone will travel at sixty miles per hour. "I have a governor on the gas pedal," Sudduth says. "It only lets you go so fast."

When the bell rings, students stream from "the trailers," as Sudduth's area is known, to a brick, three-level building that opened in 1915 as one of the first junior high schools west of the Missouri River. Sudduth follows to attend the daily meeting of seventh-grade teachers. In the sharp cold, she unlocks the main building doors by punching in a code. Security here is serious business; the main entrance has a metal detector and a friendly, armed officer.

At the meeting of ten teachers in a basement room, Sudduth notes that it's Kansas Day, and the reading teacher asks if she might suggest a relevant online film or resource to show in her class—a gesture in kind, perhaps, for all the reading comprehension that social studies teachers have been asked to integrate into their lessons. Another teacher shares that a twelve-year-old female student has been kicked out of her home. "So a little understanding, please," she says.

Back in the trailers, Sudduth reflects on what civics education means for this student population: survival. She aims to connect lesson plans to real-world skills and contemporary community resources such as health clinics, abuse hotlines, public-assistance programs, and other available support mechanisms that might help students and their families navigate. Her gaze goes distant as she recalls a delinquent student from her front row whose mother turned to the school for help when he beat her; Sudduth and others connected her with area social services, but a month later the boy was shot dead in front of the elementary school next door.

Second-period students are further along in the mapping exercise and break into groups. Sudduth introduces a new kid, who sits on the stained gray carpet with two other girls, peeling plastic binders, notebooks, and atlases; the crescent of a red-purple bruise fades below one of their eyes. Next to them sits a trio of boys, one of whom has wound masking tape around the stems of his reading glasses to adjust their fit. Spanish slips in and out of discussions about highways. One kid with a round face and a shock of orange in his hair recalls stopping in Wichita on a trip to visit family in Mexico; if his mom's employer transfers her from a Kansas City factory to one in Atlanta, he'll be moving soon.

Within district curriculum, Sudduth's task is to spend half the year on world geography and half on Kansas history, from Indigenous peoples to Eisenhower. Direct civics content includes a comparison of the Wyandotte Constitution to the US Constitution, and lessons on branches of government. But her personal goal, she says, is to make those lessons relevant to human lives. In her classroom, civics education is civic engagement; the Bill of Rights is not just read but put to work.

"If I want to further their education—everyone's education, not just a specific subgroup of kids—then I need them to know that their neighborhood should help represent them," she says. "In order to do that, you've gotta know what's out there that can help you to own it. To be a part of it, not destroy it."

While applied in different ways, civics education seemed to be thriving in the hands of every Kansas teacher I spoke with, from Wichita to Topeka and points in between, and in this, proponents of Celebrate Freedom Week's purported intent may take heart. Opponents of the legislation, meanwhile, might find some comfort in the tangled nature of the very bureaucracy that spawned it: top-down mandates have a way of dissolving in an atmosphere of silliness, sometimes disintegrating entirely before they reach places like Sudduth's classroom, the places furthest from the top. Legislators don't teach students; teachers do.

Sudduth shakes her head and squints with apparent honesty. Celebrate Freedom Week? She's never heard of it.

POOR TEETH

Aeon, 2014

I am bone of the bone of them that live in trailer homes. I grew up next to Tiffany "Pennsatucky" Doggett, the hostile former drug addict from the prison TV drama *Orange Is the New Black*. I know her by her teeth.

Pennsatucky—a scrappy slip of a woman menacing, beating, and proselytizing to fellow inmates—stole the show during the first season of the Netflix prison series. But amid an ensemble cast of similarly riveting, dangerous characters, it was her gray, jagged teeth that shocked viewers into repulsed fixation. She was the villain among villains, a monster that fans loved to hate; "Pennsatucky teeth" became a pejorative in social media.

Actress Taryn Manning's gnarly, prosthetic teeth startled viewers because, by and large, poor characters in TV and film are played by actors whose whitened, straightened, veneered smiles aren't covered up. It's hard to think of characters besides Pennsatucky through whom heinous teeth convey rather than lampoon the physicality of the poor. The first that comes to mind is the derelict serial killer in the 2003 movie actually called *Monster*; as with Manning, Charlize Theron's Oscar-winning transformation generated astonishment with fake teeth.

In my life, Pennsatucky and her teeth are entirely familiar. She's the slurring aunt who passed out in our farm's swimming pool while babysitting me, and later stole my mom's wedding band to buy the drugs that dug grooves in her cheeks. She's the stepparent whose brain, organs, and teeth corroded over the years and who now lives in a mobile-home park with my construction-worker dad.

But Pennsatucky's teeth aren't just "meth teeth." They are the teeth of poor folk, of the young grandma who helped to raise me. She had survived by working in diners and on factory lines and, ultimately, as a probation officer for the county court system in Wichita, Kansas. She was just thirty-five when I was born, so I knew her as a radiant thing; at the downtown courthouse, where I tagged along—babysitters are expensive—attorneys turned flirtatious near her green eyes, long limbs, and shiny, natural-blond bob. Then at night, in her farmhouse or the tiny brick house we fixed up in a rough Wichita neighborhood, I watched her take out her teeth, scrub them with a rough brush, and drop them into a cup of water with a fizzy tablet.

"Brush your teeth and don't eat too much candy," she'd tell me. "You don't want to end up like Grandma." She'd widen her eyes and pop her dentures forward so that they bulged from her lips, sending me giggling. In the early 1970s, a dentist had pried every one of her teeth, too far gone or too expensive to save, from her twenty-something skull. She's sixty-nine now and has worn false teeth for more than forty years.

"I had bad teeth all my life. They were straight and looked okay, but I always had toothaches," she tells me when I ask how she ended up with dentures. As I was growing up, the story fluctuated—she was in a car accident, her natural teeth just fell out, and so on. "I was excited to have them, knowing I would never have another toothache. Now I think it was pretty stupid, but at the time it was really painful, and I thought I was doing the right thing."

More than 126 million people in the US—nearly half the population—had no dental insurance in 2012, according to the National Association of Dental Plans. In 2007, the *New York State Dental Journal* reported that while only one-tenth of general physician costs were paid out of pocket, nearly half of all dental costs were settled directly by patients. This reflects spending by the uninsured but also those sharing costs with coverage providers; most plans cover routine cleanings but leave patients to pay for 20 to 50 percent of fillings, crowns, and other big-ticket visits. For those who can't afford to pay that difference, treatment is delayed and teeth continue to degrade.

But expense isn't the only barrier to dental care. Those on Medicaid find that few dentists participate in the program due to its low payout. And more than 45 million people in the US live in areas, often rural or impoverished, with dentist shortages, according to the US Department of Health and Human Services. Medicare, as a general rule, doesn't include dental.

In the past year, the Affordable Care Act, or Obamacare, has changed many lives for the better—mine included. But its omission of dental coverage, a result of political compromise, is a dangerous, absurd compartmentalization of health care, as though teeth are apart from and less important than the rest of the body.

About a decade ago, at the age of fifty, my dad almost died when infection from an abscessed tooth poisoned his blood and nearly stopped his heart. He has never had dental insurance and has seen a dentist only a handful of times when some malady became unbearable. In 2009, according to the Agency for Healthcare Research and Quality, dental issues caused about 936,000 emergency-room visits and almost 13,000 inpatient hospital stays in the US. Many of these patients had low incomes and dental coverage that restricted care to emergencies or wasn't accepted by accessible dentists.

"I notice people's teeth because mine are so bad," Dad tells me during a break from a side job renovating a fraternity house. He has long been the handsome object of crushes, but his teeth have become increasingly askew with time, one of his eyeteeth now ragged and long like a rabbit's for lack of a carrot to file it down. "Nutrition affects teeth, right?"

I point out that Gatorade, which he favors when he splurges on a bottled beverage, is full of sugar. But it wasn't sugar, heaps of which are sucked down daily by the middle and upper classes, that guided his and my grandma's dental fates. And it wasn't meth. It was lack of insurance, lack of knowledge, lack of good nutrition—poverties into which much of the country was born.

My family's distress over our teeth—what food might hurt or save them, whether having them pulled was a mistake—reveals the psychological hell of having poor teeth in a rich, capitalist country: the underprivileged are priced out of the dental-treatment system yet perversely held responsible for their dental condition. It's a familiar trick in the privatization-happy US— like, say, underfunding public education and then criticizing the institution for struggling. Often, bad teeth are blamed solely on the habits and choices of their owners, and for the poor therein lies an undue shaming.

"Don't get fooled by those mangled teeth she sports on camera!" says the ABC News host introducing the White woman who plays Pennsatucky. "Taryn Manning is one beautiful and talented actress." This suggestion that bad teeth and talent, in particular, are mutually exclusive betrays our broad, unexamined prejudice against those long known, tellingly, as "white trash." It's become less acceptable in recent decades to make racist or sexist statements, but blatant classism generally goes unchecked. See the hugely successful blog *People of Walmart* that, through submitted photographs, viciously ridicules people who look like contemporary US poverty: the elastic waistbands and jutting stomachs of diabetic obesity, the wheelchairs and oxygen tanks of gout and emphysema.

Upper-class supremacy is nothing new. A hundred years ago, the Eugenics Records Office in New York not only targeted racial minorities but "sought to demonstrate scientifically that large numbers of rural poor whites were genetic defectives," as the sociologist Matt Wray explains in his 2006 book *Not Quite White: White Trash and the Boundaries of Whiteness*. The historian and civil rights activist W.E.B. Du Bois, an African American, wrote in his 1940 autobiography *Dusk of Dawn* that, growing up in Massachusetts in the 1870s, "the racial angle was more clearly defined against the Irish than against me. It was a matter of income and ancestry more than color." Martin Luther King Jr. made similar observations and was organizing a poor people's march on Washington at the time of his murder in 1968.

Such marginalization can make you either demonize the system that shuns you or spurn it as something you never needed anyway. When I was a kid and no one in the family had medical or dental insurance, Dad pointed out that those industries were criminal—a sweeping analysis that, whether accurate or not, suggested we were too principled to support the racket rather than too poor to afford it.

My baby teeth were straight and white, and I wasn't overweight—an epidemic among poor kids that hadn't yet taken hold in the 1980s—but I had plenty of tells: crooked bangs, trimmed at home with sewing shears; a paper grocery sack carrying my supplies on the first day of school while other kids wore unicorn backpacks; a near-constant case of ringworm infection (I kept a jar of medicated ointment on my nightstand year-round); the smell of cigarette smoke on my clothes, just as cigarettes were falling out of favor with the middle and upper classes; sometimes, ill-fitting clothes, as when the second-grade teacher I revered looked at my older cousin's shirt sagging off my shoulder and said, "Tell your mother to send you to school in clothes that fit you." In fifth grade, a girl noticed my generic, plastic-smelling, too-pointy boots—a Kmart version of the black leather lace-ups that were in fashion—and for weeks hounded me before and after school, kicking dirt on my shins and calling me Pippi Longstocking.

I had moments of cool clothes and good haircuts too, and I was a confident child who earned friends and accolades. But I still think of the boy who handed me a pudding cup from his lunch box every day when a mix-up in the free-lunch program left me without a meal card for months and I was too embarrassed to tell an adult.

Common throughout those years was a pulsing throb in my gums, a shock wave up a root when biting down, a headache that agitated me in classrooms. While they looked okay, my baby teeth were cavity-ridden. Maybe it was the soy formula in my bottle when they were growing in, or the sugary cereals to which my brain later turned for dopamine production in a difficult home. Maybe it was because our water supply, whether from a rural well or the Wichita municipal system, wasn't fluoridated. But richer teeth faced the same challenges. The primary reason my mouth hurt was lack of money.

Once, around third grade, an upper molar that had menaced beyond all—the worst toothache I ever had—finally rotted so thoroughly that it cracked in half while still in my jaw. Mom took me to the dentist, somehow. The pain was tremendous, he explained, because the pulpy nerve at the tooth's center was exposed. He pulled from my skull the grayed tooth, split perfectly down the middle, and let me take it home. For years, I kept the two pieces in a tiny jewelry box, sometimes taking them out and joining them like interlocking sides of the heart-shaped friendship necklaces I coveted.

Around that time, I had my jaw X-rayed for the first time. The results were grim.

"You might as well start saving for braces right now," my mom recalls the dentist saying. We were at the outset of a post-divorce period that would include much moving and a slew of partial-coverage dental insurance plans: employer-based, which would be canceled with Mom's regular job switches, and variations on state-funded, poor-kid programs in between. Each time the policy changed, Mom had to find a new dentist who would accept our coverage. Then we'd ride out a waiting period before scheduling a cleaning or filling. My dental records were often lost in this shuffle, as was the case with my general health files in doctors' offices and school districts—I got a new round of shots just about every year for lack of immunization records on file.

There would, of course, be no saving for braces.

—

It took years to find out whether the X-raying dentist's pessimistic prediction would come true. My baby teeth were slow to fall out, their replacements slow to grow in. But at some point came the unequivocal, surprising verdict: my teeth grew in straight.

I don't just mean straight enough. I mean 99th percentile straight. I mean dentists call hygienists over to take a look.

"Doesn't she have pretty teeth?" they say, my mouth under hot lamps. "Are you sure you didn't have braces? But you whiten them, right?"

I shake my head no and in the dentist's chair tingle with the bliss of gratitude. That my environment and genes somehow conspired to shake out a bright, orderly smile is a blessing I can't explain. But I can tell you what preserved the blessing: me.

When a health teacher said brush your teeth twice a day, I brushed my teeth twice a day. When a TV commercial imparted that dentists recommend flossing daily, I flossed daily. A college roommate once remarked on the fervor of my dental regimen. After boozy nights, when other kids were passing out, I held on, stumbled to the bathroom, and squeezed paste onto a brush. However tired, however drunk, I scrubbed every side of every tooth, uncoiled a waxed string and threaded it into sacred spaces.

Poor teeth, I knew, beget not just shame but more poorness: people with bad teeth have a harder time getting jobs and other opportunities. People without jobs are poor. Poor people can't access dentistry—and so goes the cycle.

If Pennsatucky ever gets out of poverty, it will be thanks in part to a prison-yard fight in the season-one finale, when the upper-class protagonist knocks out her nasty grill; early in the second season, her rotten gums nearly toothless, she

blackmails the warden into a new set of teeth. Upon incarceration, Pennsatucky traded meth for born-again religious
fanaticism, but her new teeth are a harbinger of a more
substantive rebirth. If the eyes are the soul's windows, its
door is the mouth—the fence across which pass food, drink,
words, our very breath.

Privileged America, ever striving for organic purity, judges
harshly the mouths that chew orange Doritos, drink yellow
Mountain Dew, breathe with a sawdust rattle, carry a lower lip's
worth of brown chaw, use dirty words and bad grammar. When
Pennsatucky gets out of prison, she'll need respect, rehabilitation,
employment. To that end, for all her praying and testifying, Pennsatucky's pearly gates might be her pearly, albeit prosthetic, whites.
She cries with joy in a prison van on the way to get them, and
later shows off with an over-the-top smile during laundry duty.

"You're acting a little, like, retarded," an envious inmate
tells her.

"I'm not retarded,"* she says. "I got new teeth!"

When I was a young adult, I learned I'd been born without wisdom teeth. The dentist told me I was "evolutionarily advanced"

---

* I do not repeat this hurtful slur, even within the context of a quoted hit
television show about the supremely insensitive environment of prison,
without careful thought. Here, the regrettable language is itself significant
to my essay's argument that those without access to dentistry suffer social
persecution and unfair judgments about their aptitude; Pennsatucky feels
emboldened to defend herself from a pejorative suggesting low intelligence by pointing out the improved class indicator of her new white
teeth. A decade since its original publication, I do not recall receiving
a single objection to use of the term among the essay's vast readership.
Still, I welcome the space this book provides to explain my decisions as
an essayist who seeks to heal rather than to harm. If I have erred here or
elsewhere in that pursuit, I apologize.

since human beings, no longer in the business of tearing raw flesh from mastodon bones, don't need so many teeth now. So many TV shows, bad jokes, and bucktoothed hillbilly costumes in Halloween aisles had suggested that my place of origin made me "backwards," primitive, and uncivilized, that the dentist's comment struck me deeply, just as in fourth grade when I read the word "genius" in a school psychologist's evaluation notes to my mother and wept on the sidewalk.

Having straddled a class divide and been wrongly stereotyped on both sides of it, throughout my life I've found peace in the places and things that don't evaluate my status: nature, animals, art, books. "I sit with Shakespeare," wrote Du Bois in *The Souls of Black Folk*, "and he winces not." Social disadvantage and hazard engender what he called "double consciousness," the ever-present awareness of more than one self. For Du Bois, at the turn of the twentieth century, his most challenging two-ness in the wake of slavery was to be educated and Black—a tension of socialization still at work, to be sure, as President Barack Obama's raw first memoir attests. Today, for me and millions of people in the US living on one side of a historic income gap, the defining double consciousness is to be educated and poor.

The latter, for many of those who suffered losses after the economic collapse of 2008, is a terrifying new identity, its horror projected onto Pennsatucky's serrated mouth and hard to reconcile with the Americans they thought they were. But in my academic and professional "climbing," I learned early and often that one doesn't leave a place, class, or culture and enter another, but rather holds the privilege and burden of many narratives simultaneously.

Friends who know my background sometimes kid me when I'm drunk and mis-conjugate a verb or slip into a drawl, or when, thoroughly sober, I reveal a gross blind spot in the realm of book learning (if, say, the question involves whatever one learns in sixth grade, most of which I spent playing in red dirt outside a two-room schoolhouse near the Oklahoma state line). They smile at the pleasure I take in scoring solid furniture from yard sales or, once, for expressing delight over a tiny cast-iron skillet, a miniature version of the pan my grandma once used to fight a drunken stepfather off her mother. I sometimes even enjoy the kidding, an admission of awe over the true clichés that weave my story.

But here's the thing: Wealthy people use cast-iron skillets and bad grammar too. It's just not their narrative and thus passes without remark. I've observed fellow journalists, the same ones who made trailer-park tornado survivors famous for a loose grip on the past participle, edit dumb-sounding quotes by city commissioners to suit the speaker's stature. And while I took the education I wasn't given through libraries, encyclopedias, and a stepfather's *New Yorker* subscription, plenty of members of the middle and upper classes refuse or lack the ability to seize the opportunities handed them. It can be useful to acknowledge the cultural forces that carve us, or edifying to indulge in the tropes of our assigned narratives, but true distinctions of character, intelligence, talent, and skill exist at the level of the individual, not of the class—or the ethnicity, the gender, the sexual orientation, the religion, and so on. To claim otherwise, as we've discovered across time and countless persecutions of our own doing, is at best an insult and at worst an excuse for enslavement and genocide.

In Thomas Harris's bestselling crime-novel series, the FBI consults the imprisoned serial killer and mastermind psychiatrist Hannibal Lecter in its search for "the Tooth Fairy," a family slayer who bites his victims with dentures made from a mold of his grandmother's distorted, razor-sharp teeth. Years after that manhunt, the FBI again turns to Lecter for help; this time, the refined sociopath—a former philharmonic orchestra board member and mannerly purveyor of his victims' flesh—finds it more interesting to analyze the agent than the latest case, as in a classic scene from the 1991 film adaptation of *The Silence of the Lambs*.

"You know what you look like to me, with your good bag and your cheap shoes?" he asks the young agent Clarice Starling—who comes from the same place as Pennsatucky but whose intellect, health, grit, and ambition, presumably, landed her on the right side of the prison bars. She is, Lecter says, an ambitious rube. "Good nutrition's given you some length of bone, but you're not more than one generation from poor white trash, are you, Agent Starling?" He mocks her West Virginia accent. "What is your father, dear? Is he a coal miner?"

Lecter's condescending soliloquy from a cell decorated with sketches of the Duomo cathedral in Florence—a place Starling surely hadn't heard of when she left her family sheep farm for the FBI Academy at Quantico—hits home but doesn't derail her. His most famous line, the aggressive posturing about fava beans and good Italian wine, happens when Starling sends a psychological evaluation through the glass and tells him to look at his damn self. We should do the same in the US, where the liberal proponents of Occupy Wall Street are often the same people who think Southerners are inbred and Walmart shoppers slovenly miscreants with no social awareness.

In 1903, Du Bois wrote: "The problem of the Twentieth Century is the problem of the color line." The problem of the twenty-first century is that of the class line.* For the American dream to put its money where its mouth is, we need not just laws ensuring, say, universal dental care but individual awareness of the judgments we pass on people whose teeth—or clothes, waistlines, grocery carts, or limps—represent our worst nightmares.

---

* The echelons of American power have artfully pitted class and race concerns in opposition to one another, to disastrous effect. In the interest of rejecting that false dichotomy, I avoid framing interrelated forms of injustice as separate. Meanwhile, both race and class are specific identities in their own right. While I can recall just one or two readers taking issue with my assertion that "the problem of the twenty-first century is the problem of the class line," the sentiment warrants elucidation. My statement, and the Du Bois statement to which it alludes, names the century in which society will have no choice but to finally, collectively address a system of oppression. While racial injustice remains common in twenty-first-century America, and while Black people, Indigenous people, and other people of color resisted racial injustice for centuries prior, the twentieth century saw a post-slavery United States dismantle Jim Crow laws, give rise to the civil rights movement, codify protections for people of color, and reject White supremacist foundations in cultural ways that still reverberate. Such a moment has not yet arrived for class injustice in this country, but amid historic wealth inequality I believe it will arrive in this twenty-first century.

LEDE, NUTGRAPH, AND BODY

Aeon, 2015

In a newsroom at 30 Rockefeller Plaza, on a June day in 2000, a woman handed me a videotape.

"Log this," she said. Logging tape was a mundane task that made most interns groan, but I regarded it as glamorous. It meant slogging through hours of raw video footage to create a "shot list" of metadata, a time-coded transcription of contents for video-editing purposes. Boring? For some. But just a couple years prior I'd been slopping hogs on my family farm in southern Kansas. Sure, I'd log that tape.

Analogue film remained pervasive in newsrooms and beyond, but technologies were doing what they do—changing. Some of the boxy televisions flashing from newsroom walls had been replaced with flat slabs involving "plasma." At a rooftop party in Brooklyn, the Twin Towers sparkled behind us while a *Dateline* producer showed me her new MP3 player—smaller than her hand and capable of carrying, miraculously, twenty songs plucked from the internet.

Being of a particular class, I didn't have a cell phone or cash for long-distance calls; my first email account was just a couple of years old, and I marveled at sending immediate, digital love letters from Manhattan to my boyfriend in the Midwest while yearning to hear his voice.

Just shy of my twentieth birthday, I'd long intended to be a journalist but wasn't sure what sort. Back at my esteemed journalism school in Kansas, I was a member of the last class of budding reporters receiving a traditional, hard-ass newspaper training before a historic, technology-driven curriculum overhaul took hold. My peers and I would soon get to choose: stay on the reporting-intensive track or shift to the new one tailored to "media convergence"—diversifying know-how across disparate realms of print, TV, and radio suddenly united by the web.

Excited about the internet but sensing something more abiding in story than in the container that transmits it, I'd stay on the "old curriculum."

Nonetheless, that summer I was exploring broadcasting with an internship won via clunky, cordless telephone in my college-town apartment at the end of my sophomore year. I'd called NBC's New York City affiliate and convinced an Emmy-winning investigative reporter-producer duo to put me in its speeding, honking news van. Some days were more newsroom-bound. Following orders, I sat down at a machine and popped in the assigned tape.

The footage showed the recent Puerto Rican Day Parade, which attracts 3 million sweaty people each summer in New York City. The anonymous camera-holder had followed a pack of men strutting about the dense crowd stripping and assaulting dozens of women.

It was a big story, and I held one of the few video copies that would show it to the world. Staring at a TV screen, I stopped and started, stopped and started the tape, creating a second-by-second blueprint for producers who would cut it in the editing bay. What the nation would glimpse that evening as a pared-down, summarized, three-minute package, I watched alone in slow-motion entirety, without censorship. A bright tank top, torn. A brunette woman, raped by fingers of one hand after another. A young man's sweaty upper lip, turned down at the corners. Stretches of quiet when women seemed to accept that no one would help (or could help, as when a husband struggled to reach his wife).

I felt dizzy, physically weakened. The empathy that journalism school taught me to board up tore loose. My body felt a story and responded with what that story required: tears.

The evening news coverage I helped to create wouldn't be the excruciating close-up I'd watched. It would, instead, be a network race to precise data about what racist headlines called a "wilding." How many perpetrators? How many victims? Unacknowledged, uneasy thrills shot about the newsroom as numbers ticked upward: twenty-two, thirty-seven, more than fifty women. Ratings surely would be high too. I ran a designer's rendering of the parade route, labeled with locations and times of the attacks, from one end of the newsroom to the other. What I'd seen as graphic documentation, the nation would see as a graphic.

That's the thing that broke my tough reporter's heart that day with the tape at 30 Rock—not the horror of sexual assault but my awareness of what I was doing with it: clocking it, timing it, reducing it to bullet points for processing, the way that feedlots and fast-food corporations processed the cows who, as newborns, I bottle-fed in my family's farmhouse living room on winter mornings too cold for them to survive outdoors.

It's what my old-school journalism professors lauded as hard news—an apt term for a system that "shoots" video, "breaks" the story, "cuts" to the next shot. It emphasizes political races over candidates' platforms and explosive wars over the reasons behind them. Didactic and linear, its best product is fast, lean fact. Perhaps indicating a telling defensiveness of the shortcomings of this approach, in J-school my peers and I learned never to call ten inches of lede, nutgraph, and body an "article." True journos, we were told, call them "stories."

In the fifteen years since my internship at 30 Rock, technology has facilitated a constant feed of these so-called stories. Today you have probably encountered more news of the world outside your immediate experience than most humans did in an entire lifetime. Did you feel much? Perhaps not. Information without context strikes the mind but peters out before the heart.

When you did feel something from the news, it likely was because you recognized some facet of humanity—you saw your child in a bullet-torn body in Ferguson, Missouri, or your prejudice in the man who pulled the trigger—rather than because the news report itself was humane.

The embarrassing inadequacy of our daily-news structures never was more apparent than when reporters raced to interview traumatized children hours after the shooting at Sandy Hook Elementary School in Newtown, Connecticut, in late 2012. Social media went aflame with outrage on the children's behalf, and journalists themselves expressed qualms; the CNN anchor Anderson Cooper and others chose not to join their colleagues in putting mics in young victims' faces. The broadcast journalist Lauren Ashburn wrote for the *Daily Beast* website: "In my television reporting days, I was as dispassionate as the next news gal . . . But in the wake of what happened in Newtown, it's now clear that too much restraint fails to match the moment when kids are being killed."

We should be suspicious of a news paradigm whose integrity diminishes as story importance increases. Like most, I appreciate the ability to skim headlines, to drink in complicated events that have been watered down. We're busy people, and some news requires haste. But let's be clear: no matter what my journalism professors said, most news stories aren't stories.

I recall my grandfather's response one morning in the nineties, when Grandma explained that the toast he was chewing had been spread with the margarine product I Can't Believe It's Not Butter.

"I sure as hell can," Grandpa replied. Sensing a similar hollowness in some corners of the news media, I realigned my career path toward creating reports that, even if lean on words, might be rich with nuance.

In my first reporting jobs, whether immersing myself in a pack of skinheads or listening to a police scanner at 2 a.m., I seized any chance to write so-called human-interest stories—features that describe problems and triumphs through descriptive anecdotes of individuals rather than statistic-heavy summaries of issues. The divide between the two methods is discernible on my undergraduate diplomas: I'm a bachelor of science in journalism and a bachelor of art in English. To bridge that divide academically, I pursued a master of fine art in nonfiction writing, studying the space where storytelling might be at once factual in content and artistic in form.

Along the way, information went online. Wow, the premillennials among us thought in the early days of the web, our microfiche searches humbled: anything we want is at our fingertips! Possibilities once limited by folded paper and airtime, once corralled by editors and producers, suddenly stretched further than we could see. Like hungry children we walked into an information buffet, making many poor choices as we filled our trays. Now settled into the twenty-first century, our mobile devices pumping an endless feed into our beings, it's time to take a deep breath and look for healthier options.

Page views suggest we crave short, informative text, "click-baited" with images of half-naked or bleeding bodies—even faster variations on the TV sound bites I once helped locate on tape. The marketplace has something to tell us. But to say that the 24/7, quick-and-dirty news cycle exists because people *want* it is incomplete logic. Poor people in a blighted urban food desert—devoid of garden or grocer but riddled with Burger Kings and Dairy Queens—don't consume fast food every day because their bodies are hungry for French fries. They consume it because they're hungry, and fast food is readily available. Its lack of nutrient density often means they have to keep eating, creating a confusing twenty-first-century conundrum for the evolved human body: to be at once obese and malnourished.

In a media landscape of zip-fast reports as stripped of context as a potato might be stripped of fiber, most news stories fail to satiate. We don't consume news all day because we're hungry for information; we consume it because we're hungry for connection. That's the confusing conundrum for the twenty-first-century heart and mind: to be at once overinformed and grasping for meaning.

I've begun college writing classes by asking students to name the first image that comes to mind at the term "atomic bomb." Nearly every answer, every time, is "mushroom cloud." They've seen that black-and-white photograph in high school textbooks alongside brief paragraphs about mass death. But they can't remember much about it. Who dropped the nuclear weapon? What year? In what country and for what reason?

They memorized it all once, but it wasn't relevant enough to their lives to stick.

Then the students read an excerpt from *Hiroshima Diary*, the personal account of the Japanese physician Michihiko Hachiya, who in 1945 was enjoying his quiet garden when he saw a flash of light and found himself naked.

"A large splinter was protruding from a mangled wound in my thigh, and something warm trickled into my mouth," Hachiya wrote. "My cheek was torn, I discovered as I felt it gingerly, with the lower lip laid wide open. Embedded in my neck was a sizable fragment of glass which I matter-of-factly dislodged, and with the detachment of one stunned and shocked I studied it and my blood-stained hand. Where was my wife?"

As he runs to help himself and others, Hachiya sees people moving "like scarecrows, their arms held out from their bodies" to avoid the pain of burnt flesh touching burnt flesh. His attention to fact befits a man of science, but in rendering the sights, sounds, and smells of the bomb's wake, Hachiya is an artist. He relays the tale chronologically and with little judgment, allowing readers to find their own way to meaning.

After reading his account, students look stunned and speak softly. Though generations and continents removed, they recognize Hachiya's fears as their own. "Atomic bomb" has zoomed in from detached concept to on-the-ground reality.

We have the chance now to reach such understandings through digital journalism. Recent years have seen a surge of timely, immersive nonfiction commissioned and relayed by digital media start-ups. In academia, publications such as Harvard's *Neiman Storyboard* showcase narrative nonfiction, and research centers such as Columbia's Tow Center for Digital Journalism examine its exciting new formats.

Creative writing programs in English departments and fine-arts schools increasingly honor nonfiction as a genre alongside fiction and poetry. Such concentrations most often cater to memoir, but a handful of schools now offer robust opportunities in reportage, profile writing, the essay.

However, most journalism schools, about fifteen years after a curriculum shifted beneath my feet, show little sign of seeking the artistic wisdom of creative programs. The most formative course of my college training—a reporting wringer in which each of us wrote five news pieces per week for the lauded student paper but also labored all semester on one in-depth, investigative front-page feature—no longer exists as a core requirement. Today's multimedia training demands surely contributed to that curricular decision, which deprioritizes the craft of in-depth reportage in favor of fast reports.

True story comprises two strands, spiraling: the specific and the universal. The earthly and transcendent, literal and metaphorical, tangible and intangible. The binding agents might be description, setting, structure, metaphor, character development, narrative structure. When merely dispensing information, TV anchors awkwardly interview six-year-old witnesses to shooting rampages, or reporters convey military suicides as tallies in a descending order of deemed significance known as the inverted pyramid. This approach, though sometimes useful, ultimately desensitizes or disturbs us. It fails to match the moment.

At a recent global journalism conference bringing together about a hundred media members from across fields to discuss the future of news, the internet entrepreneur Richard Gingras called for "finding the knowledge in data." Journalists, coders, start-up investors, and storytelling innovators spent the weekend discussing how to tell true stories, connect with audiences, fund journalism, and improve society in the digital age.

The event both gained and suffered from its joining of "web-bies" and "newsies." I found it enlightening to meet members of the former camp. But conversations—with the web monolith Google and the journalism innovator the Knight Foundation as cohosts—were heavy on coding jokes and more centered on delivering "content" to consumers than with questions about quality.

At the opening session, one attendee drew a roomful of loud laughter by introducing himself as Rupert Murdoch, that ultimate pillar of story's simplification, mutilation, and commodification. I had noticed an opposite pillar, of sorts, unassumingly sipping a drink at a table next to mine. When the microphone reached me, I stood and directed attention to her, one of our finest exemplars of crafted, researched, voice-driven nonfiction.

"Hi," I said. "I'm Susan Orlean."

One person laughed: Susan Orlean.

Orlean isn't precious about storytelling's form. She has a new podcast, *Crybabies*, and a prolific Twitter account. But she later told me that she'd shared my sense of being a literary animal in a techy field. She pointed out, though, what everyone was humming about during and between sessions on the digital future of news: *Serial*, the new podcast from producers of audio storytelling juggernaut This American Life. Already the most popular podcast in history, it attempts to unravel, over multiple episodes, an old murder case.

Serial might be problematic in its media ethics (the story centers on a real-life murder, and questions of race and privilege abound), but it has this right: people like a deep, slow-burning narrative, even in the realm of current events.

Such narratives are familiar to us as magazine stories, documentaries, the occasional newspaper series. But they've been secondary, a Sunday supplement to daily news. What if they were primary? What if, by examining our news sources with the same scrutiny we afford food labels, we chose stories that were, in fact, stories? We have now the opportunity to plug our digital devices less into the fast information trough and more into whole stories that better match the moments they describe. With a conscious effort to do so, how might our world change?

Difficult realities would still dominate the news, perhaps, but we'd recognize them as human experiences rather than abstract issues. Nourished by nuance, we wouldn't crave another bite from our cell phones every minute. Our news stories would be no more or less accurate, but they'd be more true—and the human beings they feed, more full.

POVERTY, PRIDE, AND PREJUDICE

NewYorker.com, 2015

As a college senior, I studied and traveled in Western Europe during the fall of 2001, following the September 11 terror attacks. The most memorable of the many political demonstrations that I witnessed was a mess of disemboweled small mammals that I found smeared and strewn on an outdoor ATM in Venice. While I couldn't piece together the details of the protesters' objections with my shaky Italian, it made sense to me that an automated teller might ooze blood from its card slot. I'd grown up poor in Kansas—the sort of poverty that qualifies for welfare, though my proud family didn't apply—and was the first to go off to university. I'd spent my life trembling at banks and in checkout lines, first with childhood caretakers and then as a young adult, over a certain question: Was there enough money in the account? To my mind that fall, the banking machine could well have just eaten a child.

I remembered that ATM in Venice when, in May, Kansas state legislators voted to impose nationally unprecedented and sharply punitive ATM withdrawal limits on welfare recipients. A family of four can receive a maximum of $497 per month from state assistance in Kansas, and perhaps a comparable amount in "food stamp" funds. The money is electronically credited to a state-issued debit card. The pending ATM cap of twenty-five dollars a day would increase the number of withdrawals required to obtain the same amount of money, with each transaction siphoning funds—one dollar to the state's electronic-benefits contractor, in addition to a given machine's standard fee—from public money into private bank coffers. (Even the cash-back option for point-of-sale transactions in Kansas comes with a forty-cent fee after the first two each month.) Compounding the pinch, the limit would effectively be twenty dollars, because few ATMs dispense five-dollar bills.

The withdrawal limit was inscribed in an amendment to a bill, passed earlier this spring, that made Kansas among the twenty-five states with laws restricting the use of benefit cards given to recipients of the federal government's Temporary Assistance for Needy Families (TANF) program. In 2012, the federal government announced that states must prohibit welfare recipients from using the cards in casinos, "adult entertainment venues," and liquor stores. Some states have expanded that list to include firearms or lottery tickets, but the Kansas law goes even further, forbidding expenditures on jewelry, tattoos, massages, spa treatments, lingerie, tobacco, movies, swimming pools, fortune-telling, bail bonds, arcade games, amusement parks, and—that frequent indulgence for families living under the poverty line—ocean cruises.

It was the legislature's latest exhibition of scorn for low-income Kansans, eleven thousand of whom receive public assistance under TANF, and far more of whom rely on public schools and health programs. Since Governor Sam Brownback's historic tax cuts in 2012—which implemented a free-market dream that he shares with two of his longtime campaign funders, Charles and David Koch, of the Wichita-based Koch Industries—Kansas's education and health programs have seen their resources diminished. In May, at least eight public-school districts shut down their institutions early, on the heels of a 2014 state Supreme Court ruling that education allocations were unconstitutionally inadequate. State hospitals are struggling, and federal Medicaid funds for uncompensated care, which totaled $45 million this year, are at risk as long as the state continues to refuse to expand Medicaid coverage in accordance with the Affordable Care Act. To address a general budget shortfall of $400 million, a record-length legislative session dragged into June; that funding impasse was resolved with a bill that raises sales and cigarette taxes (by a hefty fifty cents per pack) while mostly preserving the business income-tax exclusion that has devastated state revenues.

Similar fiscal irresponsibility was evident in the withdrawal-fee amendment. The ATM limits, originally set to take effect on July 1, are on hold while the state Department for Children and Families addresses a federal requirement that TANF beneficiaries have adequate access to funds—more than $100 million in Kansas's case. Should a withdrawal cap pass muster with the US Department of Health and Human Services, the state's electronic-benefits processor, Fidelity National Information Services—which has received incentives to keep a divisional headquarters in Kansas, and presumably has benefited handsomely from the state's business-tax cuts—stands ready to collect the additional fees. It is hard to think of a more twisted irony than a corporate-welfare recipient being paid by a state government to oversee a single mother's access to public-assistance funds.

As James Baldwin wrote, and as much research being

published during this moment of historic wealth inequality demonstrates, it is expensive to be poor. There are the overdraft fees, the maintenance costs of ramshackle houses and cars, the credit-card debt accrued for necessities that low wages don't cover, the interest paid on loans for college educations. Poverty's highest costs are often psychological, though, born of stress and of sociopolitical values that equate financial failures with moral ones. Laws creating barriers between impoverished families and public assistance intended for food and shelter represent a particular form of contempt for the poor—we'll help you, these measures suggest, but we won't trust you with that help. And they are imposed in the pall of hypocrisy and self-interest. Emily Badger, of the *Washington Post*, neatly summed up the institutionalized classism that underlies the new Kansas law:

> *We rarely make similar demands of other recipients of government aid. We don't drug-test farmers who receive agriculture subsidies (lest they think about plowing while high!). We don't require Pell Grant recipients to prove that they're pursuing a degree that will get them a real job one day (sorry, no poetry!). We don't require wealthy families who cash in on the home mortgage interest deduction to prove that they don't use their homes as brothels (because surely someone out there does this). The strings that we attach to government aid are attached uniquely for the poor.*

I once worked as a development director for a social-services agency that provides job training and creative outlets for disadvantaged kids. Every holiday season, the founding director of the organization took up a collection from her staff and asked the social workers to pick a family to receive the gift, which amounted to a few hundred dollars. There was consternation on this point, because the families that most needed the money often were rife with addiction and dysfunction. Some of the staff worried that the cash would be spent on cheap gin and smokes for the parents rather than on new shoes for the kids. Perhaps instead, some suggested, we should purchase a gift card to ensure that the money would buy groceries, or make a rent payment directly to the family's landlord. I considered that they might be right. But our boss insisted that the gift be given as cash, with no strings attached. What the family did with it was their business, she said.

I recalled then the difference between how I felt, as a child, when I showed my free-lunch card at school—in line, my cheeks would burn, and I often chose to skip lunch rather than display my poverty—and how I felt, as a young adult, when I deposited need-based scholarship checks into my bank account at the beginning of college semesters. After making those deposits, every August and January for four years, I would go to what my family calls "a sit-down restaurant," eat a big meal, and leave a big tip. By the end of the semester, I'd be living on eggs and discount-bin bread, but for the moment I had a thousand dollars to my name and a twenty-dollar bill in my wallet. When I paid for my meal with cash—"I don't need any change," I relished telling the waitress, whose tired look I understood well—I felt not just fed but free.

LINGUISTIC NOTICE FOR HOMO SAPIENS HERETOFORE KNOWN AS "PUSSIES" AND "LITTLE BITCHES"

McSweeney's, 2015

Since the Pleistocene, when you tagged along on mammoth-hunting expeditions and complained about the flaps in your sealskin booties coming loose and the snow freezing your sensitive little tootsies, you have been among us. In those early days, when the survival of Homo sapiens hinged upon physical grit, your bullshit endangered our very lives. Dudes were lifting their spears, running toward woolly beasts—*their* feet weren't warm either, mind you—while you were a safe distance behind, mumbling that you had something in your eye. Lest your feeble ass get the rest of the pack killed, they needed a word for you, a way to communicate what you are.

While we couldn't have known it then, at this linguistic juncture our young species faced a conundrum as political as your fragility was burdensome. The hunters did the best they could. They asked themselves, what represents the smallest and weakest among us?

The *ladies*, they thought.

To be sure, woman humans could be quite swift; have impressive aim with a dart; spend entire days on their feet processing carcasses into hides, meals, and tools; and survive newborn Homo sapiens craniums tearing through their bleeding perinea. Heck, over in the Neanderthal camp, boss cave-femmes went hunting and cave-gents made clothes. But, smaller than their male counterparts as a rule, woman humans couldn't shoulder as many supplies into a hunt or drag as much bleeding meat back to camp. While powerful with finesse, endurance, and childbearing, they generally weren't to be called upon for tasks of brutish violence.

So, while packing for one fateful, perilous journey into the blowing snow, man humans looked over at you, clutching your upset tummy. One of them nodded your way and whispered, "Oog isn't going, is he? He's a fucking pussy." Another agreed, "That little bitch is staying here."

Such gendered pejoratives would suffice with little challenge until well into the next epoch. Now, however, like wisdom teeth and chest hair, they no longer benefit a species whose Holocene survival has less to do with mastodon-slaying, meat-gnashing, and blizzard-hiking than with mental acumen. It turns out woman humans have that in spades—at least as much as do man humans—and they're just kind of *over* being on the crap side of a gender-binary metaphor, especially when so many of them have been on the crap side of a gender-binary reality.

One such woman human we might call "Me" recalls a pickup game of H.O.R.S.E. in a Kentucky gym where she shot hoops after spending long newsroom shifts being ostracized by an otherwise entirely male, entirely dull copy desk. She'd spent hours rescuing man-wrought infinitives from splitting and modifiers from dangling, and she just wanted to cash some jumpers, do you know what I mean? Then a stranger, a middle-aged man human with his son in tow, showed up.

"Game of H.O.R.S.E?" man human said.

"Sure!" Me said.

They fired free throw after free throw and, as the game wound down, each had four misses and thus carried the dreaded count, "H.O.R.S."

Me stepped up to the line, dribbled the ball. She aimed, sank it.

Man human stepped up to the line, dribbled. He aimed. If he missed, that would be game.

"Dad," boy human said, "if you lose to a girl, you're not my dad anymore."

Me felt kind of sorry for man human. But then she remembered an entire service station being scandalized the previous week when she topped off the oil in her car, and she thought, *Fuck that noise. Miss it.*

The shot went up.

BRICK.

Boy human stomped toward the gym door and slammed its metal handle like a little—well, you know.

"Good game," Me said to man human and reached out her hand.

But man human left her hanging, turned, and walked out like a—I'm not sure what, and here's the trouble.

We need for you a new word, one that denotes weaknesses detrimental to important twenty-first-century tasks such as shaking hands after a loss or finding milk in its natural habitat, the refrigerator, without asking, "Honey, where is the milk?" "Pussy," "little bitch," "sissy," "pantywaist," "little girl," "like a girl," and all vulva correlatives will no longer stand, even among those of us who have bandied such terms ironically heretofore. Conversely, the figurative having of "a pair," "balls," "nads," and all other scrotum correlatives will no longer do for denoting merit.

Your kind appears in all gender forms, and language will catch up to you. We haven't found the word just yet. But know that Me is hunting for it.

BELIEVE IT

Creative Nonfiction, **2015**

In any social order, you will know the powerful by who is believed and the subjugated by who is doubted. Today in America, for instance, a woman who accuses a celebrity of rape is presumed to be seeking money and attention, and a dark-skinned man who insists he's minding his own business is wrestled to the ground by police officers when a White finger points his way. Meanwhile, a White male news anchor's inflated battlefield tales are piped, unchecked, into millions of living rooms amid network negotiations for a multimillion-dollar contract renewal.

Perhaps it's no coincidence, then, that the most democratic of nonfiction genres—memoir, in which any citizen might be the ultimate authority on her own experience—is the one most scrutinized for veracity. The accuracy of memoir, for centuries the sport of affluent White men, became of grave concern around the time that women, racial minorities, and the poor stopped dipping mops into buckets long enough to dip quills into inkpots. Until the eighteenth century, Ben Yagoda writes in *Memoir: A History*, "truth was of a general quality; it wouldn't have occurred to anyone that every detail happened precisely as described." Yagoda ascribes the shift toward more modern sensibilities to *Robinson Crusoe*—initially presented as nonfiction, soon unmasked as fiction. But our collective fixation on memory's fallibility and truth's subjectivity also became fashionable just as formerly silenced groups gained the freedom and literacy to document their lives.

Crying "Fiction!" is often a convenient first line of self-defense against stories that blow the whistle on unjust structures. Men balk at women recounting harassment, White people insist racism is over, and the wealthy discount tales of poverty not just because they can't fathom realities they haven't witnessed firsthand but because those narratives threaten systems from which they benefit. Belief is a choice, however unconscious, and it self-sustains: we believe what serves our purposes, and the world we're thus open to seeing validates those beliefs.

In my German-Catholic farming community, we believed in Jesus. The crucifixion story, in particular, resonated: someone had given up his body for a cause. Jesus suffered on a cross for someone else's soul, and we suffered in wheat fields for someone else's bread—maybe even for the wafers we accepted on our tongues after priests transformed it into the body of Christ.

Some features of Jesus's story were more difficult to swallow—his dark skin, say, or the oil-rich deserts of a Middle East to which we'd soon send our small-town children with Stealth bombers. He had been rendered White on the crucifix and, like us, came from peasants. Near the altar of our tiny country church rested a sculpted scene of carpenter Joseph, teenage Mary, and the baby Jesus. When I was very small, I thought my dad, who built houses for a living, was Joseph; my grandfather had hammered together the steeple above us and carved the Communion rail from a walnut tree on our land. Females weren't allowed to stand, let alone preach, at the altar beyond that rail; at the nearby Pietà, dusted with care by elderly women, I recognized in Mary's face the emotional anguish of my mother, who became pregnant with me at seventeen.

Not unlike how statues of Brown people were made White to enhance their credibility, Sojourner Truth's dictated testimony of slavery went to press with "Certificates of Character," provided by such upstanding White men as her former owner, John Dumont.

"This is to certify, that Isabella, this colored woman, lived with me since the year 1810, and that she has always been a good and faithful servant; and the eighteen years that she was with me, I always found her to be perfectly honest," Dumont wrote for the 1850 text dictated by Truth. "I have always heard her well spoken of by every one that has employed her."

Harriet Jacobs, whose *Incidents in the Life of a Slave Girl* was, in 1861, the first published "slave narrative" actually written by a Black woman, knew her burden of proof all too well. She wrote in the preface:

> *Readers be assured this narrative is no fiction. I am aware that some of my adventures may seem incredible; but they are, nevertheless, strictly true. I have not exaggerated the wrongs inflicted by Slavery; on the contrary, my descriptions fall far short of the facts.*

Jacobs's sympathetic editor, Lydia Maria Child, forewent blurbs from male landowners but, in her introduction, told readers that Jacobs lived for seventeen years "with a distinguished family in New York and has so supported herself as to be highly esteemed by them. . . . I believe those who know her will not be disposed to doubt her veracity, though some incidents in her story are more romantic than fiction." (Child did also publish fictionalized slave narratives, an important literary genre.)

Child's introduction went on to address another barrier to credulity: negative assumptions about the storyteller's capabilities. "It will naturally excite surprise that a woman reared in slavery should be able to write so well," she wrote. She explained that a mistress had taught Jacobs to read and write in childhood, that Jacobs was now in the mix with smart Northerners, and that "nature endowed her with quick perceptions"—a bold assessment, at the time, for a White person to make of a Black woman.

More than a century and a half later, memoirs from underprivileged ranks continue to challenge readers' credulity. Linda Tirado, whose online account of missing teeth and government peanut butter went viral, received a torrent of support but also a fast backlash of accusations. For some, Tirado's handful of unearthed advantages—say, grandparents who sent her to an expensive school—rendered her poverty tale a scam. They couldn't reconcile what Tirado's subsequent 2014 book, *Hand to Mouth: Living in Bootstrap America*, shows: class isn't static or definitive. More vexing, for many, than Tirado's message was the messenger herself; her brilliance challenges the widespread understanding of financial struggle as the result of stupidity and laziness.

Skepticism's friendly cousin is amazement, and even sympathetic readers sometimes reveal their prejudices through laudatory wonder. "This book is so good I thought about sending it out for a back-up opinion. . . . It's like finding Beethoven in Hoboken," Molly Ivins wrote in her review of Mary Karr's 1995 memoir, *The Liars' Club*. "To have a poet's precision of language and a poet's instinct into people applied to one of the roughest, ugliest places in America is an astonishing event." Astonishing, maybe, to readers of the *Nation*. Mary Karr knows that Groves, Texas, is lousy with poets of the highest order.

Such surprise over a writer's abilities is a stone's throw from distrust over her ideas, as acknowledged by a blogger reviewing Jeannette Walls's 2005 blockbuster memoir, *The Glass Castle*: "I can't help but wonder if [Walls] fabricated some elements of her life story in her memoir. . . . Not because in the wake of the James Frey scandal, I am immediately suspicious of all memoirists, or because I think all non-fiction writers automatically take some liberties with the truth, but because her life is so incredibly amazing, I cannot imagine experiencing some of the things she describes and coming out with my sanity, let alone my sense of humor, intact."

Memoirists from least-heard places are accustomed to suspicion (the Americans among them enjoying the protections of the Constitution, which places the burden of proof on the plaintiff in defamation suits). Yet, the most infamous abuse of contemporary memoir readers' trust—the Frey scandal—came from the affluent, White, male author of *A Million Little Pieces*. As when Brian Williams was revealed to have lied about being aboard a helicopter shot down during the 2003 US invasion of Iraq, the controversy gave rise to a million forgiving discussions about the ambiguity of memory and the creative pursuit of emotional truth.

Mary Karr told the *Paris Review* in 2009, "It pissed me off when I saw James Frey on *Larry King* saying, 'You know, there's a lot of argument about the distinction between fiction and nonfiction.' You know what? There isn't. If it didn't happen, it's fiction. If it did happen, it's nonfiction."

Objective hardship hones a keen sense of the difference, and those for whom reality has been the least pleasant are often the most loyal to its preservation.

"I've been vigorously encouraged by various editors," Karr said in the same interview, "to fictionalize. . . . And I remember reading that Vivian Gornick said to her students, 'Just make it up, and see if it's true.' Bullshit."

The most poignant aspect of Frey's fabrications was that his internal pain apparently outstripped external causes he could offer for explaining it. A White guy from the suburbs—what did he have to moan about? Plenty, perhaps, and we know this not by the content of his life but by the agony with which he rendered it. Paradoxically, the revelation of the book's embellishments created, for the author, a dramatic true story of punishment and shame.

This, perhaps, is the deepest challenge in articulating and considering the stories of our lives: not that they force us to admit our privileges but that they force us to admit our suffering. If we see something, it must be real, and some realities hurt to look at. Therefore, our harshest critics are often those with whom we share the most common ground.

The first person I heard say she didn't believe Anita Hill was my hard-luck grandma, a longtime employee of the courts system who herself had experienced considerable sexual discrimination and harassment—though it would be decades before she spoke of it. Frank McCourt's few but staunch detractors, in the wake of his Pulitzer Prize–winning 1996 memoir, *Angela's Ashes*, included people from his native Limerick. When, in my own writing, I bear witness to my native class's woes of circumstance, the only discrediting I fear is from my own family—many of whom handle remarkable circumstances by deeming them unremarkable and by projecting their pain onto history's most famous martyr. If they believed what Karr's daddy said, that "Jesus is a trick on poor people," they might experience a reckoning with grief and injustice so profound that Christ would climb off the cross and start marching in the streets.

In matters of truth, much has been said of the memoirist's responsibility in wielding accuracy; much less has been said of the reader's responsibility in wielding belief. Belief is a form of reverence; disbelief, a form of rejection. Both can be destructive when unexamined: blind faith might give power where it's not due, while blind doubt might strip away power where it's needed most. Whether we stick out our tongues to deny or savor another person's claims, the revelation is about ourselves.

In one such revelation, I decided as a young adult that Catholicism was no longer for me. Around the same time, the church changed too: girls could serve at the altar. One needn't believe in a church's tenets to be moved by the efforts of its parishioners; even after I stopped taking Communion, I sometimes went to Mass to marvel at the new altar girls— white-robed and ponytailed, carrying gifts where someday they might even be priests.

Belief and doubt are inevitably selfish things. But beyond our limited ability to judge a story is something transcendent: our ability to receive it. Memoirists aren't making an argument. They're making an offering.

THE FIRST PERSON ON MARS

Vela, 2015

Somewhere near Kazakhstan, the 1980s: At nighttime, sur-
rounded by goats, a little girl lay on her back in a pasture and
pointed a small telescope toward the stars. Of all the places in
the sky, she focused on a steady, defined, crimson dot—easily
identified as a hunk of rock among blinking stars. The planet
Mars. She had one dream: to be the first person to walk on it.

So goes the premise of "Evghenia Is on Mars," the Twitter
account of a self-proclaimed female scientist who purports to
communicate with Earth from the red planet. Revealed in short
bursts of broken English, it's an "account" in the best sense of
the word: a plot-rich tale of an engaging character with a strong
voice and a triumphant arc.

Growing up on her grandma's goat farm, Evghenia gave
her life to studying and training for a voyage to Mars. She was
born under Soviet rule, Twitter followers can piece together, and
came of age in the wake of the dissolved superpower that beat

the United States to outer space—forces that surely shaped her as she assembled a ramshackle rocket of car parts and salvaged pieces from a nuclear dump. ("Every year from age of six I ask grandmother for rocket fuel for my birthday," she has tweeted.) Then, last year, around age thirty, Evghenia loaded her space jalopy with protein bars and poetry books and launched herself into the heavens. Four months later, according to her story, she landed on Mars. Like a hungry immigrant in a galactic land rush, the farm-girl pioneer beat government space programs and billionaire space-travel investors to stake an entire planet.

That's usually where the movie ends: the victorious arrival that would seem to conclude a journey. But Evghenia's Twitter account begins there, already on Mars—from atop the proverbial mountain instead of at the bottom, from the achieved destination rather than from the humble start. Thus, her musings often convey not a gazing forward to some goal but a gazing back at her origins.

"Favourite childshood memory: lie in paddock of goats at night with telescopes," she once tweeted of her childhood, "and look at Mars and think of how I will be on it first." She was raised, she says, by a tough, loving sage of a grandma whom she misses dearly and after whom she has named Martian mountains and caves. "If you see my grandmother please for to tell her that I just did 103 pushup in a row," Evghenia has tweeted. "I beated her record."

Somewhere in Kansas, the 1980s: At nighttime, surrounded by cows, a little girl lay on her back in a pasture. She had no telescope but sharp vision. She watched the sky and imagined being lifted from Earth—flying out her farmhouse bedroom window, zooming in flight across sparkling nighttime cityscapes

*she'd seen only in movies. She knew reaching them would mean
going where no one from her family had gone before.*

So went my life. It was my grandparents' farm, and I first
lived there when I was three, in the early 1980s. Through that
icy winter, my dad hammered together a house for us a few
dirt miles away during the day; at night, my young parents and
I nuzzled together on a stained mattress. I relished sharing a
bed there with them—a tactile memory that endures, perhaps,
because touch between my young mother and me was rare,
just as it might have been rare for my mother when Grandma
Betty was the teenaged parent. That winter, Mom and Dad
made my brother, Matt. The old ladies at Sunday Mass had
thought I myself would be a boy, Mom later remembered. I
kicked low in the womb, near the pelvis, rearing for a chance
to tear free.

When my dad, Nick, finished building our house, which
stood between a wheat field and a lake, we moved off my
grandparents' farm. My mom, Jeannie, was often cruel and
unhappy in those years, my dad frequently drunk. Mom felt
trapped, it seemed, but not for long; she never lost the gypsy
spirit she inherited growing up. Her biological dad was a dangerous figure who was in and out, but mostly out. By the time
Betty married a farmer and settled down when Jeannie was
a teenager, the mother-daughter pair had changed addresses
nearly fifty times. Just over a decade later, Mom and Dad split
(I was turning nine, and Matt was four), and all of us went
on the move. I'd rack up twenty residences before I finished
high school.

Throughout those moves, fortunately for me, the farm
remained a constant: the 1910 house of concrete block painted
white, the rows of hay bales full of snake holes, the metal shed

containing sharp objects, the cats lapping blood from the cement floor of an outbuilding where we butchered cows and pigs. It wasn't a safe place, but it was a fun one, with wide spaces into which I often disappeared for long stretches, unmissed and happily feral.

One weekend night at the farmhouse in the late eighties, my cousin Shelly and I sat next to an open single-pane window upstairs while grown-ups drank beer and Canadian whiskey in the kitchen. Outside the old metal screen, moths died trying to reach the light bulb above us. Even air had trouble coming through the screen—heavy and warm, no wind to move it—but still we breathed more easily there than in the loud cigarette-smoke cloud downstairs. We sat cross-legged, our ankles stuck to our sweaty thighs, on a twin bed that sat high off the wood floor on a creaking metal frame bought at a farm sale. The wrinkled quilt was strewn with generic candy, Uno cards, and a Hoyle deck so soft from hundreds of hands of call-your-partner pitch that it felt like sand when I shuffled it into a bridge. When Shelly and I finished playing cards we opened a big hardback book called *Ripley's Believe It or Not*.

Shelly, four years older than I was, usually didn't care about books. She liked this one, though, which made me happy, that we could share liking a book. In my parents' tense households, or at the elementary school in the small town where Dad unloaded wheat at the co-op on Main Street, books were my teachers and friends. This one had pictures of constellations and extraterrestrials, sea monsters and pyramids, circles seared into crops—recalling for me the time Dad called me outside to watch a mysterious light move back and forth in the night sky above our wheat fields.

I read aloud from the book as though I were giving a report. Shelly and I pointed a flashlight out the window and aimed binoculars at the night sky as we consulted our revelatory text. Our eyes widened while we whispered "whoaaaa" about alien visitors and the paranormal myths of the twentieth century.

"Aaaooooo!!" a drunken grown-up let loose somewhere downstairs, followed by a big group laugh.

Shelly crawled over the candy and cards and turned off the light so we could see outside better. We let our eyes adjust.

Beneath our window was the swimming pool that, when I was a toddler, Grandpa Arnie had dug out with a tractor scoop, and for which my dad had poured the surrounding concrete. In the darkness, the water had the moon in it.

Beyond the pool was a row of coniferous trees planted to block the brutal, year-round Kansas wind; we couldn't see them in the dark, but we could hear them take the wind through their needles and exhale a long shhhhhhh.

Beyond the trees, farther west, was the field where I helped Grandpa feed the cattle that congregated in fenced corners or at the edge of the pond, where lurked snapping turtles, black snakes, and spent rubber tractor tires.

Half a mile beyond that, just across the blacktop that led north to Amish country or south to the fine red dirt of Oklahoma, was the tiny Catholic church we attended. During Mass, grown-ups in Wranglers and home-sewn dresses clutched rosaries and sang of praise, but in the low vibration of their voices I could hear what they truly felt: a heavy burden.

"LOOK—what is that?" Shelly whispered. We watched something—a light—move above the shadowed trees, more quickly than we could track. Like a sun-sized light bulb, it lit up the vista of drought and cow, tree and pool. Then it receded in a blink, and the sky went back to dark.

What are the odds that one would see a spaceship while reading about spaceships? Had our minds been so impressionable that together we conjured a reality from a book? Probably. But it was a reality all the same. An electric feeling ran through us. We joked about aliens—they came, they saw, they didn't want to abduct our broke-ass family—and I laughed so hard I peed my shorts and ruined the playing cards under my sweaty legs.

I discovered the supposed space-feed about Evghenia last spring and was taken by the parallels between her story and mine. I'm hardly the first person on Mars, but I was the first person from my family to go to college. Grandpa Arnie quit school after sixth grade to work his dad's wheat farm, Grandma Betty left after ninth, my mom got a GED, my dad got a high school diploma. That I eventually would become a university professor amounted to something like interplanetary travel.

Beyond such a metaphorical resonance, Ev and I share literal commonalities: long blond hair (as she's pictured in her Twitter profile), a love of science, wayfaring parents, a beloved grand-mother for a caregiver, having been "borned in place of flat land and grasses," a matriarchal working-class family in which men come and go and women name their daughters after themselves. And we both know a thing or two about striking out alone.

For companionship on Mars, Evghenia reports, she fashioned a quirky robot named Goatbot—sort of Pixar's Wall-E in the form of livestock—that evokes the dominant animal of her Earth home. (I too have distinct goat memories, if less sentimental. One of ours stuck his head through an open pickup window and ate my dad's construction paycheck off the dashboard; another time, he tried stomping my toddler self with his devil hooves while my laughing family ran to get the camera.) When I started writing this story, I went into a dive bar along the Kansas River on a whim, and hanging on the wall was a piece of art for sale called *Goat*. The image involved a giant goat head against an outer space background—purple, Ev's favorite color—including moons, planets, and a cartoonish rocket ship with hologram sparkles trailing behind it. I bought it, of course.

While following Evghenia's reports and musings, I've often thought that she and I would be good friends. So one day, I replied to one of her tweets.

"What your favorit movies," Evghenia wrote. "My is that one of a woman who fly to mars alone and is there on it first. Wait that my life."

"Same," I tweeted back. "You're a genius."

Having seen that I'm a journalist, apparently, she replied, "Dearest sarahs. if for want make it firstest interview with first person on mars email onmarsfirst@hotmail.com."

Intrigued and amused, I sent an email, and she replied in her Twitter persona (and never wavered from it in weeks of correspondence): "Yes you are the person who can tell it my story for Earth humans because our story is very same in some ways. You is first to become famous and great writer of your town. I am first become first on mars of my town (and whole planets Earth)."

My grandparents' Kansas farmhouse was far enough into the countryside, away from city lights, that on moonless summer nights the Milky Way glowed like a ghost ship heading my way. I wrote short stories about visitors from other planets; one, printed in my fifth-grade class's annual magazine, involved setting off homemade bombs in an alley with my all-male pack of friends until a tiny alien, glowing red, accidentally flew up my nose. To me, the story wasn't scary but hilarious, an adventure worth longing for.

It wasn't that I disliked where I was or the people I was

with. I just knew on some level I was meant to leave—a knowing rooted, perhaps, in the pain of never quite being understood.

My closest friend in elementary school lived a mile down our dirt road in an A-frame house, and we'd walk to meet each other in the dust and explore the tall cattails of water-filled ditches along fields. Once, I mentioned to her that I sometimes narrated my own actions in my head, in real time—thinking everyone did this. She gave me a confused look. Another time, I told a school friend that I sensed a different animal in everyone in our class; her laugh told me that this too was strange (she wanted to know her animal, though, and seemed disappointed when I offered that she was a bear). These reveries suggest the cliché of the antisocial "nerd," but I was outgoing and friendly; I doubt my childhood pals would remember me as the strange thing I deep down felt myself to be. I wasn't an outcast but something less revocable: a true outlier.

The chasm was in my own family as well. Once I asked my mom if she knew what I meant by feeling the very edge of a thought and needing to stay in the feeling to reach the thought. She considered this seriously and said, "No." When I was in middle school and hadn't yet learned how to hide my mind, I overheard my grandma at the bottom of the farmhouse stairs talking about me to a friend on our rotary phone: "Half the time I don't understand what she's saying." That even she—the funny, kind, energetic forty-something who so often had taken me in, the person with whom I felt the most comfortable bond in my family—on some level didn't "get" me was devastating, and I cried silently at the top of the steps.

Then there were the substances—mostly booze and smokes, but much harder drugs beyond my immediate family—that sometimes carried them even further away. I didn't feel like I was so odd as if to be from Mars; rather, I often felt I was more grounded on Earth than anyone around me.

In sixth grade I moved altogether back to the farm, into the same bedroom where my parents and I had snuggled when I was small, the one with the chimney collapsing into the closet. Mom and Dad had other places and partners—often mean, sad ones, and when Grandma Betty asked if I'd like to move in with her and Grandpa, I said yes. Mom had custody of me and Matt then, and she said yes too. Matt stayed behind, and I joined them or my dad in Wichita most weekends and over summers, but throughout adolescence the farm was my permanent address. I turned into a woman in that farmhouse west of Wichita, my bedroom walls covered with posters and magazine covers of *The X-Files*.

One night in 1996, just after school let out in May (the countdown to my August birthday—sweet sixteen—already underway on a Renaissance-angel wall calendar), I was wiping dust from my farm-sale dresser when a cool, damp breeze moved from one open window to the other. I felt every hair on my arms. I looked out the window at the night sky. That year, every home had a print of Van Gogh's *Starry Night*, every tchotchke was celestial, every key chain represented a Zodiac sign. My drugstore perfume was called Sun Moon Stars, its bottle the color of night with a round gold cap. In coming months I'd tape to my dresser mirror a magazine ad for something I couldn't afford, a new Chanel nail polish called Ciel du Nuit, a dark blue with flecks of silver glitter.

At that moment, as I was holding my dusting rag and smelling the air, a pop song unlike anything I'd ever heard came across my boom-box radio. It was three chords over and over, like a country song, and it sounded like locusts and mud holes, a bass line and what I thought was a man's voice. I hoped the DJ would give the singer's name rather than roll right into another song. He did, and I was delighted to find that the deep-voiced singer was actually a woman. "Give me one reason to stay here," she sang in what, to my ears, was a rhetorical tone. The song was timely, because my longing to fly away—to be seen, heard, understood, I hoped, in cities of opportunity—had become a fever, my books and movies about pioneering women striking out on adventures a conceptual map in my mind.

That summer, I'd leave home for the first time. My family wasn't of a class that sent kids to camp; for us, summer meant harvesting wheat and peddling firecrackers from a roadside tent for extra cash. But I'd gotten a scholarship to attend an academic honors academy at the University of Kansas a few hours north. Grandma Betty bought me a battery-operated handheld fan to battle the humid summer, and I packed it alongside my journals and stuffed lion. We didn't have air-conditioning at the farmhouse, so I knew I'd fare better than some kids in the old college dormitories. The journeys for which I'd long prepared, if inadvertently, by reading books and hammering out stories on a yard-sale typewriter, were beginning.

The camp's theme that year was astronomy. More impressive to me than my textbooks about the stars, though, was the setting in which I carried them. For a month I lived in the dorm with teenagers whose families spoke languages perhaps never uttered in the small town where I went to high school. Our core course, Anthropology of the Nighttime Sky, was held in the lecture hall of a grand, limestone structure on a hill, and taught by a Zen Buddhist who was emerging as the eminent Homer translator in the world—a different animal from any man I'd ever known. He and the other students used the language I'd stifled in classrooms back home: the language of books. I learned new words, like "epistemology." A ruddy-faced girl with long, reddish hair stood up in the back of the lecture hall one class period and said, "I mean, what if we're all living inside a giant chicken?" I was enthralled.

But, for all my intellectual wonder, even on a college campus I was a thing apart. Most of the city kids there, it turned out, smoked dope the way my country friends at home drank beer; in both places I had too much at stake to act my age and had never felt my age anyway. I gave myself not to dorm-room parties but to the academic tasks I organized in the camp-issue folder. Like our camp-issue T-shirts, it was midnight blue, printed with a gold-ink version of the Flammarion engraving—the famous image of a man kneeling at the edge of the cosmos, his head ripping through to a vaster dimension by way of knowledge.

Our professor took us to the university football field at night with flashlights, binoculars, star charts. We craned our heads and together found the same spot in the sky: From the North Star, look left. See that little cluster that looks like a triangle? See that square? A little right. A little left and down. While many students groaned I approached this and all assignments with fervor. Impressed, the professor took me and only me to the top of the unlighted football stadium to learn more constellations through a telescope. I felt uncomfortable but wasn't sure why; my naivete allowed me to believe I'd been chosen for this extracurricular moment solely for my mind.

I had to leave camp early for my next adventure, which took me thousands of miles away from Kansas: the national level of a communications contest that I'd qualified for by taking tests in a high school organization called Future Business Leaders of America. The national competition that year was in New York City, a place my family had never been. Grandma Betty and Grandpa Arnie drove hours across Kansas to take me from the university campus where the camp was hosted to the Kansas City airport.

On the way to New York, my small band of teachers and

students would fly first to Philadelphia, then take a bus to Washington, DC. These, I felt, were places I was long overdue, huge places where huge things happened. Of all the things I sensed about the world that summer, I sensed nothing more strongly than the size of things and the space between them. They were big or small, close or far.

The places that called to me were the big and far ones, even as the night sky reminded me that I was small, smaller than the man-made satellites that eventually fall like rocks into our oceans. I'd spent my childhood pretending to touch faraway things, skipping rocks across our pasture pond, where the night's sky was reflected. Now, instead of reflections in library books or movies or cattle-watering holes, I wanted real, tangible things. That meant traveling where no woman from my family had walked: a graduation stage, a college campus, a sober life, an exit from childhood without a baby of my own.

When the summer ended, my junior year in high school nigh, my grandparents picked me up at the airport. I could see how much they'd missed me. I'd missed them too. They, my parents, and my little brother had mailed cards and letters; we'd talked only a few times all summer, across landlines between the farm and a dorm lobby. But what did we speak of during the long, cigarette-smoke-filled drive back to the farm? Not Homer. Not the celestial origins of ancient myth. Not Broadway. Not epistemology. The amorphous strangeness I'd lived with my whole life now had discernible shape, the distance between me and my family not larger but more perceptible. We didn't talk about where I was going, but we all knew that I would go.

Unusual destinations require unusual routes, and an unusual route is by definition an unpopulous one. Big or unorthodox goals therefore require a trade-off: the closer you get to them, the farther you are from other people—if not in terms of geography, then in terms of understanding. With whom could Neil Armstrong, first person on the moon, share memories of walking in lunar dust? Very few people—but only he will ever be first. The more exceptional the achievement, the more supreme the trade-off. With whom might Oprah, who journeyed from poor, rural Mississippi to historic heights of media influence, specifically relate? Only one person—Oprah—who I'd wager has grappled with loneliness despite a career built, ironically, on her relatability.

The people lonely at the top by way of its sparse population were probably lonely at the bottom for different reasons. One who takes a strange road likely was strange to her home. Her disconnect from her tribe—by intellect, interests, spirit, or something else—is what propelled her into the journey, perhaps, and her ability to tolerate the discomfort of loneliness is precisely what qualified her to get where few can go. To be emotionally apart, somehow, from one's family or hometown is to live in constant awareness of contrast between oneself and the very group in which one most naturally might belong. For all the love in the world, that belonging can never be fully achieved. But in the space where it might have been, something rarer has a chance to grow: a deep, indelible knowing of one's individual power. If you can survive a gulf with the very womb that brought you, you can survive the gulf between the comfort of the familiar and the terror of any unknown, between where you came from and where you're going.

People ask me about my socioeconomic border-crossings, *Weren't you afraid to do that?* Frankly, no. Alcoholism, verbal abuse, and intermittent neglect—symptoms of poverty's profound stresses—among the people I love most? That was scary. Repeating those cycles was so unthinkable to me that I only considered alternatives. My ambitions were so strong that I had no choice but to let them steer me.

Along the way, my family neither encouraged nor discouraged me but rather just let me be—a rare gift, I learned, compared to many more "successful" families who smothered their children with expectations. Often I didn't share what I was up to at school, for lack of common ground, but when awards ceremonies came around my parents and grandparents showed up with cards and hugs. They took pictures with pride.

While my goals and destinations didn't scare me, space debris often threatened me in reaching them. First, there was my own ignorance and a lackadaisical high school guidance counselor busy coaching the boys' track team. En route to college, I knew only to keep straight As and tally a list of leadership roles; before the internet era's accessible information troves, I applied to one school—the state university where I'd attended the honors academy, the most prominent school whose registrar was within reach. Once I got to college, I still didn't know what "graduate school" meant by my senior year, but I was encouraged by professors to apply.

Other people's ignorance was perhaps harder to get past. In grad school, in an Ivy League classroom, some peers made fun of my cultural references; at a television network where I was an intern, a producer suggested that my "daddy" had gotten me the gig. Still, there wasn't room to sit around feeling insecure or frustrated. There was only room for another step forward—steps that eventually landed me gigs as a successful journalist, an English professor, a homeowner, a mentally and physically healthy, happy person. As Evghenia once tweeted, quoting Kansas's favorite daughter: "Amelia Earhart: 'The most effective way to do it is to do it.' Evghenia: 'I flew to Mars in a rocketship I build it myself and on it first.'"

One needn't attend astronomy camp to know Mars is the planet we've long associated with would-be alien life-forms. In the 1960s, at the height of our social investment in and cultural preoccupation with space, "Martian" was synonymous with "alien." We still use the planet to represent strangeness or lack of relatability. For instance, "He looked at me like I was from Mars." Earth is home—blue as the blood in our veins appears. It's an anagram for "heart," nearly all of the word "hearth." Mars, meanwhile, is the color of blood spilled, its landscape potentially harboring life yet perilous for a human being.

An astrologer once told me I had in my natal chart the rare planetary aspects of "starseed"—New Age–speak for souls fresh to Earth, maybe after lifetimes on other worlds, while most spirits have been recycling as energy on this watery planet for millennia. While I don't believe or disbelieve the details of this or any other story about unknowable things, the general theme felt so right that it sent a jolt through my body. *Yes!* the goose bumps on my neck shouted. *I'm an alien on Earth!* Indeed, I realized recently, you can't spell my last name without "mars" in the middle.

But my name, Smarsh, couldn't be more humbly rooted in this planet. It means mushroom, perhaps for mushroom foragers that were my paternal ancestors in Central Europe—Prussian stretches of a Germanic region a couple thousand miles west of where Evghenia grew up.

I am, of course, a human being, but one who has long sensed that we're all less-containable things too. Walking on the earth with that particular feeling—an all-encompassing awareness that can't be measured, as can smell or sight—is at once wondrous and difficult. Growing up, I was so sensitive that I could hear in my friends' voices fears, desires, cruelties, and joys they didn't know they had. I enjoyed a robust popularity that entailed student government and homecoming ceremonies, but I often chose to be alone rather than stand next to the unconscious, precarious storm that is many human psyches. A psychologist once told me—saying, perhaps, the same thing as the astrologer but with a PhD—"You came in at a different frequency."

Emitting that strange frequency, I've learned how far a signal might have to travel before it's heard. I spent most of my childhood feeling like there was an actual lump in my throat; our German-Catholic farm-scape tamped emotional expression and often shamed aspirations in a place where it's safer not to dream. It's no surprise, then, that I relieved my throat by becoming a writer—a one-woman transmitter of the stories of my people, like an explorer on a dusty planet with a microbe-detector made of tinfoil.

So too is Evghenia an overt hustler of her own story. Soon after landing on Mars in August 2014, she hosted a twenty-minute Twitter "press conference" attended by a few early account followers but, well, no press. She is a hustler of the most direct, admirable order, forever tweeting at, say, *National Geographic* to do a write-up on her accomplishments. Whoever is behind the Evghenia account and its Russian syntax—a potentially offensive shtick in less underdog-cheering hands, with a less tongue-in-cheek wit—has rendered the character impeccably on this point. A more privileged tweeter seeking a bit of press might email a friend who knows a connected friend, and might view public horn-tooting as gauche. But Evghenia, a woman from the margins of society, has no choice but to blast her space-horn in case anyone might be listening.

What better representative than she for Earth, a planet at the margins of the universe? We've been sending our signal into space for decades, through international space programs and less intentionally through earthly radio transmissions. To public knowledge, at least, no one elsewhere in the universe has yet said, *I hear you*. This longing is particular to our species—messages in bottles sent to sea and posts to social media we hope will be liked, amid divisions of our own construction: gender, ethnicity, class, nationality, race.

Is there life here? each of us is asking. *Is it like me?*

Yes, and here's one way I know.

Every time I push past the discomfort of sharing what we were taught not to share—the dreams and horrors of our childhoods, our adult yearnings, our most vulnerable selves—some reader hears my voice and sends a message back. *Me too!* the reader says, in essence, *me too!*—relieving the most persistent, harrowing illusion of space and time: that she and I were ever separate things.

In memory of Jeannie Getz
March 27, 1962–September 24, 2015

THE NEW MIGRANTS

Texas Observer, 2016

The night before Thanksgiving, Dad's silver Ford F-150—bought used but dent-free—pulled up in front of my new place in Austin. He'd driven all day from a construction site in Monroe, Louisiana, where he was building, he'd reported, "some joint that serves fried chicken."

I went outside to greet him like I had when I was a kid, when his truck would roll down the gravel drive to our redbrick house, which he'd built with his own hands next to a Kansas wheat field. In those moments at dusk, his shirt smelled like oil and sweat when I jumped into his arms; field dust coated the lashes over his blue eyes, and bits of sawdust stuck to his light-brown beard. For today's long haul, though, he'd cleaned up. He was wearing his good black cowboy boots, and his beard, now completely white, was closely trimmed. He was smiling but looked tired in a deep way.

"Look," he said after we hugged. "I'm going to have an adult beverage. That's the real reason I stopped at Burger King—to get a Coke to mix."

"I have some hooch inside," I said.

"But look right here," he said, revealing a bottle of Kentucky Gentleman in the metal toolbox behind the pickup cab. Once inside, he pulled a few presents from Monroe out of his bag: a jar of local honey, a brass unicorn from an antiques store, a feathered red toy for my cat.

Since July, he had driven to sixteen job sites in Kansas, Iowa, Oklahoma, and now Louisiana. In October, a particularly hard work month, he had finished four convenience stores and one bar and grill in five towns across two states; during that month, he had worked eighteen overnight shifts and had just four days off. This was his new life in the post-2008 employer's economy. The upcoming week without labor was a rare gift.

Born to Kansas wheat farmers in 1955, the youngest of six children, Nick Smarsh was a natural with personal finance. His work ethic and money-saving impressed even his salty parents, who came of age during the Great Depression. Before he was old enough to drive, he owned more head of cattle than his dad did. By his early twenties, he'd already owned a foundation-building business. But it folded when the record-setting winter of 1978 left him without work for too long. You can't pour concrete when the temperature is below freezing.

Recession struck in the early 1980s, and work in the construction industry slowed. A few years later, when I was in elementary school, he took a job hauling chemical waste from industrial sites; his second week on the job, he was almost killed by faulty ventilation in his work truck. In 1989, he and my mom divorced and sold our brick house in the country. Dad moved to an apartment in Wichita to be near construction work. I wore his company-logo T-shirts, stained and torn, as nightgowns when my little brother and I stayed there twice a week.

Having just sold the house he'd planned to grow old in, Dad resisted the American urge to buy another one. In the early 1990s, he and his second wife found a clean, modest rental home for $375 a month—even less when he did handy work for the landlord. He, my brother, and I threw a football in the backyard there for sixteen years.

By 2007, though, the rent had gone up enough that he looked into the zero-down mortgage craze, whereby millions of Americans were approved for home loans with interest rates that ballooned and repayment plans that scarcely touched the principal. The bank said he qualified to borrow $150,000.

"I knew that my income was not going to be able to pay for that," he told me recently. "So we selected a $125,000 home."

I was in my twenties by then, working a couple hundred miles away as a development director for a nonprofit that helped at-risk teens, and preparing to buy my own first home. I drove south to help Dad and his wife, whose health had gone bad, move into their new place.

The next year, in 2008, the debt-driven housing bubble burst. Banks stopped lending to low-income homebuyers and big-shot developers alike, and the construction industry halted. After seventeen years, Dad was laid off by the contractor whose T-shirts I once slept in. So too were thirty-four other workers who, like my father, were older and higher-paid.

Suddenly Dad had a home loan, no equity, an ailing wife who couldn't work—and no job. While looking for work at age fifty-three, he exhausted his unemployment benefits and cashed in the 401(k) plan he'd paid into for years at his old company. Soon that was gone too.

Walking into interviews where résumés were piled two inches

high, he found himself settling for lower wages and titles than he'd earned years prior—eighteen dollars an hour as a carpenter, say, instead of twenty-two dollars an hour as a superintendent. And his new bosses were more likely to bid on faraway projects and put him on the road. If jobs don't come to builders, builders go to the jobs.

In 2010, Dad took a position with a small subcontractor that often works under a national general contractor based in the Dallas area. They sent him from Wichita to San Antonio, Mobile, Birmingham, Dallas, for months at a time. The company offered no per-diem wage for food and lodging, instead booking rooms for him in dirty roadside motels filled with dangerous characters. And his paychecks often came up short.

"He said he would pay X amount, and then paychecks were two dollars per hour less than that," Dad told me. "When you're five hundred miles from home and desperate for work, what're ya gonna do?" The company overworked him—"me alone on a job that in the past would have taken four men," Dad said—and didn't pay overtime wages on what he now calls "ungodly hours." It's an experience that, when he was living it, would choke him up when we talked.

Facing payments for his house and health insurance—which rose to $750 a month after his wife got sick—Dad argued with his boss but couldn't quit. Like millions of Americans in similar binds, he maxed out credit cards buying groceries. He tried and failed to get through the red tape of the Obama administration's mortgage-refinance program. His house was foreclosed on. On a sunny January day in 2012, I helped him move into the Wichita mobile-home park where he still lives.* We had lived in a

---

* More recently, he and his wife moved into another rental, an old house with a porch in a working-class neighborhood.

trailer on a patch of dirt for a couple years when I was a kid, so I wasn't daunted. Dad was pleased to have snagged a city lot with good south sun for a garden.

About a year ago, after bouncing among several companies, Dad got on with a good Wichita-based contractor. He's still on the road just about every week, a toothbrush in the pocket of his Carhartt jacket and a portable grill in the bed of his truck. But he's pleased with his hourly wage, relatively handsome in his profession. Money still being tight, he sometimes saves part of his ninety dollars per diem for food and lodging by sharing rooms with guys from his crew. That took setting aside some pride but ended up being kind of special; he bonded with a Filipino kid who told him in limited English about his family and culture. Dad's face has gotten its color back and has relaxed with the relief of having a steady job where his work is respected.

In Austin, I offered to give Dad my bed, but he wouldn't take it, so I put quilts on the sofa instead. The next morning, he pronounced my consignment-store couch the most comfortable bed he'd ever lain upon and the mild Austin air the best sleeping weather he'd ever breathed. He ended up staying for six days, his whole break.

I was glad to have him. My mom had recently died from a long, hard cancer. Aside from the appreciation such loss engenders, Dad and I align on a number of interests: history, beer, politics, live music, sports, structures. On those points my new city offered plenty and, between Dad's long sleeps on my couch, we spent the week exploring.

We climbed Mount Bonnell, ate Thanksgiving dinner in Hyde Park, inspected architecture, watched football, saw a blues band at the Continental Club. We revealed our Midwestern roots by ordering red beers at a sports bar. We climbed past the do-not-enter chains of a hilltop brewery and took in fall-foliage views of Lake Travis.

Most days, Dad wore a black blazer over a button-down shirt tucked into belted work jeans, which were cuffed above brown work boots faded by Sheetrock mud. A gray stocking cap covered his ears. I posted a photo of him to social media: "Hipsters long for this authentic workman style."

We went to a movie, Dad's first time in a theater in the near decade since he'd last had disposable income. I got mad when he wouldn't let me give some poor bastard a jump in the dark cinema parking lot. Later, I realized he had been worried about connecting a stranger's busted car to his truck—without which, as a traveling construction supervisor, he had no livelihood.

One afternoon, Dad slammed two Bud Lights and I drove us to the capitol.

"Look, that used to be the 'governor's business office,'" I said in the grand lobby.

"Where's the governor's urinal?" Dad said. "I gotta pee."

As we made our way through the 1888 building, Dad described the cantilever methods used to hang stairs and the inlay methods used to decorate terrazzo floors. Downstairs, in the agricultural history museum, we solved the mystery of a rusty tool he'd found while digging the foundation for my childhood home back in Kansas: It was a nineteenth-century hub wrench, once used to keep the wheels on the wagon.

We drove past that home many times over the years. Dad's parents' place was just across the dirt road, and in middle school I moved back into my maternal grandparents' farmhouse a few miles away. Dad seethed when we passed our old house and bit of land, where the family who bought it for a song still fished in the pond he and my grandpa had dug.

His last morning at my place, I helped him strategize the

timing for his retirement and calculate how much money he could bring in before diminishing his returns on Social Security. I also shared a dream of mine that might affect his life: I would own a big place in the country. Lots of space for horses and chickens and dirt bikes. Next to the main house there'd be a guest house for Grandma Betty, I said. Another for him too, if he wanted.

Dad nodded but didn't intend to take anything for free. If I could afford the land and the materials, he'd build the place. It would be a gift to himself, he said, to know his daughter had her dream home built right. He'd bring in the mail, feed the animals, and chop wood while I traveled for work.

I knew that such an arrangement would be a gift to me too. Though he's been relegated by the market to uninspired commercial construction, my father is the increasingly rare country carpenter trained by his own dad, who learned from his. For decades, they and his brothers hammered together countless buildings in rural towns west of Wichita.

He's worked on grand projects too; in the booming 1990s in Wichita, he helped turn nineteenth-century warehouses into an entertainment district, renovate a dramatic 1920s boathouse on the Arkansas River, and construct luxury movie theaters. More recently, he built the concrete forms for a new baptismal pool at the magnificent downtown cathedral where we used to go to Mass.

I told Dad I loved that plan—him helping me build a place in the country where we'd both live—and would make it my mission, though we both know well enough how plans often go.

"Still, you gotta have one," he said.

Before he left, he fixed the dead bolt on my front door and showed me how to do it myself. Then he put his small bag in his truck for the day's journey east, during which he planned to meander toward a couple of casinos and a famous pecan farm.

Back in Monroe, Dad would work on the fried-chicken joint, Slim Chickens, into the new year. During those weeks he learned the nice people and bad smells of the paper-mill town, found a decent motel with a fair weekly rate, ate his first po'boy sandwich. In January, as he wrapped up the job, he and a coworker named J.D. splurged on a giant coconut cake from his favorite café.

"We give it to Slim Chickens employees for a house-warming gift," he texted me.

He hadn't really built the restaurant workers a house, of course, but he knew they would spend most of their time there. When so much labor is required to pay the bills, work itself becomes a sort of home.

THE WIND DOESN'T STOP AT CUSTOMS

On Being, 2016

This past weekend, communities around the world celebrated Earth Day with fairs and projects in myriad languages. As with any day or week officially designated for a cause, Earth Day is only as effective as the action and awareness it prompts locally.

Still, we face an ecological crisis so profound that working together across borders is our only chance at a remedy. One state might pass laws banning fracking, say, but if a neighboring state doesn't do the same, both of them will shake with fracking-induced earthquakes.

An ecosystem, after all, is about connectivity. Mother Earth cares nothing for our political boundaries. The wind doesn't stop at customs.

Perhaps the most heartening event this Earth Day, thus, was the United Nations signing of a historic environmental pledge by 174 countries and the European Union. With those symbolic signatures, the Paris Agreement—negotiated last year to curb global warming—moves closer to coming into force. Unlike with similar efforts in years past, major carbon-emissions offenders China and the United States are on board this round.

We have little precedent for such massive-scale, preventative teamwork. It's reactive teamwork, to be sure; the scientific community has long been warning governments to take such climate action. There does seem now a semblance of forward thinking that, while potentially stymied by conflicting economic interests, suggests a humble reckoning with our reliance on the planet that we've for so long mistreated.

Without great care, such a revolutionary dialogue could fall apart before meaningful action takes place. Where might world leaders look for a model path forward?

Frozen inside a mountain in the Arctic Circle, hundreds of millions of seeds rest in crates marked by country: Kenya, Canada, North Korea. The Svalbard Global Seed Vault, construction of which began near Norway in 2006, houses the world's largest seed collection; there, nearly every country in the world is represented in protective permafrost.

It is, as I think of it, an epic, global version of the rural grain co-op I worked at during the summer wheat harvest in Kansas.

Also known as "the Doomsday Vault," the seed project is concerned not with political units but with the planet and humanity they all share. If global crisis strikes—say, famine brought on by climate change—one cold mountain holds the keys for regenerating agriculture and life.

Cary Fowler, a Tennessee-born agriculturalist who helped create the seed cache as head of the Global Crop Diversity Trust, sees it as an "insurance policy for world agriculture" on a planet where plant life endures the unprecedented effects of the Anthropocene.

In the 2012 short documentary *In the Vault*, Fowler pauses deep inside the vault to point out what he described as one of the most interesting rows of containers, labeled for the world's largest agricultural gene bank in Aleppo, Syria.

"They have a safety duplicate of their collection here in Svalbard, which is a great thing since the city and the area is in a state of war right now," Fowler says. "Doomsday happens every day. It happens in small bits and pieces. It happens quietly. So here is a very quiet solution."

Indeed, the Syrian gene bank would make the first-ever major withdrawal from Svalbard—due not only to climate change but to war. As the Syrian civil war and the drought that exacerbated it threatened their work and their lives in Aleppo, scientists heroically moved many thousands of seed and plant samples to Lebanon. To replace what was lost in the chaos, they retrieved their duplicates from the Svalbard vault. The vault exists at the eye of a global political storm but reminds us that the act of protection can be cooperative and life-affirming rather than combative and destructive. It can take the form of seeds rather than bullets.

Brian Lainoff of Crop Trust, an international organization based in Germany working to safeguard crop diversity, told Euronews, "When you're inside the vault, politics don't matter. What matters is keeping the seeds safe."

Outside the vault, though, the personal is always political. I grew up among farmers who saved seeds for generations. In recent decades, that ancient practice has butted up against corporate interests. The US court system has consistently upheld the patenting of living organisms such as plants and seeds, paving the way for corporations such as Monsanto to successfully sue small farmers.

Litigious, profit-driven entities by definition are selfish and have a short-term focus. Their impulses have driven our environmental policy since the industrial revolution.

By contrast, in establishing the Svalbard vault, people from such disparate places as the Fertile Crescent and the Blue Ridge Mountains accomplished an enormous feat toward a common goal. The vault's seeds, thousands of which were saved from extinction, will still be there centuries from now, barring cataclysmic catastrophe upon the mountain itself. Those reading this may long be dead when humanity makes its most critical withdrawals from this biodiversity trove.

Like the oft-cited "seven generations" wisdom of the Iroquois people, the Svalbard project's intentions supersede immediate profit. As it happens, part of the Iroquois Confederacy, the Onondaga Nation, lies about two hundred miles north of New York's United Nations headquarters.

Onondaga leader Oren Lyons said of inherited tribal wisdom, during an interview for the 2007 documentary *The Eleventh Hour*, "Make your decisions on behalf of the seventh generation coming so they may enjoy what you have today. . . . If you take care of the future, you'll be taking care of yourself. You yourself will have peace."

If you had access to a vault that could protect something from the dangerous forces of modern society—politics, war, capitalism—to be enjoyed by our grandchildren's grandchildren, what would you put there?

Regardless of country, party, or religion, we are all primal creatures of this earth who rely on nature for both survival and beauty. I suspect that most of us therefore would choose many of the same things for such preservation: clean air, drinkable water, wild animals, trees, grass, flowers.

Toward such a goal we might continue to act locally and

think globally, as goes a familiar bumper sticker. Now we also must call upon our leaders to act globally. Together, as both communities and nations, we must take responsibility on behalf of ourselves, our planet, and its inhabitants to come—an ecosystem that spans not just national borders but the illusory boundaries of time.

DANGEROUS IDIOTS

The Guardian, 2016

Last March, my seventy-one-year-old grandmother, Betty, stood in line for three hours to caucus for Bernie Sanders. The wait to cast her first-ever vote in a primary election was punishing, but this didn't deter her. Betty—a White woman who left school after ninth grade, had her first child at age sixteen, and spent much of her life in severe poverty—wanted to vote.

So she waited with busted knees that once stood on factory lines. She waited with smoking-induced emphysema and the false teeth she's had since her late twenties—both markers of our class. She waited with a body that in the 1960s, before *Roe v. Wade*, she paid a stranger to thrust a wire hanger inside after she discovered she was pregnant by a man she'd fled after he broke her jaw.

Betty worked for many years as a probation officer for the state judicial system in Wichita, Kansas, keeping tabs on men who had murdered and raped. As a result, it's hard to faze her, but she has pronounced Republican candidate Donald Trump a sociopath "whose mouth overloads his ass."

No one loathes Trump—who suggested women should be punished for having abortions, who said hateful things about groups of people she has loved and worked alongside since childhood, whose pomp and indecency offends her modest, Midwestern sensibility—more than she.

Yet it is White, working-class people like Betty who have become a particular fixation among the chattering class during this election: What is this angry beast, and why does it support Trump?

Hard numbers complicate, if not roundly dismiss, the oft-regurgitated theory that income or education levels predict Trump support, or that working-class Whites support him disproportionately. Last month, results of eighty-seven thousand interviews conducted by Gallup showed that those who liked Trump were under no more economic distress or immigration-related anxiety than those who opposed him.

According to the study, his supporters didn't have lower incomes or higher unemployment levels than other Americans. Income data misses a lot; those with healthy earnings might also have negative wealth or downward mobility. But respondents overall weren't clinging to jobs perceived to be endangered. "Surprisingly," a Gallup researcher wrote, "there appears to be no link whatsoever between exposure to trade competition and support for nationalist policies in America, as embodied by the Trump campaign."

Earlier this year, primary exit polls revealed that Trump voters were, in fact, more affluent than most Americans, with a median household income of $72,000—higher than that of

Hillary Clinton or Bernie Sanders supporters. Forty-four percent of them had college degrees, well above the national average of 33 percent among Whites or 29 percent overall. In January, political scientist Matthew MacWilliams reported findings that a penchant for authoritarianism—not income, education, gender, age, or race—predicted Trump support.

These facts haven't stopped pundits and journalists from pushing story after story about the White working class's giddy embrace of a bloviating demagogue.

In seeking to explain Trump's appeal, proportionate media coverage would require more stories about the racism and misogyny among White Trump supporters in tony suburbs. Or, if we're examining economically driven bitterness among the working class, stories about the Democratic lawmakers who in recent decades ended welfare as we knew it, hopped in the sack with Wall Street, and forgot American labor in their global trade agreements.

But, for national media outlets composed largely of middle- and upper-class liberals, that would mean looking their own class in the face.

The faces journalists do train the cameras on—hateful ones screaming sexist vitriol next to Confederate flags—must receive coverage but do not speak for the communities I know well. That the media industry ignored my home for so long left a vacuum of understanding in which the first glimpse of an economically downtrodden White is presumed to represent the whole.

Part of the current glimpse is J.D. Vance, author of the best-selling new memoir *Hillbilly Elegy*. A successful attorney who had a precarious upbringing in an Ohio steel town, Vance wrote of the chaos that can haunt a family with generational memory of deep poverty. A conservative who says he won't vote for Trump, Vance speculates about why working-class Whites will: cultural anxiety that arises when opioid overdose kills your friends and the political establishment has proven it will throw you under the bus. While his theories may hold up in some corners, coastal media members have repeatedly asked Vance to speak for the entire White working class.

His interviewers and reviewers often seem relieved to find someone with ownership on the topic whose ideas in large part confirm their own. The *New York Times* election podcast *The Run-Up* said Vance's memoir "doubles as a cultural anthropology of the white underclass that has flocked to the Republican presidential nominee's candidacy." (The *Times* teased its review of the book with the tweet: "Want to know more about the people who fueled the rise of Donald Trump?")

While Vance happens to have roots in Kentucky mining country, most impoverished Whites are not conservative male Protestants from Appalachia. That sometimes seems the only concept of them that the American consciousness can contain: tucked away in a remote mountain shanty like a coal-dust-covered ghost, as though White poverty isn't always right in front of us, swiping credit cards at a discount store in Denver or asking for cash on a Los Angeles sidewalk.

One-dimensional stereotypes fester where journalism fails to tread. The last time I saw my native class receive substantial focus, before now, was over twenty years ago—not in the news but on the television show *Roseanne*,* the fictional storylines of which remain more accurate than the musings of comfortable commentators in New York studios.

Countless working-class progressives, including women

---

* Not long after this essay's publication, I was dismayed to learn of Roseanne Barr's political stances and racist statements in the modern era. However, her television show in the 1980s and '90s, replete with progressive working-class characters, remains in my view an overall gift to the culture.

such as Betty, are thus rendered invisible by a ratings-fixated media that covers elections as horse races and seeks sensational B-roll.

This media paradigm created the tale of a divided America—red vs. blue—in which the 42 percent of Kansas voters who supported Barack Obama in 2008 are meaningless.

This year, more Kansans caucused for Bernie Sanders than for Donald Trump—a newsworthy point I never saw noted in national press, who perhaps couldn't fathom that "flyover country" might contain millions of Americans more progressive than their Clinton-supporting friends.

In lieu of such coverage, media makers cast the White working class as a monolith and imply an old, treacherous story convenient to capitalism: that the poor are dangerous idiots.

The twofold myth about the White working class—that they are to blame for Trump's rise, and that those among them who support him exemplify the rest—takes flight on the wings of moral superiority affluent Americans often pin upon themselves.

I have never seen them flap so insistently as in today's election commentary, where notions of poor Whiteness and poor character are routinely conflated.

In an election piece last March in the *National Review*, conservative writer Kevin Williamson's assessment of poor White voters—among whom mortality rates have sharply risen in recent decades—expressed what many conservatives and liberals alike may well believe when he observed that communities ravaged by oxycodone use "deserve to die."

"The white American underclass is in thrall to a vicious, selfish culture whose main products are misery and used heroin needles," Williamson wrote. "Donald Trump's speeches make them feel good. So does OxyContin."

For evidence of classism beyond opinion pieces, look no further than a recent *Washington Post* series that explored spiking death rates among rural White women by fixating on their smoking habits and graphically detailing the "haggard face" and embalming processes of their corpses. Imagine wealthy White women examined thusly after their deaths. The outrage among family and friends with the education, time, and agency to write letters to the editor would have been deafening.

A sentiment that I care for even less than contempt or degradation is their tender counterpart: pity.

In a recent op-ed headlined "Dignity and Sadness in the Working Class," David Brooks told of a laid-off Kentucky metal worker he met. On his last day, the man left to rows of cheering coworkers—a moment I read as triumphant but that Brooks declared pitiable. How hard the man worked for so little, how great his skills, and how dwindling their value, Brooks pointed out, for people he said radiate "the residual sadness of the lonely heart."

I'm hard-pressed to think of a worse slight than the media figures who have disregarded the embattled White working class for decades now beseeching the country to have sympathy for them. We don't need their analysis, and we sure don't need their tears. What we need is to have our stories told, preferably by someone who can walk into a factory without his own guilt fogging his glasses.

One such journalist, Alexander Zaitchik, spent several months on the road in six states getting to know White working-class people who do support Trump. His goal for the resulting new book, *The Gilded Rage*, was to convey the human complexity that daily news misses. Zaitchik wrote that his mission arose from frustration with "'hot takes' written by people living several time zones and income brackets away from their subjects."

Zaitchik wisely described those he met as a "blue-collar middle class"—mostly White people who have worked hard and lost a lot, whether in the market crash of 2008 or the manufacturing layoffs of recent decades. He found that their motivations overwhelmingly "started with economics and ended with economics." The anger he observed was "pointed up, not down" at those who forgot them when global trade deals were negotiated, not at minority groups.

Meanwhile, the racism and nationalism that surely exist among them also exist among Democrats and higher socioeconomic strata. A poll conducted last spring by Reuters found that a third of questioned Democrats supported a temporary ban on Muslims entering the United States. In another, by YouGov, 45 percent of polled Democrats reported holding an unfavorable view of Islam, with almost no fluctuation based on household income. Those who won't vote for Trump are not necessarily paragons of virtue, while the rest are easily scapegoated as the country's moral scourge.

When Hillary Clinton recently declared half of Trump supporters a "basket of deplorables," Zaitchik told the *Washington Examiner*, the language "could be read as another way of saying 'white-trash bin.'" Clinton quickly apologized for the comment, the context of which contained compassion for many Trump voters. But making such generalizations at a $6 million fundraiser in downtown New York City, at which some attendees paid $50,000 for a seat, recalled for me scenes from the television political satire *Veep*, in which powerful Washington figures discuss "normals" with distaste behind closed doors.

When we talked, Zaitchik mentioned HBO talk-show host Bill Maher, who he pointed out "basically makes eugenics-level arguments about anyone who votes for Donald Trump having congenital defects. You would never get away with talking that way about any other group of people and still have a TV show."

Maher is, perhaps, the pinnacle of classist smugness. In the summer of 1998, when I was seventeen and just out of high school, I worked at a grain elevator during the wheat harvest. An elevator fifty miles east in Haysville, Kansas, exploded—grain dust is highly combustible—and seven workers died. The accident rattled my community and reminded us about the physical dangers my family and I often faced as farmers.

I kept going to work like everyone else and, after a long day weighing wheat trucks and hauling heavy sacks of feed in and out of the mill, liked to watch *Politically Incorrect*, the ABC show Maher hosted then. With the search for one of the dead workers' bodies still under way, Maher joked, as I recall, that viewers should check their loaves of Wonder Bread.

That moment was perhaps my first reckoning with the hard truth that, throughout my life, I would politically identify with the same people who often insult the place I am from.

Such derision is so pervasive that it's often imperceptible to the economically privileged. Those who write, discuss, and publish newspapers, books, and magazines with best intentions sometimes offend with obliviousness.

Many people recommended to me the bestselling new history book *White Trash*, for instance, without registering that its title is a slur that refers to me and the people I love as garbage. My happy relief that someone set out to tell this ignored thread of our shared past was squashed by my wincing every time I saw it on my shelf, so much so that I finally took the book jacket off. Incredibly, promotional copy for the book commits precisely the elitist shaming Nancy Isenberg is out to expose: "(the book) takes on our comforting myths about equality, uncovering the crucial legacy of the ever-present, always embarrassing—if occasionally entertaining—poor white trash."

The book itself is more sensitively wrought and imparts facts that one hopes would dismantle popular use of its titular term. But Isenberg ultimately can't escape our classist frameworks in her analyses.

When *On the Media* public radio host Brooke Gladstone asked Isenberg, earlier this year, to address long-held perceptions of poor Whites as bigots, the author described a conundrum: "They do subscribe to certain views that are undoubtedly racist, and you can't mask it and pretend that it's not there. It is very much a part of their thinking."

Try to imagine such a generalization being made about any other disadvantaged group, and you might begin to see how rudimentary class discussion is for this relatively young country that long believed itself to be free of castes. Isenberg has sniffed out the hypocrisy in play, though.

"The other problem is when people want to blame poor whites for being the only racist in the room," she told Gladstone. ". . . as if they're more racist than everyone else."

That problem is rooted in the notion that higher class means higher integrity. As journalist Lorraine Berry wrote recently for the progressive news website *Raw Story*, "The story remains that only the ignorant would be racist. Racism disappears with education we're told."

As the first from my family to hold degrees, I assure you that none of us had to go to college to learn basic human decency.

Berry points out that Ivy League–minted Republicans

shepherded the rise of the alt-right. Indeed, it was not poor Whites who passed legislation segregating people by race.

It wasn't poor Whites who criminalized Blackness marijuana laws and the "war on drugs."

Nor was it poor Whites who conjured the specter of the Black "welfare queen."

These points should not minimize the horrors of racism at the lowest economic rungs of society but should remind us that those horrors reside at the top in different forms and with more terrible power.

Among reporters and commentators this election cycle, then, a steady finger ought to be pointed at Whites with economic leverage: social conservatives who donate to Trump's campaign while being too civilized to attend a political rally and yell what they really believe.

Based on Trump's campaign rhetoric and available data, it appears that most of his voters this November will be people who are getting by well enough but who think of themselves as victims.

One thing the media misses is that a great portion of the White working class refuse to consider themselves victims as a point of pride. Right now they are clocking in and out of work, sorting their grocery coupons, raising their children to respect others, and avoiding political news coverage.

Barack Obama, a Black man formed by the Black experience, often cites his maternal lineage in the White working class. "A lot of what's shaped me came from my grandparents who grew up on the prairie in Kansas," he wrote this month to mark a White House forum on rural issues.

Last year, talking with author Marilynne Robinson for the

New York Review of Books, Obama lamented common misconceptions of small-town middle America, for which he has a sort of reverence. "There's this huge gap between how folks go about their daily lives and how we talk about our common life and our political life," he said, naming one cause as "the filters that stand between ordinary people" who are busy getting by and complicated policy debates.

"I'm very encouraged when I meet people in their environments," Obama told Robinson. "Somehow it gets distilled at the national political level in ways that aren't always as encouraging."

To be sure, one discouraging distillation—the caricature of the hate-spewing White male Trump voter with grease on his jeans—is a real person, of sorts. There were more than a few in my town: the good ol' boy who menaces those with less power than himself—running people of color out of town with the threat of violence, denigrating women, shooting BB guns at stray cats for fun. They are who Trump would be if he'd been born where I was.

Media fascination with the hateful White Trump voter fuels the theory, now in fashion, that racism is the only explanation for supporting him. Certainly, financial struggle does not predict a soft spot for Trump, as cash-strapped people of color—who face the threat of his racism and xenophobia, and who resoundingly reject him, by all available measures—can attest. However, one imagines that elite White liberals who maintain an air of ethical grandness this election season would have a harder time thinking globally about trade and immigration if it were their factory job that was lost and their community that was decimated.

Liberal analysts, though, have a way of taking a systemic view when examining societal woes but viewing their place on the political continuum as a triumph of individual character. Most of them likely inherited their political bent, just like most of those in red America did. If you were handed liberalism, give yourself no pats on the back for your vote against Trump.

Spare too the condescending argument that disaffected Democrats who joined Republican ranks in recent decades are "voting against their own best interests," undemocratic in its implication that a large swath of America isn't mentally fit to cast a ballot.

Whoever remains on Trump's side as stories concerning his treatment of women, racism, and other dangers continue to unfurl gets no pass from me for any reason. They are capable of voting, and they own their decisions. Let's be aware of our class biases, though, as we discern who "they" are.

A recent print-edition *New York Times* cutline described a Kentucky man: "Mitch Hedges, who farms cattle and welds coal-mining equipment. He expects to lose his job in six months, but does not support Trump, who he says is 'an idiot.'"

This made me cheer for the rare spotlight on a member of the White working class who doesn't support Trump. It also made me laugh—one doesn't "farm cattle." One farms crops, and one raises livestock (though one might refer to a place involving both operations as a cattle farm). It's sometimes hard for a journalist who has done both to take the *New York Times* seriously.

The main reason that national media outlets have a blind spot in matters of class is the lack of socioeconomic diversity within their ranks. Few people born to deprivation end up working in newsrooms or publishing books. So few, in fact, that this former laborer has found cause to shift her entire writing career to talk specifically about class in a wealth-privileged industry, much as journalists of color find themselves talking about race in a Whiteness-privileged one.

This isn't to say that one must reside among a given group or place to do it justice, of course, as good muckrakers and commentators have shown for the past century and beyond. See *On the Media*'s fine new series on poverty, the second episode of which includes Gladstone's reflection that "the poor are no more monolithic than the rest of us."

I know journalists to be hardworking people who want to get the story right, and I'm resistant to rote condemnations of "the media." The classism of cable-news hosts merely reflects the classism of privileged America in general. It's everywhere, from tweets describing Trump voters as inbred hillbillies to a Democratic campaign platform that didn't bother with a specific anti-poverty platform until a month out from the general election. Poor and working-class Whites against Trump may not be the voting majorities in their areas, but they are a meaningful faction whose misrepresentation and invisibility threaten to turn them away from civic engagement.

The economic trench between reporter and reported-on has never been more hazardous than at this moment of historic wealth disparity, when stories focus more often on the stock market than on people who own no stocks. American journalism has been willfully obtuse about the grievances on Main Streets for decades—surely a factor in digging the hole of resentment that Trump's venom now fills. That the term "populism" has become a pejorative among prominent liberal commentators should give us great pause. A journalism that embodies the plutocracy it's supposed to critique has failed its watchdog duty and lost the respect of people who call bullshit when they see it.

One such person was my late grandfather Arnie. Men like Trump sometimes drove expensive vehicles up the gravel driveway of our Kansas farmhouse looking to do some sort of business. Grandpa would recognize them as liars and thieves, treat them kindly, and send them packing. If you shook their hands, after they left Grandpa would laugh and say, "Better count your fingers."

In a world where the Bettys and Arnies have little voice, those who enjoy a platform from which to speak might examine their hearts and minds before stepping onto the soapbox.

If you would stereotype a group of people by presuming to guess their politics or deeming them inferior to yourself—say, the ones who worked third shift on a Boeing floor while others flew to Mexico during spring break; the ones who mopped a McDonald's bathroom while others argued about the minimum wage on Twitter; the ones who cleaned out their lockers at a defunct Pabst factory while others drank craft beer at trendy bars; the ones who came back from the Middle East in caskets while others wrote op-eds about foreign policy—then consider that you might have more in common with Trump than you would like to admit.

THE JUMP

Scratch: Writers, Money, and
the Art of Making a Living, 2017

The winter after I quit my tenured professorship, I couldn't afford a haircut. I stood at the mirror with a pair of scissors to my long hair and cried.

What had I done?

When I had resigned a few months earlier, giving up a lifetime of assured income, insurance benefits, research support, and professional belonging to which so many academics aspire, some acquaintances had hinted that I was making a mistake. I'd received cards from friends saying they were worried about me; from colleagues, eyebrows raised in silence. One old pal warned that we weren't in our twenties anymore.

To be fair, I was barely thirty-two. And, thanks to my working-class background, I'd already been in the workforce for almost twenty years. I'd never had the irresponsible twenties some enjoy. If quitting my day job had anything to do with age, it wasn't immaturity but the opposite, the ubiquitous American midlife crisis arriving a decade early.

Those who knew me the best fretted the least. A handful of close friends and family nervously supported my unorthodox move, knowing they couldn't rightly question my history of good judgment. That judgment had taken me from a prairie farmhouse to an Ivy League graduate school to a middle-class income in air-conditioned classrooms far from the hand-blistering wheat harvests of my youth. I'd carved a life from being disciplined, even self-denying, in a family that tended toward the impulsive.

So why then the desire to leave, to dismantle what I'd built?

Behind such a monumental decision was a confluence of reasons and events—most of which others couldn't know because I myself was still struggling to articulate them. According to the grapevine, some thought I was running away from, not toward, something. In that way they were wrong. I offered my department, the one party I believed deserved an explanation, the only true reason I fully understood at the time—accurate, if incomplete: my mother's health. Two months after I had received tenure and promotion, my fifty-year-old mom had been diagnosed with a rare, aggressive breast cancer.

The enormity of her prognosis, in the midst of an already auspiciously difficult year, evoked in me that feeling I sometimes get at funerals. You know the one—when you're stunned into clarity, rung by humble reckoning with mortality, a dead body at the front of a chapel. When you look around and ask, *What the hell are we all doing with our lives?*

I'd climbed out of hard-soil origins by being intentionally pragmatic, but my nature was a wilder thing. I quit my job to be at my mother's side in another state, yes, but also to heed a more selfish call: the old creative yearnings of a girl who hadn't

yet worked herself raw to pay for college, married her high
school sweetheart, fought for employment, fixed up houses,
planned to have a baby. Before all that, I'd had a different
life vision—adventure, travel, and the ultimate Holy Grail:
publishing what since childhood I'd quietly thought of as My
Book.

I'd never given up those dreams. They had become an amorphous longing, though, as I did what so many of us do in the
real world: eke out an authentic enough life that, first and fore-
most, paid the bills and theoretically allowed me to write My
Book in the crevices between other demands. By the time Mom
was diagnosed, I'd been chipping away at it for more than a
decade. My Book had been a research project when I was an
undergrad, my thesis when I was an MFA student. Even then
I hadn't been able to prioritize it while I labored to pay the
bills. Soon I found myself in a coveted position with a teaching
load of four courses per semester. In such an occupation, a sick
mother might be visited over a long weekend, and a book might
be written over a summer.

With the sound of my mother's bell tolling from the near
future, my usual order of priorities—job first, then my loved
ones and my dreams, wherever they might fit in—felt all wrong.
I'd woken back up to the beautiful, savage, heart-ripping reality I once knew as a child, in which moments are to be seized
because the next paycheck is never assured. Somehow, not even
the promise of decades of salary pay and benefits in a society
built around money could lull me back to sleep.

For years I'd behaved as a people pleaser—putting everyone else's needs and feelings above my own. Now I suddenly
had no tolerance for people or actions with even a whiff of
bullshit about them. And lo, most academic departments carry
more than a whiff. My upbringing as a Midwestern farm girl

perhaps had honed my sense of smell. In *The Uses of Literacy*, cultural critic Richard Hoggart described the experience of being a "scholarship boy" who is "at the friction point of two cultures": "He has left his class, at least in spirit, by being in certain ways unusual; and he is still unusual in another class." I was a scholarship girl. Hauling lesson plans across a college campus as a professor a mere decade after I'd hauled feed across a cattle pasture was one hell of a friction point.

As chair of my university's diversity initiative, I'd found that academia wasn't the occupational promised land for women, minorities, and other historically marginalized groups that it might have been for middle-class White men. I'd always felt relatively comfortable as a woman in academia, though. It meant jumping through all the usual unfair hoops, but those hoops I knew existed not just at universities but also behind the bars where I'd poured whiskey for tips. Same shit, different pay grade.

What vexed me more was an otherness of socioeconomic class. I was a woman in a man's world not as a female professor but as a female professor who was the first woman in her family to stay in school past eleventh grade.

My blue-collar origins meant the risk I was taking in leaving my job was more foolhardy than even my most cynical critics knew. I had no firm plan about another job, just a handful of creative project leads, a small retirement fund I could cash in if I had to, and a feeling that couldn't wait.

When I quit my professorship, it wasn't the first time I'd taken an economic risk that to some might seem outlandish. My undergraduate college tuition was covered by scholarships, and I worked to pay the rent. But after a low-paying stint at a newspaper, in 2003 I was accepted to an elite graduate degree program. The annual tuition was around $40,000, more than the annual income of anyone in my family. The school offered a small fellowship, and the government would provide up to $18,500 a year in subsidized loans. The rest would have to come from private lenders. I hesitated over the loan documents in my mom's apartment—aching to go to Columbia but wrecked by the repercussions.

"You'll regret it if you don't go," Mom said. Ultimately, I agreed. For a kid with my origins, I figured, the financial debt was worth the social capital. When it comes to economic risk, what appears reckless to the privileged is often the smartest bet to the poor. By the time I graduated from Columbia and left New York, my bet was upward of ninety grand.

In recent years many have questioned a degree's value and chastised those who take out big loans to buy one. Most of those critics, I'd wager, never worked a wheat field. Debt burden and being overeducated in an employer's market is psychologically and financially crushing, yes, but an assured lifetime sentence to manual labor can be more crushing—ask my dad, a brilliant thinker who has given me poems written in carpenter's pencil on scraps of two-by-four lumber. Most college graduates who are underwater financially at least have fish to eat, and though I loathe debt, I indeed would choose it over starving. It takes a toll but buys a chance.

What would justify my student loans, I'd always told myself, would be a book deal that allowed me to pay them off with one big check. Like those loans, to leave tenure with little cushion to fall back on was a horrible decision on paper. I wasn't delusional on that point and faced a healthy host of reasonable fears: the primitive terrors of starvation and homelessness, the more luxurious concerns of disappointing colleagues and leaving students.

But at my deepest core, I felt the departure was necessary.

Spending much of my life in economic poverty—a sort of freedom in that one has little to lose—had afforded me a wealth of
self-knowing. The painful requirements of following through
on the feeling were, perhaps, less scary to me than they would
have been for someone more privileged. I'd gone without before
and survived. I figured I could do it again—though I foolishly
imagined I wouldn't have to.

The university, for its part, wondered how much money
I'd need to stay. This response startled me. I'd never in my
life considered manipulating an employer for a raise, let alone
leveraging the matter of my mother's health to do so. There
was no amount, I said.

They'd hold my position for a year and a half, they said.
Grateful, I thought on this, but still the clarity rang through
me. I was resigning, I said.

Would I at least sign a letter merely calling my departure a
leave of absence rather than a resignation, they asked, so as to
preserve department funding for my tenure line in a dangerous
fiscal climate?

Here I paused. Amid my flush of individualism I still felt protective of and responsible to the writing curriculum I'd helped
build. Signing such a letter might behoove that curriculum and
my colleagues, on whom my departure placed the burdens of
picking up classes and reassigning my many duties. I was leaving
one month into a new school year, putting my files in order as
best I could for whoever would inherit them. Within a couple
of weeks I'd be rambling across the West toward my mother
and a host of adventures. Surely I could sign a letter bending
language for the sake of a place, people, and mission I held in
high regard. Doing so, I realized, would benefit me too—a way
to hedge my bets. If I signed the letter, the job would be waiting
for me for a year and a half.

As a child, I liked to reenact a climactic movie scene in which Indiana Jones ducks, runs, and maneuvers through a gauntlet deep inside an ancient temple. He gauges each step to avoid death, only to arrive at a ravine so deep he can't see the bottom. It's far too wide to jump. He reads from a diary of secrets guiding him toward the Holy Grail and sees he has no choice but to cross. "Nobody can jump this," he says, sweating. He's up shit creek at that point, his dad back at the entrance bleeding out next to a cluster of greedy Nazis.

"It's a leap of faith," he says and groans at the pun from God. He puts his hand on his heart like he's taking an oath, steadies his breath, stretches one leg into the abyss, and sways forward, appearing to the naked eye to be falling to his death. But a stone bridge catches him—invisible by way of optical illusion, it had been there all along. Pretending I was Indy, I used to run and jump along rows of hay bales at the corner of our alfalfa field.

In those years, by necessity I trusted no voice but my own. I believed in myself precisely because so little was expected of me. The knowing that would take me over so many chasms amounted to hearing my highest voice and being true to it.

I considered the requested letter stating a leave of absence. It would mean calling what I was doing temporary when the tuning fork inside me said it was permanent. To sign such a letter, I knew, would not be true.

"I got the silver, but I'm going for the gold," I had told my mom, who somehow understood. "Silver," to me, was an economically stable life. "Gold," to me, was a fulfilling one.

Mom nodded seriously.

"Go for the gold," she said.

I didn't write a letter about a leave of absence. I wrote a letter of resignation. I did not apologize. I was intentionally dismantling every aspect of my constructed identity, killing the darlings of a secure life in order to find the story I needed to live. It felt terrifying and grand.

Months later, there I was, standing before a mirror with a pair of scissors, not even ten bucks to spare for a trip to Great Clips. The project leads I'd thought would pan out as income hadn't. Mom had finished surgery, chemotherapy, and radiation with excellent results in Colorado and had decided to move, at least temporarily, to the Kansas town where I still owned a house. None of my reasons for leaving my job had been justified, it seemed. I was a woman crying while cutting her own hair—a familiar image in popular culture denoting madness. Had I in fact lost my mind when I left my job?

Just over a year earlier I had been eating dinner with my husband, putting an extensive tenure application in three-ring binders, paying into a retirement fund with a handsome match by my employer, renovating a dream house perched on a hill in a college town. It was an unhappy marriage, a sometimes inhospitable work environment, and a too-big house that I both paid for and cleaned. In those middle-class discomforts, though, I'd at least been in sync with the rest of society, I realized, feeling like a self-made pariah.

Now, at age thirty-two, I had no money, no job, no health insurance, no mate, no plan for a roof once the one I was under sold. There hadn't been a single offer on the house anyway. I'd cashed in my small retirement fund to pay the mortgage, and now my savings were gone. I didn't even own a car, since mine had broken down one morning on the way to campus not long before I resigned, like even *it* thought the job was no longer the right place for me. My grandma was letting me borrow her truck, like she had when I was in high school. She had a limited stash of hard-earned savings and had loaned me money to cover bills. It seemed that I had ruined, not saved, my life.

Familiar generational woes were close by, lapping at my feet like the fire of poverty I'd labored to escape. Dad's house was foreclosed on; he moved into a trailer with his wife, whose painkiller prescription after a car wreck decades prior had led to worse health problems. A close family member confessed to a longtime gambling addiction. Mom and her partner were on the outs, but her health insurance was through his employer, and I worried that she would be uninsured if they broke up. My grandma, dismayed by her daughter's cancer and exhausted from caregiving, moved into my place and had emotional and physical breakdowns for which I drove her to emergency rooms.

More than one person said to me, in apparent seriousness, "If I'd had the year you've had, I would kill myself."

Indeed I was so beleaguered that I sometimes prayed to leave earth. Of all my troubles, I'd most underestimated the psychological trauma of relinquishing a professional title that commands respect and confers identity in a culture that values productivity above all else—a trauma likely exacerbated by my having been born, by class and gender, to little respect. As a woman who had worked nearly every day since adolescence for some employer, I'd never had so much time on my hands. I felt lost, crushed by the weight of open space and infinite possibility I'd longed for. I wouldn't hurt myself, I was sure, but I wasn't opposed to dying in my sleep.

It took a lot to break my spirit. It had never been done. But after that year—the divorce, the cancer, the gossip, the family, the resignation, the return to poverty—I was broken.

So when my former university advertised a search to fill my old position, I did what seemed the only rational thing to do: I tried to get my job back.

A former colleague generously assured me that, while the department legally had to conduct a public search, it was a no-brainer that the gig would be mine if I applied. I wrote a cover letter saying I'd been wrong to leave and sent it, my pride the cost of postage. Like the woman who sells a brooch to buy potatoes in wartime, I cared nothing for pride.

For weeks I awaited word from the search committee, imagining the joys and horrors of returning to gainful employment I'd brazenly walked away from, should I indeed be welcomed back. Then word came:

The search had been canceled.

Amid other budget priorities, the tenure line had been on the chopping block since I vacated it. Funding for the hire hadn't been approved. I couldn't return if only because the job no longer existed, for the moment. I myself had vaporized it by declining to sign a letter saying that I might come back.

This news was distressing but also, somehow, a relief. The paradoxical turn of events was so preposterous that it was comical. Rather than feeling destroyed by a final blow, I felt renewed.

I remembered that funeral feeling, recalled the sureness with which I had jumped. I had an eerie sense that some hand had known what it was doing when it signed a letter saying exactly what I intended. It was my own hand.

I'd been a sprinter and a long jumper in high school track—good at running fast and taking flying leaps. This one had turned out to be a very long leap, I thought. The leap of a lifetime. It wasn't that I'd landed in ruin. It was that I hadn't landed yet.

In that scary, stomach-turning moment of suspension, I saw, I still had the power to stick my landing. I did so as the only identity that remained after I shed all the others: writer.

I was drawn back to the sort of pages I hadn't written since before I earned a living by reporting for newspapers or writing grants for nonprofits. I sat down and did the writing that I hadn't been able to do in a life with the wrong husband and eighty students per semester and office dramas and perpetual committees needing tending. I wrote not to pay the bills, as I had for years as a journalist and professor climbing away from the early shames and pains of my life, but to say what I had to express—which, predictably, were those very shames and pains.

In that moment looking in the mirror with the scissors, in the throes of not just poverty but a return to it by my own action, painfully untethered from the solidarity of the rat race and its comfortable trappings, the world questioning my sanity, I wasn't sure I trusted myself. I didn't know what was coming in the next few years: my mother's health declining, months of caregiving and writing at her side, the repair of ailing family connections, the long-dreamed-of book deal, the paying down of debts. I didn't know where I'd land—in a bed next to Mom, three days before she died, telling her that I'd dedicate my book to her.

When troubled by uncertainty, though, I'd remember how I felt when I spoke the hardest, most necessary words: This marriage is over. This house is for sale. I resign. I—that woman—had never felt stronger or more clear. She was the one who wouldn't sign a letter even pretending she might return to her old job if only to keep the option of going back. Perhaps she sensed that, in my proverbial darkest hour, I would try to turn back. She knew I was setting out on the most difficult, rewarding journey of my life. *I might not trust myself*, I'd think, *but I trust that woman.*

BLOOD BROTHER

*Tales of Two Americas: Stories of Inequality
in a Divided Nation,* **2017**

VQR, 2017

Your brother has a hole on the inside of each arm that never quite closes. A blood tap, really, like an oil well for drilling. He is a tall, strong man in his early thirties—an ideal source for plasma.

A woman calls his name. She takes his temperature and blood pressure. He gets to skip the full-blown health screening since he's been coming here twice a week, off and on, for almost ten years. She pricks his finger to make sure his blood is okay today.

Some of the other regulars take iron pills for fear they'll become anemic and be turned away. There's a weight minimum of 110 pounds, so the smallest, frailest women, sometimes elderly or under-fed or both, put on extra clothes or wear ankle weights to pass.

A technician wearing a white lab coat, a name tag, and a clear-plastic shield over her face puts a needle in one of your brother's inner-arm holes. He's in a "donating bed," a high-tech recliner of sorts that elevates the legs and leans him way back.

Rows of these chairs on the donor floor hold people whose

faces he sometimes recognizes. They look at cell phones, magazines, or televisions hanging from the ceiling while maroon fluid drains from their veins. Some of them are homeless. Some of them are like your brother: college graduates with beat-up cars, insurmountable credit-card debt, federal and private student loans. The state university where he worked and borrowed his way through undergraduate degrees is just four blocks away. Plasma centers like to set up shop near universities, where the blood is young and the wallets are light.

When your brother finally graduated, the economy was in the tank. As a first-generation college student he had no connections in the professional world, and no one to tell him that communications and history degrees were bad bets to begin with. A good job never turned up. For years he has worked at call centers, leasing agencies, shipping companies. Those paychecks don't cover basic living costs, though. Thus, his face has aged a decade going in and out of this place by necessity.

The plasma center, though, like hundreds of similar businesses across the country, always looks the same: The fluorescent lights. The rows of quiet people lying back with one arm hooked to a whirring machine. The white lab coats and the clear-plastic face shields. The signs about what to eat the day before, the day of, and the day after giving plasma in order to keep your strength up.

Your brother's blood follows a tube to a centrifuge that separates out what they want: liquid plasma the color of Mountain Dew.

The materials around the place tout the lifesaving service he's providing others; the plasma stripped from his blood will be turned into pharmaceuticals. Very expensive pharmaceuticals, ones he could never afford were he diagnosed with hemophilia or an immune disorder. He doesn't have health insurance and could use a trip to the doctor himself. The promotional pamphlets and websites call what he's doing a donation, but it's really a sale.

The buyers are corporations with names like BioLife, Biotest, Octapharma. Plasma brings thirty, fifty bucks a pop depending on how often you go and how much you weigh. Your brother is in the highest weight class, which means he gets twenty dollars for the first donation of the week, forty-five dollars for the second. Sometimes there are bonuses: prize drawings, scratch-off tickets. The place your brother frequents is running a recruitment special: UP TO $400 THIS MONTH. Applicable for eligible, qualified new donors. Fees vary by location. Check with your preferred CSL Plasma donation center to see if they are participating in any other special promotions.

Regulars like your brother are already on the donor loyalty program called Z Rewards. The more plasma given, the more points and the higher status they attain—bronze, silver, gold. If you're away too long, they want you back. "Lapsed donors," who haven't given plasma in six months or more, get fifty bucks each for their first five return visits.

Plasma is big business, a monopolized industry composed mostly of five international corporations. After the 2008 economic crisis, when Americans lost their jobs and homes during the Great Recession, the plasma industry suddenly had a swelling source of eager plasma sellers. New centers popped up across the country, and total donations—transactions, really—nearly doubled in five years, rising from 12.5 million in 2006 to more than 23 million in 2011, according to the Plasma Protein Therapeutics Association.[*] In 2008, plasma was a $4 billion industry. In 2015: $20 billion.[**]

[*] In 2019, plasma centers in the US received 53.5 million donations, about triple the number during the Great Recession, according to a University of Michigan–Ann Arbor study on the link between plasma donation and poverty.

[**] In 2023, market analysts projected the industry would be valued at $45.7 billion by 2027.

The sort of drugs made with your brother's plasma came onto the market during the 1950s and have a grim history. During the sixties and seventies, private plasma companies siphoned their product from the veins of American prison inmates, paying them five or ten dollars a hit.* From the late seventies to the mid-eighties, US officials estimated, about half of all diagnosed hemophiliacs contracted HIV from infected drugs derived from the plasma of such a high-risk population. The resulting class-action lawsuits revealed that one company knew it was flooding the market with dangerous supplies.

During the nineties, China turned poor, rural areas in Henan Province and elsewhere into springs of plasma. Chinese farmers' blood, it turned out, was worth more than their labor in the fields. In the process, dirty needles, other bad practices, and the resulting tainted plasma supply infected thousands, maybe hundreds of thousands, of Chinese people with HIV and hepatitis C. Every plasma station in the country would be shut down, but in the last few years they've blossomed again across the country. In 2012, a doctor who discovered the 1990s contamination published a letter warning of the dangers involved when "plasma collection once again becomes a profit-seeking route for some unscrupulous health officials and medical professionals on local levels, thus having devastating consequences for some of China's most vulnerable people."

What if your brother came across this information in a magazine while hooked up to the plasma machine? Would he feel a kinship with the US prisoners and the Chinese farmers? As it happens, your brother's grandpa went to prison a time or two;

* In early 2023, Massachusetts legislators proposed a bill directing the state Department of Correction to establish a program reducing incarcerated individuals' sentences by up to a year upon donation of their bone marrow or organs.

on the other side of his family he is the first man in generations
not to be a farmer. He worked hard to go to college instead of
to prison or the fields, but here he is, selling out his veins. If he
knew the history of plasma as a product, would he feel afraid
for his health, cheated by an economy?

Today in regulated markets like the United States, where
collection methods are sterile and technology has gotten sophisticated in cleaning contaminated supplies, plasma donation and
plasma-based drugs are considered exceedingly safe. On the
receiving end, transfusion of whole blood, which enters recipients much the same way it left its donors, is more likely to spread
disease. That's why blood is donated while plasma is purchased:
the chance to make fast cash might incentivize disease carriers to
lie about their health when showing up to give blood or plasma,
but disease would be destroyed during industrial processing
of the latter. The Food and Drug Administration thus requires
paid-for blood, frowned upon by the medical industry, to be
labeled as such. Paid-for plasma, most of which is transported
to drug factories, doesn't have to be labeled.

Laws about what body parts can be sold as goods are complicated. The year your brother was born, 1984, the National
Organ Transplant Act made it illegal to buy and sell organs.
Since a 2011 federal court decision, "donors" of some kinds of
bone marrow can be paid. People in budgetary binds legally sell
pieces of themselves for cash every day: sperm, eggs, hair. The
poor have long been valued for how much work their bodies
can do. Today, the body itself is a commodity.

The flow reverses and your brother's blood, its plasma gone
like panned gold, is pumped back into him: red cells, white
cells, platelets, sodium citrate mixed in as an anticlotting agent.
Promotional materials insist the process is harmless, but it isn't
always. Some donors, including your brother, get fatigued and

lightheaded. Occasionally people black out. The anticoagulant bonds with calcium in the blood and, in rare cases, can lead to dangerous calcium depletion.

A healthy body rebuilds the plasma that's been sold, but that takes time. Plasma can't be given more than twice a week, per FDA regulations. The United States is the only Western country that allows even that frequency. Lenient regulations and financial desperation amid historic wealth inequality means American plasma accounts for about 70 percent of collections worldwide. The holes that don't heal in your brother's arms are in thousands, maybe millions of American arms.

He's your brother because you share a country, an economy, a land, a species. If you met him, you'd probably think he was witty. He'd reach out to show you pictures of his pit bull on his cell phone, and you'd pay little mind to the hole in his arm near his short sleeve.

If he were your *brother-brother*, though, you would know him so deeply that the thought of him laying his arm down to sell what's in his veins would make you wince. His blood and all its parts would represent to you something that cannot be assigned a monetary value.

You'd remember the first time you saw it run down his body. He was two, you were six. You were taking a bath together. Your parents had left the bathroom, so you were alone in the soapy water entertaining him with plastic toys. He tried to stand up and slipped, hitting his face so hard on the side of the tub that it split open the smooth, delicate skin under one of his gray eyes. The cut opened up in the shape of a third eye. The blood that welled out of it was the brightest red you'd ever seen. The damp flesh around it went white.

You'd remember the sound of his cry, primal and scared, and how bad you felt—like it was your fault. He had to get stitches.

Your mom told the doctor they were sewn too tight in his soft
baby skin, but the doctor didn't listen. She was right. He still
has a scar under his eye that looks like the laces of a football.

After an hour in the recliner, though, while they take the
needle out of his arm, your brother isn't fretting about what
his blood means. He isn't regarding himself as a precious thing.
He isn't thinking about the hemophiliacs who need medication,
the drug corporations that will manufacture it, or the insurance
companies that will pay for it after someone pays them. He is
deciding what expenses to prioritize with forty-five dollars.

On his way to the checkout desk, he takes one of the cook-
ies set out on a tray for staving off nausea. He gets the money
he made applied to the prepaid debit card. His first purchase
will have to be at the gas station, as the gauge in his beater is
below E. When he gets behind the wheel he'll shake his head
to lose the dizziness and pray he has enough fuel to make it to
the pump.

THE UPRISING OF WOMEN IN "RED STATES" IS JUST BEGINNING

The Cut, 2018

O f the many groups rendered invisible by political stereotypes—liberal working-class men, conservative people of color, progressive Christians, and just about any instance of complexity within demographics viewed as monoliths—there is one I have long thought poised to be revolutionaries: reasonable women in so-called red states.

Public school teachers in particular, three-quarters of whom are women, have long held the line for democracy. While their state governments have swung right toward privatization, they have forged ahead with the pragmatic work of educating children, while ideological lawmakers, three-quarters of whom are men, cut their state budgets.

Today those women lead a labor uprising in places national media and Democratic politicians have erroneously written off as hopeless isles of angry, conservative White men: West Virginia. Oklahoma. Kentucky.

In recent weeks, West Virginia teachers closed down every

public school in all fifty-five state counties and won each of their five demands: a 5 percent raise, preserving seniority, stopping expansion of charter schools, blocking unfair means of calculating health insurance costs, and defeating a union-busting bill to prevent dues collection from paychecks.

Since then a wave of conservative-led states have seen their teachers organizing to demand what their state governments have threatened or taken away: a livable wage, respect, adequate funding for delivering on their mission. Some may be surprised by those teachers' stances in places currently represented by far-right politicians. But the fire in those women's chants echoing through capitol domes is no surprise to this daughter of southern Kansas—where undervalued, uncompromising women in public school classrooms were my first heroes and models of principled defiance.

In fourth grade, Mrs. Coykendall gave me lotion for my chapped hands and, unlike some teachers, called on ragamuffin me when I raised my hand. In fifth grade, Ms. Dunn explained her breast cancer to the class before boldly removing her wig because, she said, she hated how the thing itched. In seventh grade, a blustering male administrator lectured Mrs. Strothman in front of her own classroom and stormed out. She turned to us, smiled, and rolled her eyes. Watching from my desk, I imagined that someday I would roll my eyes when a male boss condescended to me. Through their actions, these women modeled a strength that they might not have called "feminism," but that's for damn sure what it was.

Women like my teachers, from places misleadingly painted by cable news graphics with monochromatic strokes of red, have been "resisting" since before it was cool—if not in organized action, then by the very act of surviving under state and local governments that have remained hostile to women regardless of Title IX and *Roe v. Wade*. Today, with their male allies, they are fighting back against extreme conservatism as Democrats, Republicans, and independents alike.

Meanwhile, women in jobs overlooked by our narrow, sexist definition of "working class," such as the service and caregiving industries, are challenging this country to expand its vision of labor beyond White men with tool belts, and make good on the promises of democracy.

Nationally, they're demanding higher wages through the Fight for $15 campaign as service-industry workers and pressing for universal health care as unionized nurses. In Kansas, whose administration shifted from moderate Democrat Kathleen Sebelius to far-right Republican Sam Brownback less than a decade ago, they are rising up as coalitions of lawmakers, first-time congressional candidates, activist groups, and underpaid public employees to push back against governments that would dismantle public health care, schools, and assistance for the children, elderly, and poor. With the US Supreme Court poised to decide a landmark case on dues collection by public-sector unions—a decision that could make way for union-stomping laws in states that have held them off thus far—millions more female public workers have cause to join this fight.*

You wouldn't know it from following national headlines for the last couple years, when safari reporting from poor and working-class areas beget countless stories of backward Bubba at the diner on Main Street. Those tropes have crystallized so thoroughly that "blue-state" liberals can't seem to square that millions of people in Republican-governed states vote Democrat, and vice versa. CNN's Joy Reid sarcastically tweeted during the West Virginia teachers' strike, "If they start voting for

---

* In *Janus vs. AFSCME* in 2018, the Supreme Court ruled it unconstitutional to collect fees from non-union public employees who receive union benefits. The decision was a major blow to public-sector unions.

politicians who actually support those things, look out GOP."
This simplistic take, like so many others, insulted the many
West Virginians who do vote for such politicians. It's a historically Democratic-leaning state, a seat of the American labor
movement, and one of many working-class bastions where a
socialist won the Democratic primary in 2016.

We overlook the history and nuance of "Trump country"
at our nation's peril. Every place that coastal media loves to
assign a tidy red narrative has a complicated history and willfully obscured past that those who seek change today should
remember.

In 1921, two hundred Kansas coal miners died in two counties, while earning a dollar a day. Miners went on strike, the
company bosses brought in scabs to replace them, and the
women of mining households—mostly German and Slovenian
immigrants—took to the street. They marched to the mines
carrying guns, babies, and American flags. They threw rocks at
the scabs and beat the bosses with brooms. The governor called
in the National Guard. A *New York Times* editorial wondered
whether police officers should start clubbing these female protesters over the head. Labor tensions would continue, but the
women of Kansas had ignited a national debate over not just
union rights but women's place in society. It is a debate we can
help settle by acknowledging that women's efforts for labor
rights help workers of all genders.

Last month, a woman wearing a red shirt in Charleston, West
Virginia, held a homemade poster-board sign declaring that her
own teachers had taught her she should know her worth. The
last line on her sign: "Today I lead by example." Joining the
teachers stopping work, she at once honored those who went
before her and walked the line for future generations of workers.

Today's labor movement among traditionally female occupations like teaching, nursing, and the service industry is not a ghost rising from the past, but a spirit that has always coursed through hardworking women by necessity, from a miner's wife who threw a rock to a teacher who held a sign. This movement shows the country that the members of a mostly female profession are more powerful than a mostly male legislature.

Why? They have been underpaid by male bosses and over-looked in national conversation since the beginning. They have toiled in places where "feminism" is less a cultural badge of honor than a high-stakes operation. They have been rolling their eyes for decades.

THE WINTER WHEAT I HELPED RAISE

Pacific Standard, 2018

The red winter wheat I helped raise west of Wichita was modified by man. Selected for a high yield come harvest, it grew in chemicals sprayed by low-flying planes that as a child I chased along the fields' edges. We were in those fields while powerful people discussed farm subsidies at restaurant tables. They researched and debated "the issues." Grandpa Arnie, who left school in sixth grade because his German-American dad said it was time to work, had a hole in his face where the skin cancer got cut out after decades on the tractor. So I reckon he knew quite a lot about the issues.

But there was a distance between what we knew and what we had the language or access to express. The people who taught me how to talk about America didn't talk much about it at all. They instead exuded a tacit, unemotional cynicism about so-called democracy and the painful void where our purchase on it might have been.

We were starved for someone to even feign to care about

us. In my lifetime, Republicans have done the feigning, to great effect. But, in my experience, rural areas are a flight risk to either party.

Free from allegiance to definitions that so often constrain the civically engaged, my family's politics are more like prairie grass than neat rows of wheat crops—independent, wild, overlooked. During the 2016 presidential primaries, like many working-class Americans, they supported a democratic socialist from Vermont.

Kansas politics, while presumed "deep red" in modern times, in earlier years were among the most progressive in the nation. The prairie populism of those times is largely forgotten, but I see it sprouting where CNN isn't looking. The greater divide in America today is not between red and blue but between what is discussed in powerful rooms and what is understood in the field.

WRITING ASSIGNMENT

The Guardian, 2018

Fourth grade should've been the hardest year of my early life.

My parents had divorced during the previous summer and sold the house my dad built with his own hands next to a wheat field. Economic opportunity lacking in rural Kansas, we moved to Wichita. I'd be back in rural schools in a couple years, but in 1989 I started the academic year in an urban district.

A new school, new place, newly divorced parents with new romantic partners—big challenges for a nine-year-old whose mom and dad were toiling on construction sites and in retail stockrooms as opposed to volunteering with the parent-teacher association.

Yet this began one of the happiest periods of my childhood: the year and a half when Mr. Cheatham was my teacher.

In the basement of an old brick building without air-conditioning, where teachers handed out ice chips at the hot start of the school year, Mr. Cheatham had built a creative paradise for learning: Art supplies for creating "magazine covers" that bound our writing. A piano to accompany the plays Mr. Cheatham—by then a veteran teacher in his fifties, with a thick walrus mustache—wrote for us to perform. A shuffleboard court painted on the concrete floor, for practicing math as we kept score. A tent that, with a flashlight shone through it, revealed a night sky of constellations for memorizing. A loft, reached by a wooden ladder, stuffed with bean bags and books.

Mr. Cheatham was the teacher designated for advanced learners—an opportunity that hadn't existed in my previous, rural school district—and I thus was in his class again in fifth grade.

Around 1990, I wrote my first bit of memoir in his class. I was from a family of Midwestern, German-Catholic farmers that wasn't much on reflecting. The demands of labor kept our eyes looking forward toward the next chore, the next bill, and our stoic culture frowned on self-expression.

But Mr. Cheatham had assigned us to write a story. For some reason, rather than making something up, I described a scene from my family, embedded with what I longed for someone to know: that my mom was unhappy, that money was tight, that I felt untethered from my home.

Mr. Cheatham mailed the raw tale to a national children's magazine, which published it as a two-page, illustrated spread. No one I knew had ever had their name in a magazine, let alone as the writer.

By the time the story made it into print, I had already changed schools again. Largely owing to the chaos of poverty, I would attend eight schools by the time I finished ninth grade—from a two-thousand-student Wichita high school, for just one semester, to a creaking two-room schoolhouse on the prairie containing thirty-three kids.

The winter I left Mr. Cheatham's classroom, my mom took me to the elementary school during holiday break to tell him goodbye. I was wearing a navy wool coat from a discount store and felt embarrassed that my fine blond hair was wild with static from the cold, dry air. It was the last time I saw him.

Around that time—the recent publication of my story an unimaginable joy and validation—I started telling my grandma, who was my primary caretaker for much of my upbringing, that someday I would write a book about our family.

In some ways, my family has more in common with the farmers and laborers who often voted against school-district bond issues—proposals to fund school renovations with a small tax increase—than they do with me, a first-generation college graduate and former English professor.

But, seeing how education gave me opportunities they never had, they are defenders of public education.

"Betsy DeVos is trying to get the Fed government to pay for GUNS for teachers," my grandma texted me recently. "How insane is that?"

I shared with her that Secretary of Education DeVos, who would begrudge dollars to public schools and predatory-loan forgiveness to defrauded college students, reportedly owns ten yachts. Someone recently untied one of them, valued at $40 million, from an Ohio dock, setting it adrift on Lake Erie.

"Too bad she wasn't in it," Grandma texted back.

The privatization DeVos seeks at the federal level began in my home state years ago. School districts sued the state in 1999 and 2010 for failing to provide adequate funding, the Kansas Supreme Court repeatedly ruled in their favor, and legislators refused to comply—a constitutional crisis that Democrats and moderate Republicans have fought to resolve by ousting conservative representatives.

Those who profit from the dismantling of public schools do so not just with tax dollars funneled into private school vouchers but with their control over information and ideas. One of the most overlooked threats to democracy is classroom curricula shaped by private interests for their own political, ideological, and financial benefit.

The current Kansas gubernatorial race reflects the state's twenty-year school-funding battle. Republican candidate Kris Kobach, best known for helming Donald Trump's busted voter-fraud commission and for unlawfully suppressing the votes of thirty thousand Kansans as secretary of state, has said current public school funding is excessive, evidenced by what he claimed are "Taj Mahal" buildings that "look like Fortune 500 companies." Meanwhile, Democratic candidate and state senator Laura Kelly, endorsed by the state teachers union, has pledged to be the "education governor" and undo damage wrought by recent governor Sam Brownback's deep tax cuts.*

Whatever their party allegiance, teachers in "red states" like mine aren't waiting for politicians to save them. Last spring in West Virginia, Oklahoma, and Kentucky they went on strike to demand better funding. In this year's midterm primary elections, Oklahoma educators organized to defeat Republican state House incumbents who voted against raising taxes to fund teacher pay raises. Of the nineteen Republicans who voted against the tax increase, eight have been defeated, seven didn't run, and just four have advanced to the general election.

---

* Kelly won that election, as well as reelection in 2022. During her governorship, she prioritized education and oversaw growth of previously depleted state funds.

Amid such a battle over public schools—the sole institution through which children of all backgrounds converge and receive opportunities that most families could not afford in a private system—I sometimes wonder what sort of classroom experience I would have had if born twenty or thirty years later than I was. Teachers may be as committed as ever, but the system in which they work has been strategically chipped at, falsely discredited, and at times underfunded since I graduated from high school in the late 1990s.

Those fighting to protect that system, though, are winning again. Last spring, the more moderate legislature voted in during the 2016 election approved $500 million in additional funding for Kansas schools, allowing districts to raise teacher salaries and restore cut positions.

Looking back, I see that public school teachers are not just educators but civic soldiers on the frontlines of democracy. They told me I was smart and could be anything—an overreaching statement in a country that has proven to be a plutocracy rather than a meritocracy but one that I gained something from believing. Armed with the education and encouragement they had given me, I boldly set my eyes on college and the sort of vocation no one from my family had ever known: to get paid for my ideas and creativity rather than for backbreaking or unfulfilling labor.

A book I started writing many years ago, about working-class women, being broke, and the gritty home I love, will be published this month. Mr. Cheatham is not just thanked in the acknowledgments but appears in a passage about the crucial role public education played in my life.

He doesn't know that. He's eighty-four, and I've not seen him in nearly three decades. But recently he appeared on Facebook, commenting about my upcoming book launch at Wichita's independent bookseller, Watermark Books.

There he was, the bushy mustache now thoroughly grayed, in a thumbnail photograph on my laptop screen. There was no "hello" or "it's been a long time," as though it was yesterday that I sat in his classroom, when computer screens were green and I had no access to them outside of my public school.

This was all he typed: "I'll be at Watermark with a story you wrote in 1990."*

---

* Cheatham attended the 2018 launch event for *Heartland*, hosted by Watermark Books at a large event venue in Wichita. When he appeared in the book-signing line, he had the story with him as promised.

LIBERAL BLIND SPOTS ARE
HIDING THE TRUTH

The New York Times, 2018

I s the White working class an angry, backward monolith—
some 90 million bigoted Americans without college degrees,
all standing around in factories and fields thumping their
dirty hands with baseball bats? You might think so after two
years of media fixation on this version of the aggrieved laborer:
male, White, conservative, racist, sexist.

This account does White supremacy a great service in several
ways: It ignores workers of color, along with humane, even
progressive White workers. It allows college-educated White
liberals to signal superior virtue while denying the sins of their
own place and class. And it conceals well-informed, formally
educated White conservatives—from middle-class suburbia to
the highest ranks of influence—who voted for Donald Trump
in legions.

The trouble begins with language: elite pundits regularly
misuse "working class" as shorthand for right-wing White
guys wearing tool belts. My father, a White man and lifelong

construction worker who labors alongside immigrants and people of color on job sites across the Midwest and South working for a Kansas-based general contractor owned by a woman, would never make such an error.

Most struggling Whites I know live lives of quiet desperation feeling angry at their White bosses, not at their coworkers or neighbors of color. My dad's previous three bosses were all White men he loathed for abuses of privilege and people, including himself.

It is unfair power that my father despises. The last rant I heard him on was not about race or immigration but about the recent royal wedding, the spectacle of which made him sick.

"What's so special about the royals?" he told me over the phone from a cheap motel after working construction hundreds of miles from home. "But they'll get the best health care, the best education, the best food. Meanwhile I'm in Marion, Arkansas. All I want is some chickens and a garden and place to go fishing once in a while."

What my father seeks is not a return to times that were worse for women and people of color but progress toward a society in which everyone can get by, including his White, college-educated son who graduated into the Great Recession and for ten years sold his own plasma for gas money. After being laid off during that recession in 2008, my dad had to cash in his retirement to make ends meet while looking for another job. He has labored nearly every day of his life and has no savings beyond Social Security. He does bear some individual responsibility for those outcomes, in my view, but for decisions and behaviors that financially comfortable people make every day with far less consequence.

Yes, my father is angry at someone. But it is not his coworker Gem, a Filipino immigrant with whom he has split a room to pocket some of the per diem from their employer, or Francisco, a Hispanic crew member with whom he recently built a Wendy's north of Memphis. His fury, rather, is directed at bosses who exploit labor and governments that punish the working poor—two sides of a capitalist democracy that bleeds people like him dry.

"Corporations," Dad said. "That's it. That's the point of the sword that's killing us."

Among White workers, this negative energy has been manipulated to great political effect by a conservative trifecta of media, private interest, and celebrity that we might call Fox, Koch, and Trump.

As my dad told me, "There's jackasses on every level of the food chain—but those jackasses are the ones that play all these other jackasses."

Still, millions of White working-class people have refused to be played. They have resisted the traps of racism, sexism, homophobia, xenophobia, and nationalism and voted the other way—or, in too many cases, not voted at all. I am far less interested in calls for empathy toward struggling White Americans who spout or abide hatred than I am in tapping into the political power of those who don't.

Like many Midwestern workers I know, my dad has more in common ideologically with New York's democratic-socialist congressional candidate Alexandria Ocasio-Cortez than with the White Republicans who run our state. Having spent most of his life doing dangerous, underpaid work without health insurance, he supports the ideas of single-payer health care and a universal basic income.

Much has been made of the White working class's political shift to the right. But Donald Trump won among White college graduates too. According to the Pew Research Center in

2016, 49 percent of Whites with degrees picked Trump, while 45 percent picked Hillary Clinton (among them, support for Trump was stronger among men). Such Americans hardly "vote against their own best interest." Media coverage suggests that economically distressed Whiteness elected Trump, when in fact it was just plain Whiteness.

Stories dispelling the persistent notion that racism is the sole province of "uneducated" people in derided "flyover" states are right before our eyes: A White man caught on camera assaulting a Black man at a White supremacist rally last August in Charlottesville, Virginia, was recently identified as a California engineer. This year, a White male lawyer berated restaurant workers for speaking Spanish in New York City. A White, female, Stanford-educated chemical engineer called the Oakland, California, police on a family for, it would appear, barbecuing while Black.

Among the thirty states tidily declared red after the 2016 election, in two-thirds of them Clinton received 35 to 48 percent of the vote. My White working-class family was part of that large minority, rendered invisible by the Electoral College and graphics that paint each state red or blue.

In the meantime, critical stories here in "red states" go under-discussed and underreported, including:

Barriers to voting. Forces more influential than the political leanings of a White factory worker decide election outcomes: gerrymandering, super PACs, corrupt officials. In Kansas, Secretary of State Kris Kobach blocked thirty thousand would-be voters from casting ballots (and was recently held in contempt of federal court for doing so).

Different information sources. Some of my political views shifted when my location, peer group, and news sources changed during my college years. Many Americans today have a glut of information but poor media literacy—hard to rectify if you work on your feet all day, don't own a computer, and didn't get a chance to learn the vocabulary of national discourse.

Populism on the left. Today, "populism" is often used interchangeably with "far right." But the American left is experiencing a populist boom. According to its national director, Democratic Socialists of America nearly quadrupled in size from 2016 to 2017—and saw its biggest one-day boost the day after Ocasio-Cortez's recent primary upset. Progressive congressional candidates with working-class backgrounds and platforms have major support heading into the midterms here in Kansas, including the White civil rights attorney James Thompson, who grew up in poverty, and Sharice Davids, a Native American lawyer who would be the first openly lesbian representative from Kansas.

To find a more accurate vision of these United States, we must resist pat narratives about any group—including the working class on whom our current political situation is most often pinned. The greatest con of 2016 was not persuading a White laborer to vote for a nasty billionaire with soft hands. Rather, it was persuading a watchdog press to incompletely portray the American working class. The resulting national conversation, which seeks to rename my home "Trump country," elevates a White supremacist agenda by undermining resistance and solidarity where it is most urgent and brave.

Author's note: About a month after publishing the above essay, the New York Times *published the follow-up below, under the headline "Our Blind Spots Often Hide the Truth About America," with their editor's note at the top.*

—

Editor's note: An op-ed by Sarah Smarsh, "Liberal Blind Spots Are Hiding the Truth About 'Trump Country,'" received more than fifteen hundred comments from readers. Here are a selection of the comments, which raised questions that we put to the author.

Mary V., Virginia: I had a conversation last week with a woman I had recently met. We were talking about the importance of supporting women in all types of roles—as professional chefs, doctors (she is an emergency-room physician), and throughout all levels of society, including politics. I casually mentioned how cool I thought it was that Alexandria Ocasio-Cortez had won her race in the Bronx. My companion's demeanor immediately changed, and she flatly replied, "As a Christian and a capitalist, I have absolutely no interest in anything that socialist has to say."

The speed with which this happened was both startling and disturbing. Our friendly conversation was wiped out in a matter of seconds by her swift application of labels—her own self-identification, and to Ms. Ocasio-Cortez.

Q: To what extent do labels prevent productive dialogue?

Sarah Smarsh: A couple of years ago, over beers at a bar in Texas, my dad—a White construction worker from rural Kansas, described in my piece—shocked me by saying, "If you get past everything you've been told and really read up on it, 'socialism' doesn't sound all that bad." Soon after that, a democratic socialist, Bernie Sanders, won the Democratic caucus or primary for president in twenty-two states, including our home state of Kansas.

Not everyone is so open-minded. The weaponization of terms such as "feminist," "liberal," and "socialist"—and thus the vilification of those who claim those labels—has long been a successful strategy for preserving power. Labels always oversimplify, but at their worst they dehumanize: "illegals," for instance. You are right to be disturbed by the negative charge with which your acquaintance said "that socialist."

Diminishing a perceived opponent or an inconvenient fact through name-calling—say, "fake news"—is a hallmark of the current Republican administration, but dangerous labels work in all directions. Envisioning a "red state" as a field of "deplorables" leads some self-righteous liberals to say those states "get what they deserve"—as though everyone suffering for lack of Medicaid expansion voted for their conservative state officials, as though everyone even gets to vote. In most states, the losing political party receives 30 to 40 percent of the vote. Those millions of people, along with the disenfranchised, are no more represented by their state administrations than liberals nationally are represented by our current president. Calling their home "Trump country" is thus a childish misnomer.

Labels even err when self-ascribed. Into my early twenties, I inaccurately called myself "conservative" with little understanding of what that meant. One of the most destructive assumptions we make in political discourse is that people's parties and votes align with their beliefs. In fact, a better indicator of political behavior is one's place, culture, and social group—conditions we're born into, by no virtue or fault of our own.

Productive dialogue requires that we set aside our assumptions about other people and places and refuse to reduce them to labels—even ones that they themselves embrace. We must remain vigilant against easy, reductive frameworks, perhaps especially those that appeal to our own biases.

———

Leonard Ray, Baton Rouge, Louisiana: I live in the area that you might think people describe as "Trump country" (our state voted 58–38 for Donald Trump). To be honest, most of the White people I know don't have many African-American neighbors . . . sometimes coworkers, yes, but many times not even that. "Trump country" (as well as "non-Trump country") isn't exactly racially integrated to a great degree . . . there are pockets where it is, but not many. So I'm not sure there's much opportunity to be, in a personal sense, mad at coworkers or neighbors of color.

Q: You say your father works alongside minorities, but what about people who have few interactions with people outside their race?

Smarsh: I grew up mostly in a small town that was overwhelmingly White. The handful of students of color were embraced—not because White students were liberally minded, I think, but because by virtue of our shared home a minority student was "one of us." As the researcher Brené Brown has written: "People are hard to hate up close. Move in."

I am certain, however, that some of the White students in my hometown who loved their individual Brown peers harbored racist views about those minorities as a group. Similarly, my father's positive working relationship and friendships with laborers of color does not preclude him from racist thoughts or actions.

Where the limitations of individual experience beget tribalism, we might summon the power of information and education to help us transcend our own groups and narrow visions of the world. What if *An Indigenous Peoples' History of the United States*, by Roxanne Dunbar-Ortiz, were required reading in a

public school's social studies curriculum? What if public college
were available to everyone, tuition-free? One doesn't need a
degree to know the difference between love and hate, right and
wrong. One does, in a world of racist messages, need unbiased
facts to form a worldview that does not favor Whiteness.

While we work toward systemic justice and integration, we
can strive at the individual level to break free from our proverbial bubbles. My humble attempt at this involves attending
public events, celebrations, and church services in communities
outside my own, and following and reading people of color,
whose wisdom for answering your question likely exceeds mine.

Sean C., Charlottetown, Prince Edward Island, Canada: Sarah
Smarsh's article is one part anecdotal and one part wishful
thinking (it would be nice if economic populism was the key to
reaching Trump voters). There has been extensive polling and
social science assessment of Trump voters, and White racial
grievance is overwhelmingly the biggest predictor of support
for him. Indeed, White racial grievance has been driving the
White working class toward the Republicans since the 1960s.
She is correct to note that Trump also won plenty of White
college graduates, but that is a different issue, as the well-off
have always supported Republicans. It's easy to see what they
get from Trump—a big tax cut.

*Q: Are White racial grievances deciding factors for higher-
earning Trump supporters as well, just more easily hidden in
their votes for a tax cut?*

Smarsh: I agree that motivations among different income brackets of White Trump voters surely differ, but only in the version

of power they seek to preserve. Ultimately, though it might be harder to see in one group or another, they all reap both racial and economic advantage.

However, your point is misplaced here. You seem to be responding, as did a number of commenters, as though I wrote a piece about Trump voters—a group that has, by my estimation, enjoyed too much attention. I wrote instead about people like my White, working-class family who are presumed, based on their place and identity, to be Trump supporters but are, in fact, something else—apathetic or disenfranchised nonvoters, Democrats, newly minted democratic socialists, independents.

As I wrote, "I am far less interested in calls for empathy toward struggling White Americans who spout or abide hatred than I am in tapping into the political power of those who don't."

Yet from another comment recommended more than thirteen hundred times: "To the author: If your father and good people like him hate unfair power, corporations, and bosses that exploit workers, then wouldn't supporting Trump be against their own interests?" To which I answer, yes, it would. That's why the people I wrote about don't support Trump.

This dissonance between my story and a large portion of the reaction (*Me: Not everyone in "Trump country" is for Trump. Them: Then why are they all for Trump!*) proves the point of my piece—that the dominant narrative about much of our country is not just inaccurate but willfully blind.

Lissa, Virginia: "The trouble begins with language: elite pundits regularly . . ." This article gives all of us a lot to ponder. But I cannot get past the number of times I have written a comment asking for an explanation of the word "elite" in the context in which the word is used in a specific article. Extrapolating terms incorrectly and otherwise generalizing is at the core of what Sarah Smarsh is arguing. She begins by doing the very thing she goes on to lament. I don't want to take away from her very real points, but the word "elite" is one of the words that has been misused as a tool for division and often as a tool for deriding high levels of education.

Q: Does the term "elite" get misused and applied too broadly, just as "working class" often is?

Smarsh: The term "elite" is successfully leveraged by conservative propagandists seeking to cast coastal liberals as condescending snobs. A native of rural Kansas, I've lived in blue urban places, where some of my dearest friends and most staunch professional advocates reside. Having straddled that cultural divide, as a writer and citizen, I resist the stereotyping of either side.

However, objections to valid class critiques—feeling outraged when working-class people express their grievances toward wealth without pausing to point out all the virtuous people who possess it—often strike me as the class equivalent of Whites accusing people of color of reverse racism, or men accusing feminists of misandry. The prevailing narratives of our media and culture operate in service to those male, White, or financially comfortable people who claim equal offense. So we must listen with particular concern to the protests of those for whom inaccurate portrayals represent not just distasteful generalizations but economic and even mortal danger. If articulating that injustice comes with an edge of anger, well, try being on the losing end of a narrative every day of your life and see how patient it makes your language.

My piece uses the term in question once: "elite pundits

regularly misuse 'working class' as shorthand for right-wing White guys wearing tool belts." Here I am describing political commentators who hold the immense privilege of being called upon for their opinions in national media. That is, by definition, an elite platform, and its rarefied stature is relevant to my discussion of classist narratives. I'm not generalizing but rather specifying a real power structure in our country.

Steve Paradis, Flint, Michigan: I wonder what the newspapers are like in Wichita, Kansas. I grew up watching my parents reading the daily paper and picked up the habit from them. Front to back page, too, just as it was delivered, scanning every page, even the boring local stuff about zoning boards and school board meetings. That same paper now has about three pages of local news—mostly crime or mayhem—and the obits. The rest is homogenized stories from the various wire services; the paper itself is a mid-state edition covering about a hundred-mile radius. That means the local political news coverage is gone, and there's only a page or two of state news. So you don't see your life in the paper anymore, no more than you see on television, broadcast, or cable. You don't see yourself or people like you in the media, and it's easy to think that the media doesn't think you matter.

Q: Does your father seek news outlets different from that of other working-class members of his community? Does he feel he is incorrectly portrayed by more "liberal" news outlets?

Smarsh: Like most newspapers in midsize cities, the *Wichita Eagle* staff and print product has shrunk since my childhood in the 1980s and '90s. I grew up at the tail end of the newspaper era and still "take the paper," reading it front to back each morning. I was a member of the last class of my journalism school to receive an old-fashioned newspaper training before the digital era altered curricula toward "media convergence." The demise of local news was the backdrop of my early career, increasing my awareness of how a dearth of local reporting resources is inextricably woven into today's divisive political climate.

My piece names disparate information sources among the electorate as one of the most overlooked influences on political ideologies, party identification, and voting habits. I have spent much of my career developing strategies to counteract that civic media crisis. It's one reason that I still live in my home state of Kansas rather than a major media center—a sense of responsibility to live in the place about which I write.

Coastal media is often criticized for inadequate "parachute journalism" into Middle America, but it shouldn't be New York's job to understand Nebraska. Nebraska understands Nebraska. I am sure that state is teeming with qualified journalists who still have local contacts and understandings, who were laid off in the last fifteen years, and who would gladly report for duty if someone paid them to do so.

Until then, as you say, people there and in so many places are left with wildly biased and polarized social media "silos," national outlets that rarely mention their home, and—if they're lucky—cash-strapped local outlets for their information. For those in rural America, I know firsthand, the resulting sense of not just isolation but misrepresentation and even invisibility is profound. That's shifted some in the last few years, but now when they're written about, it's all Trump or opioids or economic despair.

There's a lot more to those communities. There's joy, heroic community problem-solving, and even some liberals. To remain unseen and unheard in national conversation is an invalidation. It's no surprise that some might be suspicious of "the media" and vulnerable to messaging that journalists aren't trustworthy.

As for my dad, he believes his best news source is folks on the ground—his fellow construction workers on job sites, locals in line at gas stations, and, as he traverses the Midwest and South for the next job, cashiers he chats up at the grocery store. He makes a point of asking them what's going on in their communities and what they think about current events, and he shares his information in kind. Even with a daughter for a journalist, he most prizes stories straight from the mouths of those who live them. So do I. As he put it when I asked him, "I get my news from the people I talk to, not Sean Hannity."

Liz, New York City, New York: As a native Arkansan, I so deeply appreciate what Sarah Smarsh is saying about seeing the complexity of people's experience, and the urgent necessity for working people of all races, sexes, and locations to band together. As an adopted New Yorker, I felt stabbed by the word "elite," which has become a catchword by which conservatives dismiss and disparage everything that folks in this great city think and feel.

I am a queer theologian, a single mother of two who works three jobs and, like most New Yorkers, struggles every month to pay the exorbitant rent. I am nearly desperate for a movement to take hold along the lines Smarsh describes: those of us who struggle refusing to be duped by the powerful and wealthy forces that pit us against one another for their own gain, seeing one another as we really are, as we really struggle, as we really hope and dream for a better life, for all of us. For that reason, I'll tamp down my visceral reaction to the unfortunate word "elite." Ms. Smarsh, thank you for this eloquent piece. We have more in common than even you may know, and I hope we can keep building that mutual understanding.

Q: *What would you say to those who feel hidden behind a label?*

Smarsh: I told my dad to never read the comments, but he did—and yours was the one he wanted me to read. It moved him deeply, so I'll let him respond: "This person is what the world needs. I am inspired by her grit, determination, hope, unity as an answer. Her life should not be like this in America."

AT THE PRECISE GEOGRAPHIC HEART
OF THE DARK-MONEY BEAST

The Guardian, 2018

In a dim corridor backstage, Vermont senator Bernie Sanders looked down at Kansas congressional hopeful James Thompson's denim jeans and black boots. "Hey, James," Sanders said without cracking a smile. "Could I borrow your cowboy shoes?"

Thompson took just a second to recover from the razzing.

"I wear them because the shit's so deep around here," he replied.

Through the thick cement walls of this downtown Wichita convention hall, we heard the roar of four thousand Kansans awaiting speeches by Sanders, Thompson, and progressive rocket ship Alexandria Ocasio-Cortez in support of Thompson's run for Congress. It was Ocasio-Cortez's first political appearance outside New York after her remarkable primary win in June, when the twenty-eight-year-old democratic social-ist defeated one of the most powerful House Democrats in

Washington. Here in the lower Midwest, Thompson—who also has never held office—has tapped into similar yearning for a representative who has more old friends at the local pub than in DC.

The choice of location for Ocasio-Cortez's debut outside New York is poetic. Like Sanders, she and Thompson have refused corporate donations, and this district is home to perhaps the greatest conservative influencers in US history—the Koch brothers, whose political network pledged to spend $400 million on conservative candidates before the midterms.

It's one thing to push the Democratic Party left in New York City. It is quite another to rabble-rouse for universal health care, wind energy, and a livable wage in Charles Koch's backyard. Doing so takes, my friends in the Northeast might say, hutzpah.

Or, as my Kansas farmer grandpa might have said: That Jim is full of piss and vinegar.

No congressional candidate has ever done what Thompson is doing in this era of unrestricted corporate campaign donations: hold a progressive sword at the precise geographic heart of the dark-money beast. When I asked whether anyone has, say, tried to break his kneecaps, Thompson let out a big laugh.

"I'd like to see them try," he said. "That's one good thing about being six foot two."

Such humor—joking in a manner that polite society might view as unseemly—is the necessary roughness that millions of Americans develop to survive on job sites, in barrooms, in their own homes while the air-conditioning window unit drips water onto the carpet.

It only makes sense that a progressive movement unifying the working class across lines of race, gender, age, religion, and location would contain candidates like Thompson, who is both a civil rights attorney who represented detained immigrants and victims of police brutality and a former bouncer at a Wichita country-western nightclub called InCahoots.

A hard story often comes with hard language. During a period of homelessness, Thompson bathed, washed clothes, and fished for food in a canal. He fought for emancipation from an abusive parent and attended sixteen schools before finishing high school. This is not a man who, in the face of rising authoritarianism, will be "civil" to please pearl-clutching political leaders on either side of the aisle.

This is precisely his appeal in southern Kansas. Thompson might be a new star for coastal reporters. But his combination of progressive ideas and unapologetically impolite language has been gaining supporters—and even converting some Trump voters—for a year and a half without the National Democratic Party lifting a finger.

In contrast to a version of liberal America often criticized as, well, a bunch of wimps, his campaign slogan is "Fight for America."

Thompson told me he was first encouraged to run for office by Republican friends who felt out of sync with a party morphing into an "insanely right caricature." A pro-choice, gun-owning military veteran who supports legal weed and Social Security expansion, Thompson can kick dirt with farmers at rural events, walk in Wichita's recent Pride and Juneteenth parades, and post a photo of himself smiling with two guys wearing "Bearded Deplorable" shirts after a long conversation about the issues.

He nearly won a special election last year. Now Ocasio-Cortez and Sanders—who won the Kansas Democratic caucus for the 2016 presidential nomination two to one—are here to make sure he gets it done in the midterms, thus flipping this district blue for the first time in twenty-six years.

The eager crowd, which outgrew its original venue and was relocated at the last minute to accommodate thousands more, is mostly Midwesterners who loathe Trump and were long ago written off as a waste of resources by the National Democratic Party. Recently governed by extreme conservative Sam Brownback for eight years, they were resisting long before it was a national movement.

In contrast to red-hatted rallies that in 2016 got far more political coverage, they are both pissed off and peaceful, both riled up for change and diverse in racial makeup.

Thompson knows that, while the progress his would-be constituents seek is toward a dignified and humane world, the fire in their bellies must now be summoned.

"I had to fight all the time. Literally and figuratively," Thompson will tell them from the stage, as he asks them to fight now alongside him. "That's just part of growing up in poverty. When I see people struggling and I talk about it, I'm not talking about it from up on a hill somewhere."

Ocasio-Cortez, who has faced different uphill battles, carries herself with the same self-possession. She taunted on *The Late Show with Stephen Colbert* that the current president doesn't know "how to deal with a girl from the Bronx." She and Thompson evoke the unflagging spirit of California representative Maxine Waters, who received death threats for unapologetic criticism of the corrupt Washington regime and responded, "You better shoot straight."

This scrappy attitude is not the empty bluster of a fearful ego with a yellow comb-over seeking to preserve itself. It is a knowing of one's own strength, fortified by the mortal dangers of poverty, labor, misogyny, White supremacy.

It is the Statue of Liberty looking a bully in the eye in a barroom and saying to someone standing behind her, "Hold my torch."

To back up their talk, Ocasio-Cortez and Thompson quite literally walk the walk.

The day after the Wichita event, Ocasio-Cortez told me by phone from Missouri, where she was campaigning for congressional candidate and fellow progressive Cori Bush, that physical presence both builds support and dissolves the political polarities on which so many pundits feed.

"When someone actually knocks on your door or goes to your civic association meeting and you actually touch their hand, it really does change everything," said Ocasio-Cortez, who recently tweeted a photo of the shoes she wore door-to-door, holes worn through the soles, with the comment, "Respect the hustle."

"There are places in the Bronx and neighborhoods in Queens that look like neighborhoods in Wichita," she told me. "I walked in thinking I was in for a world of hurt. There is this impulse to just abandon it. To just say, you know what, forget it—it's a lost cause. It's just gonna be difficult or hurtful or dangerous. But I decided to go in anyway."

What she got for her leap of faith was one of the most important political upsets in modern history—and an appreciation for the extent to which working-class voters have felt forgotten.

Her forty-eight-hour tour of Wichita and Kansas City, Kansas, as well as St. Louis, Missouri, proved her instincts correct, recalling fellow community organizer Barack Obama's musings about his well-received travels through the rural Midwest as a Black liberal.

"The thing that I hear over and over and over again is 'thank you for coming here,' 'thank you for coming,'" she said, her tone implying incredulousness that, besides Sanders, other Democrats with national platforms hadn't deigned to visit. "Presence is such a basic thing to ask for."

Sanders told me by phone from Washington, a few days after his Kansas stop, that a fifty-state strategy is common sense.

"It is beyond comprehension, the degree to which the Democratic Party nationally has essentially abdicated half of the states in this country to right-wing Republicans, including some of the poorest states in America, those in the South," Sanders said. "The reason I go to Kansas and many so-called red states is that I will do everything that I can to bring new people into the political process in states which are today conservative. I do not know how you turn those states around unless you go there and get people excited."

For many in the crowd, his visit was validation of months of hard work that takes particular gumption in a place described by so many headlines as "Trump country."

Since launching his first run for the seat in early 2017, Thompson says, he and his campaign have knocked on 40,000 doors and made 330,000 phone calls. Including phone bankers across the country, the effort has included 7,000 volunteers.

That hustle has already knocked twenty-four points off the Republican Party's lead—from thirty-one points when the current secretary of state, Mike Pompeo, won in 2014 to just seven points in last year's special election won by Representative Ron Estes.

Before the rally with Sanders and Ocasio-Cortez, Thompson

reflected on the difference between his approach and that of opponent Estes when he's back from Washington.

"[He] is either in a vehicle waving or walking down the center of the street waving," Thompson said. "He had four hundred individual donations in the special election. We had twenty-nine thousand. As long as he's got his four hundred people that are willing to donate money, and the big corporate PACs giving money, he doesn't need to dirty his hands shaking hands with people."

On social media, Thompson has been challenging Estes to debate him in each of the district's seventeen counties—"show up or shut up," Thompson has said, with no response. While under a very different context, it's not so unlike when New York representative Joe Crowley kept failing to appear at primary debates against Ocasio-Cortez.

"Thinking that you can get a job without showing up for the job interview just is wild to me," Thompson said.

This is the great irony of conservative criticism of progressive candidates. Candidates such as Sanders, Ocasio-Cortez, and Thompson are accused of seeking handouts for lazy moochers, while evidence suggests they are the hardest workers in the fight.

When Ocasio-Cortez was in fifth grade, her tough teacher in the New York City public schools was a Kansas native with a fierce love for her home state. Young Ocasio-Cortez was nervous, she told the Wichita audience, when the teacher organized a state history project and assigned her Kansas.

"After reading a lot about wheat, as a ten-year-old," Ocasio-Cortez said to laughs, "I learned that Kansas was founded in a struggle over the conscience of this nation."

She referenced the Kansas-Nebraska Act of 1854, which charged the Kansas territory with deciding whether they would allow slavery. Abolitionists fought bloody border wars with neighboring, slave-holding Missouri—sparking the Civil War—and Kansas was established as a free state.

"That is the crucible and the soul of this state," Ocasio-Cortez said, articulating what many Kansans know but rarely see reflected in modern politics, national discussion, or the Electoral College that obscures their votes.

Like Sanders and Thompson, she pointed out that persistent notions of Kansas as a "deep red" state didn't jibe with the large minority she was seeing on the ground. While the Wichita crowd thundered after one of Sanders's remarks onstage, Ocasio-Cortez peeked out from behind the curtain with her cell phone. She tweeted the video, adding: "The Midwest feels pretty all right to me!"

Meanwhile, leaders in the Democratic Party from House minority leader Nancy Pelosi to former senator Joe Lieberman have been critical of this excitement, suggesting that moving left harms the party.

"If a centrist model is what works [in Kansas], then why has that centrist model not won the past twenty years, and in fact lost by twenty to thirty points in every election since [1992]?" Thompson asked me. "The idea that we need to be more like Republicans so we can beat Republicans is asinine. We need to have a clear choice. Something to vote for instead of against."

One such thing would be Medicare for all, he said, which he acknowledged isn't feasible under the current legislature but has pledged to work toward. When describing public health care or other programs that have been defunded or privatized into oblivion, he put it in language working-class voters might appreciate.

"It's like taking a car, taking the battery out, and going,

'Oh, see, it doesn't run anymore. So we need to get rid of it,'"
Thompson said. "Put the battery back in."

He laughed when I noted there are a lot of lawmakers who
would never think of a car battery as an analogy—because
they've never had to change one themselves. Thompson
explained that law school taught him to avoid legalese when
addressing a jury.

"[Voters] want to hear me talking about real solutions in
plain language that is not mealymouthed and trying to play
both sides of the fence," said Thompson, who walked onstage
to Garth Brooks's 1990 country hit "Friends in Low Places."
"Regardless of whether they agree or not, they're going to
respect that a lot more."

Thompson told me that he learned in the military both to be
willing to have conversations with people who have different
perspectives and to draw a line in the sand when someone
doesn't share your openness.

"You offer 'em a choice," Thompson said. "I would prefer
to sit down and talk. But if you wanna be an ass, all right."

While he does not identify as a democratic socialist like Sanders and Ocasio-Cortez, Thompson is perceived at the national
level as a party rebel for his stances on the minimum wage,
health care, and other basic assurances that all three candidates
insist will summon voters regardless of location in midterm
primaries and elections this year.

"They're not radical ideas—they're common-sense ideas,"
Thompson told the crowd at the convention hall. They laughed
when he added, "That's why we see a crowd of thousands here
today when there was a MAGA rally four days ago that had
fifty people at it."

But Thompson got some of the event's wildest cheers when
he spoke about the supposedly more divisive matters of wom-
en's reproductive rights. He is a defender of *Roe v. Wade* and
proponent of legal weed.

"When people talk about raising money for our state? Here's
an idea: legalize marijuana," he said, and the crowd exploded.

At another point, he called out false narratives about his
home that might cause some to be surprised by the massive
gathering at noon on a weekday, months before the election
in a midterm year: "When people wanna say this is Trump
country, I say 'hell no.'"

Video of this statement made it onto his least favorite cable
television network, later prompting Thompson to tweet with
several laugh-cry emojis, "Must be doing something right if Fox
is talking about me and causing alt-right heads to explode."

It's a herculean undertaking to fight the forces that work
against Thompson's campaign: Fox News, the Koch brothers,
his own Democratic Party. Where I'm from, there's only one
thing that might hold more sway than they do: straight talk
and an authentic handshake.

Solidarity from Sanders, Ocasio-Cortez, and other candidates
and activists across the country fortifies the progressive Kansans
doing the talking and shaking.

"If James wins here," Sanders said onstage, "this will be not
only another progressive member to the Congress. This will be
a shot heard around—not just this country—the world."

All three candidates challenged the crowd to channel the
energy of the moment into the civic action that might decide
election outcomes.

"I'm just a figurehead," Thompson said. "You are the way
that we flip this district. You are the ones that can make the
changes that you want. You are the ones that have the power

in this country. It's not with the Koch brothers. It's not with the big corporations. It's with you."

The crowd cheered so loudly that a woman behind me plugged her ears with her fingers.

"Ron Estes, I hope you look at this crowd and are shakin' in your boots," Thompson said. "Because we're coming for you."*

---

* Despite having come close to flipping Kansas's Fourth Congressional District with the 2017 special election, following then representative Mike Pompeo's departure to join the Trump administration as director of the Central Intelligence Agency, in the 2018 midterms Thompson's grassroots campaign received little financial support from the state Democratic Party and none from the national party. Thompson lost that race to incumbent Republican Ron Estes by a much larger margin of nineteen points.

BLUE WAVE IN KANSAS

The New York Times, 2018

At an open-air debate at the Kansas State Fair in September, a raucous crowd roared, cheered, and booed with such vigor that the candidates often were forced to pause before they could speak.

The Republican candidate for governor, Kris Kobach, and the independent, Greg Orman, had strong support in the packed bleachers. But the loudest cheers, to my ears, were for the Democrat, state senator Laura Kelly. She fed off the approval, delivering zingers and carrying her small stature with swagger.

The loudest boos were for Kobach, the secretary of state, who earlier in the year had been found in contempt of federal court for failing to notify unlawfully suppressed voting registrants of their eligibility.

"You're a criminal!" one man shouted several times. Kobach paused for a beat and shook his head with a laugh. The heckler was my partner, a White, male construction worker who is the most radical progressive I know.

Soon, someone behind us took up the call.

"You're a criminal!" she shouted. I turned, and a middle-aged White woman wearing a pro-teachers T-shirt smiled sweetly at me.

"So he can take a break," she said, nodding at my mate.

One might wonder how Kelly, a moderate Democrat similar to Hillary Clinton in politics, age, and strategy, decisively won a governor's race in "Trump country" against a candidate whose signature anti-immigrant tactics precisely align with President Trump's xenophobic closing argument to midterm voters. Trump and Vice President Mike Pence both traveled to Kansas to campaign for Kobach, as did Donald Trump Jr.

So, liberal Laura Kelly—how? One reason is that there never was a "Trump country" at all. Rather, like many "red states," Kansas is a gerrymandered, dark-monied place where election outcomes may have more to do with who votes and how those votes are counted than with the character of the place. In such states, Fox News and conservative talk radio have artfully prodded White fears to great effect, but about 40 percent of voters routinely reject the Republican Party. In Kansas, Trump won the general election, but Bernie Sanders won far more votes than Trump during the state's caucuses. Party tribalism has increased here, in recent years, but a legacy of independent, unpredictable politics runs deeper.

In fact, dozens of former and current Kansas Republican lawmakers endorsed Kelly, supporting what the governor-elect in her victory speech on Tuesday night called not a "blue wave" but a "wave of common sense."

To be sure, if the Electoral College is our barometer, Kansas is deep red. It hasn't gone for a Democratic presidential candidate since 1964. My home congressional district, a mix of rural counties and the city of Wichita, has been represented by a Republican for twenty-three years.

Nonetheless, as of election night, exactly one state has elected three female Democratic governors: Kansas—and all in the last twenty-eight years.

Kelly's win is notable not for being out of keeping with the political spirit of the state but for representing the end of what many Kansans woefully call "the Brownback era"—after the former governor Sam Brownback—when religious conservatism and free-market extremism made the state synonymous with far-right politics in national headlines.

Kobach is a different sort of creature than Brownback, who for all his terrible ideas comes across as a man who believes in something larger than himself. Kobach, rather, is Trumpian—from disregard for the Constitution to grotesque displays of bravado, as when he joined a suburban summer parade in a Jeep mounted with a realistic replica of a .50-caliber machine gun. But the Kelly campaign rightly linked Kobach's government-strangling economic vision to the unpopular Brownback, whose own voters turned against his 2012 "live experiment" with deep tax cuts once they saw what it wrought on public schools and roads.

Kobach ran ads that turned "liberal" into a pejorative and pledged to shield Kansas from outside forces like the federal government and immigrants. Kelly said she'd put political labels aside and work to build a better Kansas from the inside out.

At her election-night watch party, before Kelly's race was called, the crowd cheered when a fellow pragmatist and the first-time candidate Sharice Davids defeated a four-term Republican in Kansas's Third Congressional District. But a more staunch progressive did not fare as well. In the Fourth Congressional District, the civil rights attorney and military veteran James Thompson spent twenty months unapologetically championing Medicare for All and marijuana legalization. He won over leftist populists and fed-up conservatives alike but came up short in his effort to flip one of the nation's most conservative districts, home to the billionaire Charles Koch and Koch Industries.

Kansas's big Democratic wins, it turned out, were by women with less bold platforms who emphasized working across the aisle. It seems that if Midwestern states are bound for a return to their democratic-socialist roots—prairie populism, it was once called—they will first require a return to center in female form.*

Regional wins by moderate Democrats prompted one writer to suggest that the next Democratic presidential nominee be "a steaming pot of Midwestern Nice." Midwestern Nice, this woman of the lower Midwest has observed, is not necessarily lacking in radical ideas or competitive fire but is never mean or flustered. While potentially passive aggressive, it is more often plainly unimpressed. Think of the Senate Judiciary Committee hearings in September when the Supreme Court nominee Brett Kavanaugh disrespected the authority of Senator Amy Klobuchar of Minnesota. Her pained smile conveyed that she was having precisely none of it, but she avoided being reactive. Later, Judge Kavanaugh offered an apology, and Senator Klobuchar—who won reelection this week by a landslide—accepted.

Laura Kelly, whose campaign emphasized public schools, Medicaid expansion, and infrastructure, does her job with the same steadiness. So did Kansas's last Democratic governor, Kathleen Sebelius, the former Department of Health secretary and an Affordable Care Act architect. Kansas elected Sebelius twice, not so long ago, along with a lieutenant governor she

---

* In 2022, Kansas had the only Democratic-held governorship up for election in a state Donald Trump won in the 2020 presidential election; Kelly won reelection, defeating Republican Derek Schmidt. During that same election, Davids was elected to her third term as a US representative from Kansas's Third Congressional District.

poached from the Republican Party for the sake of getting things done.

If this be Trump country, it seems the only thing more compelling to its voter majority than a far-right Republican man is a no-nonsense Democratic woman, albeit not one named Clinton.

My White construction-worker dad, who can be found razzing fellow workers on job sites that they're "socialist and just don't know it," voted for Kelly in his first-ever midterm participation. The "I voted" sticker symbolically placed on the left side of his hard hat tells the overlooked story of Kansas and the nation: more people are paying attention than at any point in our lifetimes, and this bodes poorly for far-right factions propped up in recent decades by impassioned religious and ideological bases.

Moderates and progressives in conservative strongholds who lost close, hard-fought battles—competitive races largely owed to a political awakening on the left all of two years ago—know that correcting the nation's course will take time. Like Thompson, whose campaign made a special effort in rural and small-town communities, they have lost a race yet changed culture along the way such that a future race might be won.

States like mine began their battles with the far right long before much of the nation did. We are thus further down the road of recovering from its effects. By the 2016 election, in Kansas, bipartisan coalitions had formed to oust extremist legislators. Soon a band of moderate lawmakers repealed Brownback's draconian tax cuts and allocated hundreds of millions of dollars for public schools to raise salaries and restore cut positions.

There remains across the nation a rural-urban political split that newly elected Democrats such as Kelly must seek to bridge.

Both sides of the aisle remain a hot mess of diverging ideas and realignments. But moderates and progressives beyond this place might feel encouraged: Kansas just held the gubernatorial version of Hillary Clinton versus Donald Trump, and more people were with her.

BRAIN GAIN

The New York Times, 2019

For more than a century following the industrial revolution, rural and small-town people left home to pursue survival in commercial meccas. According to the American story, those who thrived in urban centers "made it"—a capitalist triumph for the individual, a damaging loss for the place he left. We often refer to this as "brain drain" from the hinterlands, implying that those who stay lack the merit or ability to "get out."

But that old notion is getting dusty.

The nation's most populous cities, those bicoastal pillars of aspiration—New York City and Los Angeles—are experiencing population declines, most likely driven by unaffordability. Other metros are experiencing growth, to be sure, especially in the South and West. But there is an exodus afoot that suggests a national homecoming, across generations, to less bustling spaces. Last year, Gallup found that while roughly 80 percent of us live in urban areas, rural life was the most wished for.

If happiness is what they seek, those folks are onto something. A 2018 study by NPR, the Robert Wood Johnson Foundation, and the Harvard T.H. Chan School of Public Health reported that despite economic and health concerns, most rural Americans are pretty dang happy and hopeful. Forty percent of rural adults said their lives came out better than they expected. A majority said they were better off financially than their parents at the same age and thought their kids would likewise ascend. As for cultural woes, those among them under age fifty showed notably higher acknowledgment of racial discrimination and commitment to social progress. All in all, it was a picture not of a dying place but one that is evolving.

The University of Minnesota Extension researcher Ben Winchester has cited a "brain gain" in rural America. Winchester found that, from 2000 to 2010, most rural Minnesota counties gained early-to-mid-career residents with ample socioeconomic assets. A third of them are returning, while the rest are new recruits.

I grew up in and wrote a memoir about a place that by many measures during my Reagan-era childhood and Clinton-era adolescence was indeed "dying." American readers love a tale of escape from such places, populated by characters who exemplify addiction, abuse, bad decision-making. My memoir instead seeks, through historical facts and cultural analysis, to reveal the immense public forces of policy and socioeconomics that shaped my family's behaviors, opportunities, and outcomes. I wrote affectionately yet unsparingly *from* that area, where I still choose to reside.

In the year since it was published, this less-common narrative has prompted thousands of people to find me at speaking events and book signings. They tell me this: *Our stories are different but the same. I know the world you wrote about—it's deep in me, and I care about it.*

From Seattle to Charlottesville, they come bearing home-grown tomatoes (that's "'maters" to us), fresh loaves of bread, small-town yearbooks, landscape photography, original paintings of big skies. They cry as they relate their own stories of departure, return, longing.

These aren't just White people lamenting the loss of the family wheat farm. They are Black women missing their families in the rural South, Muslim women organizing workers in meatpacking towns on the Plains, young gay men hoping to return to their small-town roots. This is the rural America I know and love—a place with problems, yes, but containing diversity, vibrancy, and cross-cultural camaraderie.

I explore this shift in the zeitgeist with a new podcast, *The Homecomers*, featuring rural and working-class advocates from the Black Belt of the Deep South, migrant camps of California's Central Valley, the Iowa tribe of Kansas and Nebraska, the desert Southwest, Appalachia, and the Midwest. I spoke with people who founded or help guide entities such as the Black Farmers' Network, the United Farm Workers Foundation, the Doris Duke Conservation Scholars Program, the Female Farmer Project, the Southern Documentary Fund, and the Kansas Democratic Party.

From where I sit, they are heroes of the American odyssey—seeing value where others see lack, returning with the elixir of hard-won social capital to help solve the troubles of home. In one conversation, the political scientist Veronica Womack described the metaphorical significance of her Black students at Georgia College considering work in agriculture.

"It's kind of a circle," Womack said. "When our ancestors were made free, land was their pursuit." So when she says her students are coming home, she explained, she means that they have realized that farming is a "vehicle that I can use to be free."

The *Christian Science Monitor* recently reported a prairie trend of young people, drawn by family ties and affordable entrepreneurship, returning to rural and small-town homes around college graduation. They're opening restaurants or starting small, unconventional farming operations. One college senior founded a direct-to-consumer beef company in Otoe County, Nebraska, and sold $52,000 worth of meat in the past nine months.

This return—or refusal to leave—is good news for Americans who will happily remain in cities. The future of rural is intertwined with suburban and urban outcomes by way of food production, natural resources, the economy, political movements, and beyond.

We need policymakers who understand this (and care about it). Progressive Democratic presidential candidates have unveiled a spate of rural policy plans more robust than any in recent political memory. They suggest actions for which rural advocates have argued—investing in rural people and economies to lead a Green New Deal, cutting out oppressive middlemen in moving food from producers to eaters, and much more.

Government agencies have made piecemeal efforts to attract professionals to rural America, offering loan forgiveness or other incentives to teachers, doctors, homebuyers. To make the burgeoning rural return feasible, we need big structural fixes for a big problem, such as Poland's recent scrapping of income tax for young workers in an effort to keep them in the country.

The concept of home is subjective unto the individual. But we have long interpreted it at the mercy of forces such as capitalism and industrialization. The resulting social imbalance is an objective crisis. Mobility is a virtue of freedom. Staying—or returning—is an equal virtue.

CHRONICLING A COMMUNITY, AND A COUNTRY, IN ECONOMIC CRISIS

The New York Times, 2020

As the United States awakens from one of its foundational myths—that we are a democracy without castes—the official record of our times is being written largely by people born to socioeconomic advantage. This irony, in which those on the fortunate end of historic wealth inequality attempt to chronicle a populist movement produced by that inequality, often results in dubious journalism.

Even well-intentioned urban, coastal, college-educated scribes commit obliviously condescending word choices ("flyover country"), illogical assumptions (everyone in "red states" voted for Trump), and variations on poverty porn, in which subjects are conveyed as helpless and joyless ("observe this sorry case in Appalachia"). To those who know something about, say, rural poverty firsthand, such nonfiction narratives may read as voyeuristic studies predicated on the dangerous idea that we are a nation of two essentially different kinds of people.

In fact, we are a nation of essentially similar people shaped by vastly different circumstances of place, wealth, education, and culture. Those best able to document our socioeconomic divide with humility and accuracy typically have occupied more than one class, remain connected to the one they left, and attribute any upward mobility to good fortune rather than to personal exceptionalism.

One such journalist is the *New York Times* columnist Nicholas Kristof, who grew up tending sheep on a small family farm in rural Oregon in the 1960s and '70s. In *Tightrope: Americans Reaching for Hope*, he and the journalist Sheryl WuDunn, who is also his wife, offer a litany of stories from across the country, revealing the structural causes of countless so-called personal failures among the working poor. Most of these stories come from Kristof's hometown of Yamhill, population 1,105.

Yamhill, which thrived with blue-collar industry just a few generations ago, serves as a microcosm for a nation in which life expectancy has alarmingly declined. One in four of Kristof's former peers died in adulthood from substance use disorders, suicide, accidents, or treatable health conditions such as obesity and diabetes. *Tightrope* suggests why: a corrupt and uniquely cruel economy in which millions of underpaid or underemployed Americans cannot afford education, health care, or housing. Familiar statistics on these dismal trends take on fresh urgency when juxtaposed with photos of Kristof's schoolmates who are now homeless or dead.

The authors' affection for Yamhill is the heartbeat of the book. Kristof remains tied to the strained community through friends and the sheep farm, which is still in the family, and WuDunn has been visiting the area since she and Kristof became engaged decades ago. In this way, *Tightrope* avoids a problem common among books about places authors have "escaped." Yamhill is not reflected through a rearview mirror, distorted by a removed author's guilt, resentment, or nostalgia. Rather, it is conveyed up close by way of detailed reporting on living people—intimate access achieved because the authors, while outliers with respect to their professional status and home on the opposite coast, are also of the place.*

Together, their first-person "we" has the refreshing effect of fogging the authorial "I" and keeping the spotlight on those they've interviewed or memorialized—a popular cheerleader and athlete who in middle age froze to death while homeless; a wounded veteran battling addiction and post-traumatic stress disorder; a woman who survived a homicidal husband only to bury four out of five of her adult children. The individual tales in *Tightrope* cut across race, ethnicity, and geography but share a theme of economic misfortune in a nation plenty rich enough to help if it cared to.

These stories are so numerous, in chapters addressing the destruction of unions, the war on drugs, insufficient health coverage, unaffordable housing, and other failures of public policy, that we rarely get to know one person deeply. But their number conveys the breadth of financial struggle, the exploration of which took the authors to all fifty states.

Kristof and WuDunn have written four other books together, and in 1990 became the first married couple to receive a Pulitzer Prize for journalism, for their reporting on the Tiananmen Square protests and massacre. (WuDunn was also the first

---

* In 2021, Kristof left his position at the *New York Times* to run for governor in Oregon. The following year, the state's Supreme Court ruled he did not meet the three-year residency requirement to appear on the ballot. Kristof has since returned to his work as a columnist.

Asian-American woman to win that prize.) Their partnership itself crosses cultural borders; WuDunn grew up on Manhattan's Upper West Side and is now an investment adviser at a New York securities firm. *Tightrope*'s analysis of our country's class problem reads as lived understanding.

The authors reveal their liberal stances but also validate sacrosanct conservative ideas about work ethic and individual responsibility. The book's resulting fixation on substance abuse among the working poor might turn off progressive readers who would note that wealthier people are seldom put under a microscope for the same self-destructive behaviors. However, Kristof and WuDunn show over and over how "bad choices" are rooted in problems bigger than the individual: childhood abuse, lack of knowledge, dearth of resources.

Kristof and WuDunn quote past and current leaders from both political parties who agree that capitalism is broken. Meanwhile, Republicans and Democrats alike might find themselves surprised to learn from *Tightrope* that "the needy" are their intellectual and moral equals, or that the only real difference between them and the rural poor is the opportunities they received.

Common objections to such empathy, at least toward the White people in *Tightrope* who identify as politically conservative, include "Why do they vote against their best interest?" and "Why did they vote for Trump?"

The presumed answer is often some racism or sexism unique to poor or working-class Whites—even though, in 2016, 44 percent of college-educated White women voted for Trump, according to CNN exit polls, and even though support for Trump was roughly the same across income brackets.

Historically, economic crisis breeds fear and vulnerability to manipulation by authoritarians among groups perceiving a loss of power; racism is indeed rife in a country built on White supremacy. But *Tightrope* catches what many analyses miss about struggling communities across color lines: an undercurrent of self-hatred, in which people blame themselves for bad outcomes and are loath to ask for a "handout." "One hazard of our social Darwinism," the authors write, "is that it is absorbed even by those who are themselves on the bottom, leading them to stigmatize themselves."

Kristof and WuDunn acknowledge the bravery required of their sources to share painful realities in a society that has shamed them. In one scene, as a thirty-year-old contractor is having eighteen teeth pulled at a free dental clinic in Virginia, the young dentist laments the man's case. The authors describe the man's anxious look, "sitting in the chair as he was being talked about."

Careful not to portray their subjects as one-dimensionally miserable, Kristof and WuDunn document the tireless and heroic ways in which the people they interviewed *tried*, often with greater gumption than many fortunate people will ever be asked to summon. In Tulsa, Oklahoma, a woman recalls trying to enroll herself in ninth grade after taking the necessary school forms to the prison where her mother was incarcerated on drug charges, in order to procure her signature. Kristof's rival for class valedictorian, the daughter of a county truck driver, found her studies derailed by teen pregnancy; she didn't go to college but she didn't turn to drugs, either, and through hard work with her husband has kept the family afloat.

The authors praise the particular strengths of one of Kristof's lifelong friends, who faced job loss, methamphetamine addiction, a criminal record, and obesity-related diabetes: when young Kristof "drove the tractor through the sheep shed wall (the second time), it was Clayton who helped fix the shed. Or there was the time Clayton managed to kill hundreds of yellow jackets and destroy their nest after Nick had fled in defeat."

People like Clayton exist in other wealthy nations, but statistically—thanks to greater social safety nets elsewhere—none fares so poorly as Clayton in the United States. *Tightrope* thus concludes that America's true distinction is our lack of concern for one another. To rectify such a crisis, the authors argue, we cannot rely on charity; only robust public policy will suffice. They suggest that such policies should prioritize early childhood programs, high school graduation, universal health coverage, access to contraceptives, housing, jobs, and government-issued savings bonds and monthly allowances for all children. To those who say we can't afford it, they observe, "Everybody knows about the cost of food stamps for the poor, but few people are aware that the median taxpayer is also subsidizing the corporate executives whose elegant French dinner is tax deductible."

Tightrope's greatest strength is its exaltation of the common person's voice, bearing expert witness to troubles that selfish power has wrought. But Kristof and WuDunn interviewed official experts, too, who are catching on to what marginalized people have known all along.

"The American people think this system is completely rigged," Fred Wertheimer, a longtime advocate for campaign finance and government ethics reform, tells them. "And they're correct."

I AM BURNING WITH FURY AND GRIEF

The New York Times, **2020**

Consider every moment, since the dawn of woman, when a female aspired but to no avail. She asked to attend school but was denied. She raised her hand but wasn't called on. She applied but wasn't hired. She enlisted but wasn't deployed. She created but wasn't credited. She ran but wasn't elected.

Imagine the sadness and frustration of every such instance as a spark, their combined energy the size of many suns. That is the measure of grief and fury I felt rise inside me as I watched Elizabeth Warren's bid for the Democratic nomination wane.

When Hillary Clinton lost in 2016, it hurt in similar ways but didn't surprise me. Out here amid rural and working-class spaces, it was plain to some of us that centrist ideas did not excite in times of historic wealth inequality. This election, though, I thought Senator Elizabeth Warren—a class revolutionary to match the moment—might go to the White House.

It turns out that she won't even go to the general election.

Now the same pundits who in 2016 proved they know very little will list the reasons, without realizing they're among the reasons.

Such yapping is forgettable, but a more reliable bit of political analysis from this election has stayed with me. It was March 2019, about a month after Warren had entered the race, and my father and maternal grandmother were talking politics at my kitchen table in Kansas.

"This is the best chance that a woman has ever had to become the president," said my dad, a White, sixty-something construction worker who has identified as a democratic socialist since Bernie Sanders's 2016 candidacy. "Now. It's now."

"Ten years from now," said my grandma, a White, seventy-something retiree who grew up in poverty and spent decades on the farm where I grew up.

"No, it's now. It's now," Dad replied.

"Hey, I'm game," Grandma said.

"They cannot do it wrong, and I believe that Elizabeth Warren is the chance," he said, tapping his finger on the table. I had hit record on my cell phone. The now year-old audio's rambunctious sound indicates that alcohol was involved.

"If Elizabeth would get the nomination," Grandma said, "I would bust my ass—if I had to crawl down the sidewalk to get to the neighbors: 'Vote for Elizabeth!'"

"I would too, I would too," Dad said. "That is exactly what it's going to take to make it happen."

"I hope so," Grandma concluded.

What breaks my heart about this exchange is that my grandmother, deep down, never really believed Warren or any woman would get the nomination. Maybe that's because she had watched cable news repeat a self-fulfilling prophecy about electability. Maybe it's because, as a woman who has seen so much, she knew that electability was a valid concern. Or maybe it's because it hurts so dang much to let yourself harbor a dream that you might not see come true. Whatever her motivation, you know what? Grandma was right.

Nonetheless, their conversation was a mark of progress. My previously apathetic family now votes with gusto and would consider campaigning for a candidate, and my father must not be the only man who wore a hard hat and rooted for Warren.

Two weeks ago, when she placed fourth in the Nevada caucuses—despite thoroughly winning a Las Vegas candidates debate and pulling in nearly $3 million in donations the next day—I was on the Gulf Coast of Florida. I had just given a keynote address at a Planned Parenthood fundraiser. It was the first time I'd ever toed the line of journalistic ethics by speaking on behalf of a peripherally political organization because, well, these are desperate times for women's rights.

The event organizers shared with me that their impressive new health facility, ensuring reproductive health care for regional women, had been kept secret from the broader, conservative community throughout a capital campaign and construction. The men who built the structure, for instance, were told it would be a dentist's office. Such measures were crucial to avoid blowback, vandalism, or worse from anti-choice contingents. I understood, hailing from the area where the abortion provider George Tiller was murdered by a religious zealot in 2009.

After the fundraiser and after watching Warren's dismal returns on a hotel television, I spent the next day on the beach with a Geraldine Brooks novel I'd randomly purchased at a bookstore on Sanibel Island. The book was about a bright girl in the Massachusetts Bay Colony who is indentured as a servant in Cambridge to pay for her brother's academic studies. Along the way, she tends the miscarriage of a girl whose rapist goes unpunished.

I looked out at the sea and considered that, for all our advancing on gender matters, the novel's story is alive today: a woman must step aside as a man ascends to the presidency, and a "pro-life" activist would sooner bomb an abortion facility than let a raped girl cross its threshold.

My grandma might not get to see our first woman president. Warren might not either. I'm thirty-nine—will I? I feel certain of it, yet many women have died after a lifetime of such certainty.

A few nights before the Super Tuesday primaries that ultimately squashed Warren's chances, I had a dream that I was in a crowd watching her onstage. She glowed like someone who has won in a way that has nothing to do with numbers. We spoke afterward. She was clearly at peace with whatever happened with the election.

Warren might not be bound for the presidency, but she has apparently lodged herself in another powerful place: the female psyche. The countless little girls with whom she famously "pinkie swore" that women should run for president will remember.

If this supposed democracy is worth lasting, at least one of them won't be denied.

IN DEFENSE OF POPULISM

Columbia Journalism Review, 2020

A common, specious refrain from journalists and their favored sources is that the countries hit hardest by the Covid-19 virus have one thing in common: populist leaders.

Last month, the Associated Press reported on the link between coronavirus outbreaks and anti-science sentiment in government. The story, which was picked up around the world, pits populism against democracy: "Academics have been fretting about whether liberal democracy—the political system that helped defeat fascism in World War II, set up international institutions like the World Health Organization, and seemed to have triumphed in the Cold War three decades ago—can muster the stuff to take on the new populism and address complex twenty-first-century challenges."

The terms "populist" and "populism" appear eleven times in the story, but the definition of the term the story provides is misleading. It suggests that populism is necessarily anti-science:

"Populism in politics means pushing policies that are popular with 'the people,' not the elites and the experts."

The story's sources elaborate on this theme. "Populists by nature . . . have a disdain for experts and science that are seen as part of the establishment," laments one, the head of a Washington think tank. The coronavirus "hits every blind spot that the populists have," says another, a political scientist with the Brookings Institution.

Also last month, in a *Washington Post* column that explores a drop in support for populist leaders amid the pandemic, a political scientist and an economist note that "early cross-national evidence suggests that populist governments implemented far fewer health measures and mobility restrictions when the pandemic began compared with non-populist governments." This politics piece, including the *Post* headline and subheads, uses "populism" or "populist" twenty-two times but does not appropriately qualify it with "right-wing" until its twentieth mention, in the penultimate paragraph.

Such attitudes are perhaps even more pervasive in cable news, where you're never more than a few minutes of political analysis away from misguided takes on "populism" as a treacherous force.

These are but the latest iteration of careless misuse of the term in recent years throughout the news media. Populist leaders, one would gather from headlines, are all science-denying fools, not to mention aspiring autocrats intent on bending the worst of human impulses toward a more racist, sexist, xenophobic—and, now, diseased—world.

It is true that many such rulers make populist appeals. Populism has proved, historically, a comfortable vehicle for extremists whose views—say, climate-change denial or religious fundamentalism—are challenged by science and other realms of quantifiable expertise, the experts among which may be vilified as "elites."

But populism is neither right nor left—nor anti-science—by definition. It is merely a concern, whether genuine or feigned, for the common people. Today's most prominent populists in Washington include Representative Alexandria Ocasio-Cortez, Senator Elizabeth Warren, and Senator Bernie Sanders—people who base their policies on valid evidence and have given their lives to fighting everything that the far right represents.

Indeed, the most crucial progressive political movements of our time—Black Lives Matter and #MeToo, climate marches and gun-reform rallies—are by nature populist. Founded at ground level, often by victims of racism, sexism, environmental injustice, and lax gun laws, they were then energized by the fed-up masses.

Similarly, during the 1890s, a group of Kansas farmers—bankrupt due to falling crop prices, drought, greedy railroad monopolies, and a federal government serving powerful interests—coined the phrase "populist" to describe an alliance of the people. Within a year, their People's Party, or Populist Party, was a national coalition of farmers, unions, and workers' organizations. Their radical ideas included labor rights, corporate regulation, the progressive income tax, women's suffrage, popular election of senators, and the eight-hour workday. No movement to overthrow corrupt power will get far without true unity, and the party was thwarted by racism and nativism within its own ranks. The Democratic Party platform today, though, owes much to their efforts.

Yet "populist" remains a dismissive, negative descriptor in prominent liberal discourse, a polite way of hinting at bigoted fools wearing red trucker hats. Journalists surely know what "populism" actually means, but they apply it to far-right movements far more readily than to progressive uprisings. This habitual, unchecked misuse of the term perhaps betrays an unexamined distrust of, or even distaste for, the proletariat—whose power might upend the capitalist structures from which plenty of liberals, including the most influential voices of establishment media, benefit. This is the sad grain of truth beneath working-class resentment of the so-called media elite, and it provides fodder for condemnation of our essential, often heroic free press.

If Joe Biden wins the presidency this November, I imagine some journalists will be quick to analyze, with implied relief, "the defeat of populism"—as though the sizable populist faction of Biden's own party had no hand in his victory, and as though democracy has been saved because populism was defeated.

Instead, at the very least, journalists and commentators should provide an ideological qualifier when tossing "populism" around: "right-wing populist," "progressive populist." The more precise word for describing leaders such as Jair Bolsonaro, Vladimir Putin, Boris Johnson, and Donald Trump, though, is not "populist" but "demagogue." The latter is by definition disingenuous, exploiting social fissures, manipulating media, and misleading the electorate in pursuit of selfish gain. A demagogue may use populist strategies to win support but has little or no concern for the masses.

After missing the direction of the 2016 election, a remorseful press sought to correct its blind spots. Conscious efforts have since been made, some more successful than others, at addressing the socioeconomic gulf between those who discuss the nation and those who are at best the ill-understood subjects of discussion.

Some aspects of that gulf reach beyond editorial decisions to the often subconscious realm of word choice. Many well-intentioned journalists likely are not aware of their classist handling of "populist." Words matter, not only for their effect on an audience, but for revealing our absorbed biases of class, race, gender, and beyond.

Trump laughs off the tyranny of his own language, carelessly inflicting harm while insisting "they're just words." In such a climate, we must be impeccable with ours.

HOW IS ARGUING WITH TRUMP VOTERS
WORKING OUT FOR YOU?

The Guardian, 2020

Their children hold signs that read, "God hates fags."
I myself was a child when their family, the extremist
group called Westboro Baptist Church, began picketing
in Kansas in 1991. Driven by patriarch Fred Phelps's homopho-
bic interpretation of the Bible, they quickly became infamous for
wielding shocking slogans and shouting lurid insults in public
spaces.

It would be easy to write them off as monsters—a familiar
impulse in today's political climate, particularly toward supporters of Donald Trump. But, with democracy itself on the
line this election year, we must remain open to the possibility
of transformation.

I saw Westboro for the first time in the late nineties at the
University of Kansas. I was a first-generation college student
who had inherited no family political tradition. We were working in wheat fields when better-off families were attending civic
events or reading opinion pages. In that void, I had absorbed

a vague, moderate conservatism from the prevailing culture of my Reagan-era childhood and adolescence at the dawn of conservative talk radio.

On the typically liberal campus that was challenging my ideas, Westboro was a frequent, well-organized presence at the LGBTQ+ Pride parade, music concerts, or lectures. Over the previous decade, they had traversed the country to disrupt all manner of events, including the funerals of American soldiers and the murdered gay man Matthew Shepard. But KU—"gay U," some Kansas conservatives liked to call it—was just down the road from their home in Topeka, so students like myself saw them often.

"Fags die, God laughs," read one sign. During my senior year, in response to the 2001 terrorist attack on the World Trade Center—deemed punishment for a culture increasingly accepting of queerness—"Planes crash, God laughs."

The content of their message was horrifying, but the tone with which they shared it—smiling, smug self-righteousness, casting pity on us who weren't saved—was repugnant as well. Their vitriol had the opposite of its intended effect, raising my awareness as a heterosexual, cisgender woman of the trials faced by my LGBTQ+ peers.

By the time I graduated in 2002, my politics had significantly altered. I arrived deeming affirmative action unfair; after a sociology class for which I researched the impact of one's race, gender, and economic status on life outcomes, I concluded that affirmative action was right as rain. I arrived with no concept of worker rights, all but erased from consciousness in my union-busted state; after reading early twentieth-century documents of the labor movement for an American literature class, I realized that I had been born near the bottom of a socioeconomic ladder my country kept insisting didn't exist. I arrived believing I could be at once socially liberal and fiscally conservative; after excelling on campus while paying my own way through school and then graduating into poverty for lack of social capital—while watching less motivated, less capable children of affluence walk into prestigious internships and lucrative jobs—I viewed the so-called free market, welfare reform, and the US tax system as a thoroughly rigged disaster that only progressive measures could remedy.

To be clear, for all the claims to the contrary about universities, there was no perceptible agenda to convert me to liberalism. The professors who questioned my conservative ideas did so respectfully and gave me As. Organizations such as the College Republicans were a visible presence.

Rather, my information sources and environment expanded. Upon reviewing these new discoveries, I converted myself.

Plenty of students make no such shift. Conservatism remains ever available for those attending universities, as evidenced by the numerous far-right college graduates currently running this country. According to Pew Research Center, 51 percent of men who voted for Republican congressional candidates in 2018 held college degrees. While the Westboro group is hard to pin along modern party lines, their signature argument is decidedly far-right—and most of its leaders are credentialed attorneys. Conversely, millions of Americans without college degrees develop progressive views by way of informal education: reading, observing, life experience. It was not higher education that changed me but my willingness to change.

Among those born to bad or limited information—the flawed narratives of history books, the blinders of privilege, or propaganda on their parents' televisions and car radios—there are those who will stick with existing beliefs regardless of what they are shown. But there are those who would reconsider, and we need them more than ever.

Megan Phelps-Roper would have been in her early teens, holding one of those hateful signs, when I passed her family on the way to class. Like me, she attended public schools and consumed popular culture. But where my formative years were carved by mainstream influences—Catholicism, the nightly news, waiting tables—hers was the stuff of cults.

Her grandfather was the charismatic, zealous leader demanding commitment and claiming a monopoly on truth. Doubt and dissent were discouraged, sometimes through abuse. Shame and guilt were devices of control, and those who left were cut off from communication. Phelps-Roper participated in a family protest against homosexuality for the first time at age five.

As she came of age, Phelps-Roper's ability to assess information had been thoroughly perverted. Westboro acted not out of hate but out of *love*, her elders taught her, to warn mortals of their sins so that they might repent and avoid eternal damnation.

At the age of twenty-six, however, Phelps-Roper would make a much larger and braver leap than my political shift from center-right to solid left. In 2012, she left Westboro—her lifelong idea system, her identity, and nearly her entire family.

Just as the cruel signs she once held probably convinced few who saw them, it was not angry condemnations of her ideas that moved her toward the truth. It was, rather, a handful of friendly strangers on Twitter, including a Jewish man who responded to Phelps-Roper's anti-Semitic provocation. Sensing the humanity beneath her inhumane behavior, they thoughtfully pressed her with intellectual and philosophical debate over the course of several years.

"People had grace for me when I seemed not to deserve it the most," Phelps-Roper told PBS's *Amanpour & Co.* last year after the release of her memoir, *Unfollow.* "The fact that they were able to suspend their judgments long enough to have those conversations with me completely changed my life. So now instead of me being out there with Westboro creating new victims, I'm working for healing and change to try to repair some of that damage."

I noticed that, in her writings and interviews about her experience, Phelps-Roper does not favor the term "cult." I asked her whether, perhaps, she found the descriptor accurate but not constructive.

Phelps-Roper conceded that the term is accurate enough, even though some common features of cults are not true of Westboro, such as moneymaking schemes or sexual ownership of women by the leader.

" 'Cult' is definitely a convenient shorthand that rapidly conveys the gist of the situation at Westboro and communities like it: a small, fringe group that exerts an inordinate amount of control over its members, exalting itself to special status via claims of unique access to truth," Phelps-Roper told me via online message.

All the same, she confirmed that she doesn't use the term because it shuts down communication channels.

"People tend to dismiss cult members as crazy or stupid, rather than complex human beings like everyone else," she said. "That makes compassion and real understanding more difficult, and it can give us a false sense of security that we're not subject to the same kinds of forces that draw people into these groups and keep them there."

Plus, Phelps-Roper explained, she can't get through to her family by lobbing labels that make them bristle.

"I want to reach Westboro members—to help convince them that there are other, better ways of living in the world," she said. "If I use a needlessly pejorative word like that to describe people who are earnestly trying to do what they believe is right, I'm throwing obstacles in my own path and making change even more difficult than it naturally is."

There has been much discussion in recent years about the extent to which liberal America should or should not have empathy for, say, economically distressed Trump voters. Some encourage compassion about the hard lives that made some of them vulnerable to political fearmongering. Others might point out that plenty of Trump voters are doing just fine in the coddled world of Whiteness and that, regardless of their reasons, we should practice zero tolerance toward agents of oppression.

The strongest position contains both truths. We can acknowledge that destructive ideas have roots deeper than the individuals who hold them and yet firmly denounce such ideas. To hear Mary Trump tell it in her new memoir, her uncle is severely dysfunctional in part because of his upbringing. But the purpose of her story is not to engender sympathy for our current president, whom her book's subtitle calls "the world's most dangerous man." It is to show how he was made—revealing that the problem is not the current president but, rather, what patriarchy, corporate greed, and White supremacy can make out of an innocent child born in the belly of all three.

You can be intellectually woke without being awakened to the largest truth: that we are all connected, enemies and allies alike. The United States is teetering toward authoritarianism. Are you still lecturing strangers on social media? Are you still shouting at a family member that they're wrong? How is that working out?

If you want to stop fascism, the efficient mission is not to attack the opposing side. It is, rather, to be the opposite of Donald Trump: a defiantly open heart who protects and bolsters valid information systems required for people to truly decide for themselves about all that he and his movement represent.

If you think such information is a given in the world we are living in, you are mistaken.

Many White people believe the current president is a good man. Are they irrational, some perhaps even disturbed? If they have valid news sources, then by my estimation, yes.

But many do not. They live in spaces inundated by decades of right-wing propaganda and intentional manipulation of their fears.

Not everyone targeted by disinformation falls for it, and such experiences are not an excuse for racist, sexist, xenophobic views and political choices. But they are a reason.

In March, 63 percent of Fox News regulars polled by the nonpartisan Pew Research Center's American News Pathways 2020 Project said the president's response to the Covid-19 pandemic was "excellent." Just 23 percent of average Americans—and a mere 2 percent of MSNBC regulars—agreed.

MSNBC's and Fox News' treatment of facts is not analogous. The former comments with a liberal slant, while the latter now amounts to state television for a Republican White House. But both sides of the American political divide have allegiances to information sources that affirm their existing beliefs.

Meanwhile, false information masquerading as fact is a common feature of our times. According to analysis by researchers at New York University and Princeton University, most disinformation disseminated online during the 2016 election had a pro-Trump slant. Another study, published by *Science* in 2019, suggested that misinformation during that election was most concentrated among conservative media consumers. However, researchers at the University of Colorado published a report last May indicating that a substantial number of leftists share false or misleading information too.

Let's acknowledge that today's cultural chasm is driven by social media streams and cable "news" programs. It is easy, in such a splintered media ecosystem, to maintain a closed system of unfalsifiable beliefs in which inconvenient facts become "fake news."

Some of today's most dangerous misinformation concerns a public health crisis. What accounts for those who, say, insist that the Covid-19 pandemic is a hoax and thus refuse to wear a mask?

According to a research report from the Harvard Kennedy School of Government, the strongest predictors of belief in Covid-19 conspiracy theories are not educational attainment or political affiliation but, along with partisan and ideological motivations, "a psychological predisposition" to dismiss experts and doubt mainstream narratives about major events.

But to what is this predisposition owed? We enter treacherous territory when we diagnose something inherent about a person to explain her partisan leanings. The behavioral geneticist Brad Verhulst conducted two major research studies in recent years, including one following more than eight thousand siblings for ten years, that debunked oft-cited studies claiming causality between personality and politics. It is self-aggrandizing for the well-informed, though, to declare that gullibility is innate and that proponents of misinformation are just dumb. Here we find the fatal flaw of self-congratulatory liberalism.

When presented with evidence of, say, lower salaries for

women and higher incarceration among people of color, liberals rightly reject the notion that these outcomes result from innately lower aptitude, laziness, and corrupt character. We rightly point to the oppressive conditions of a racist, sexist state to explain such data. In other words, we understand that the system failed the person, not the other way around. Yet we place ideological identities in no such environmental context.

What if our systems failed the media consumers who are, for myriad reasons, easily taken by political lies? Underfunded public schools could be emphasizing media literacy and civics but are forced to prioritize testing-driven curricula while providing basic needs such as food and health care. Under-regulated, profit-driven social media companies have focused on mining user data rather than stopping the malicious spread of false information on their platforms. Understaffed news publications have, amid efforts to adapt to the digital media economy, used salacious, conflict-driven clickbait to maintain the bottom line.

We must approach the current political crisis less like a valid debate and more like the treatment of a toxic stream along which extremist factions swirl into themselves like eddies. You and the person you're arguing with don't even share a common set of definitions, let alone discussion frameworks or world-views. No movement can win in the twenty-first century without this understanding as a foundation.

To clear that toxic stream, we need robustly funded schools with civics curricula that activate participation in democracy, tell the story of all peoples, admit our often brutal history as a nation, and incorporate twenty-first-century media literacy as an essential tool of citizenship. We need government crackdowns on big tech's complicity in the spread of misinformation. We need new, less compromised business models encouraging media members to be government watchdogs rather than generators of advertising revenue.

But information is only part of the solution for what ails our country. Political scientists have long noted the role of emotion in political behavior, and logic will not sway positions that were not formed through logic. Many Trump voters were moved not by facts but by the feelings their outrageous leader incites. As conservative analyst Bill Kristol recently tweeted, reacting to news that the Republican National Committee will merely endorse "the President's America-first agenda" in lieu of any new platform, "It's no longer the Republican party. It's a Trump cult."

Here we can learn from those like Phelps-Roper, who have freed themselves from irrational worldviews. Undoing indoctrination, as her story of unlikely Twitter friendships reveals, requires not just better information but a nonconfrontational, even respectful tone in conveying it.

Members of oppressed groups should not be expected to do this work, which is at best emotional labor and at worst physically dangerous. But what about would-be cultural bridge-builders protected by privileges such as Whiteness and wealth? Should they bother?

Yes. Nationally, according to recent *New York Times*/Siena College polls, voters are breaking ranks from Trumpism, disavowing their lifelong party or finding belonging with "never Trump" Republican groups like the Lincoln Project.

My state government contains several elected officials who left the Republican Party and became Democrats in recent years—including a viable 2020 candidate for a US Senate seat held by Republicans since 1919.

From 2014 to 2018, during which the Black Lives Matter movement successfully forced a national reckoning about race, the portion of White Republicans who said government spends too little on improving conditions for Black Americans more than doubled, rising from 14 to 33 percent, according to a report from the Associated Press-NORC Center for Public Affairs Research.

We should value justice over unity. But there is more unity to be had than you might think from watching the news. People change, and privileged Americans who can help them do so play an important role in this pivotal moment.

As Phelps-Roper says in her much-viewed TED Talk, the Twitter friends who helped her see the light "didn't abandon their beliefs or their principles—only their scorn. They channeled their infinitely justifiable offense and came to me with pointed questions tempered with kindness and humor. They approached me as a human being—and that was more transformative than two full decades of outrage, disdain, and violence."

If someone who dislikes this notion has changed someone's mind through contempt and condescension, I'd love to hear about it. The opposite is more likely to be true, in my experience. The confronted person digs in, defends, doubles down.

In a July opinion piece for the *New York Times*, Charlie Warzel described a Senegalese medical anthropologist sent by the World Health Organization to Guinea, where residents were resisting public health guidance during the Ebola epidemic in 2014. He spent a long time listening, rather than lecturing, and realized that the people "weren't selfish or anti-science. They were scared and felt stripped of dignity by officials who didn't respect them or understand their traditions."

While US "anti-maskers" of the Covid-19 pandemic are a different bunch, understanding their motives is necessary to successfully reach them.

"You cannot force public trust," Warzel wrote of the current health crisis. "You have to earn it by being humble and transparent, and by listening."

Is such humility warranted in the face of terrible actors, those who not only refuse to wear a mask but refuse to accept the value of entire groups of human beings?

If an equitable, nonviolent society is our goal, ideologies that seek to dismantle unjust power structures such as White supremacy and patriarchy are unequivocally better than those that do not. There is no moral equivalence between the neo-Nazi and the Black Lives Matter protester, or the feminist marcher and the men's rights activist. Some ideas are superior to others.

But even if your ideas are superior, I am asking you to consider that you did not arrive at them because of your innate superiority. Depending on your level of social privilege, you arrived at them because of your life experiences, your information sources, your community influences. Even a psychological predisposition toward rational thinking, if this is a valid possibility, is just a bit of good fortune you did nothing to earn.

If you had been born into the Phelps family, would you have thought your way out of Westboro? At what age? Twelve? Eighteen, when you left home? Twenty-six, by way of social media? Forty-four, better late than never? How about never? For many the answer thus far is never.

That's an extreme example, I hear you say. Children of cults are one thing, but a Trump voter has free will in their decisions.

True. Yet if you'd been born White, in a homogeneously White place, with Fox News on every television and Rush Limbaugh on every car radio for your entire life, would you be a liberal or even a centrist today? Maybe, but not without knowing the hard truth that people who think monstrous things often are not, at their core, monsters.

Nope, I hear you say. *I am better than a Trump voter. I'm sure as hell better than a Nazi.*

On the level of ideas, well, yes. But why? Is it because something about them is naturally defective? You yourself would have been one of the good ones in Germany, correct? Because something about you is inherently better?

If that all sounds right, be careful. The seed of everything you're fighting is inside you.

RURAL ROUTE

NationalGeographic.com, 2020

When I was growing up on a small wheat farm, employment by the postal service struck me as enviable. One of my best friends was the daughter of the postmaster in the small town where I attended middle school, and with my limited socioeconomic awareness I viewed their resulting middle-class stability as "rich." Once I owed my friend a bit of change and for some reason mailed the few coins to her in a stamped envelope. The next time I saw her postmaster father, he shook his head and told me the lumpy envelope had been shredded as it passed through processing equipment intended for flat letters.

Never having seen a mail-sorting machine, I misunderstood his explanation and thought the coins had set off some metal detector that screened for hazardous contents. While I felt embarrassed, the admonition only increased my reverence for the United States Postal Service.

I was deeply aware of my family's vulnerability working

in remote fields, construction sites, and factories without adequate pay, health insurance, retirement funds, or sense of belonging to some official institution. Postal work, while physical, difficult, and sometimes perilous, appeared to come with all those basic benefits—plus, I now imagined, cool machines that might keep people safe. Most of my closest family members had suffered major work injuries toiling for industries that placed little value on their lives. The postal service, though, seemed a protective force—for the mail, for mail carriers, for the American people.

Years later, when a college friend dropped other career pursuits and became a postwoman in Wichita, I felt somehow proud to know her and, even, a little pang of envy.

Her job is getting harder, though, and you can track the urbanization—and privatization—of our country through the postal service's changes and challenges.

When President George Washington signed into law the Postal Service Act of 1792, thereby establishing the United States Post Office Department, the population was overwhelmingly rural and agricultural. Soon, though, the industrial revolution changed our relationship to the land. Today, four out of five Americans live in cities.

But while we are a mostly urban people, we are a mostly rural place. Rural areas still cover 97 percent of our geography. From the fertile soils of the Black Belt to the unpaved roads of Native American reservations, from the snowcapped Sangre de Cristo Mountains to the Midwestern prairie that I now see from my window, the United States is not just a country. It's country.

Amid that vast space is the pervasive miracle of 46 million rural mailboxes.

About 29 percent of all residential and business delivery points served by the USPS are classified as rural, according to the agency's 2019 annual report to Congress. Due to population growth, encroaching cities, and dated boundaries, however, some of those areas are no longer so rustic. It is difficult to quantify how many of the USPS's almost eighty thousand rural routes involve muddy lanes, country highways, and small towns, according to Allan Jones, a labor relations analyst for the National Rural Letter Carriers' Association (NRLCA). But they wind across 3.6 million miles of this land.

Those routes can be beautiful drives through our country's abundant natural treasures, and those small post offices contain beauties of their own: interesting, even grand period architecture, perhaps, but more often the austerity of a simple box, four walls and a roof with a homely sign, efficient and resolute against the elements.

Knowing firsthand the punishing labor of agricultural life, the particular dangers of an isolated location, and the social disadvantages of being rural, I am not one to sentimentalize country life. While bountiful with pleasures, it is not a happy pop-country song about a pickup truck and a young woman in cutoff shorts. It is a reality, rather, where a pickup truck slides off loose gravel and kills the teenage girl driving it, as happened to my high school classmate.

Thus, for the 130,000 mail carriers delivering rural routes, the job looks quite different from that of their city counterparts. The routes are long, in some cases with extensive stretches of driving between stops. Rural mail carriers don't wear uniforms, and about 38,000 of them drive their own vehicles. Those vehicles often require four-wheel drive for navigating rough terrain, and carriers frequently work in remote areas. There is an online memorial devoted to rural carriers who have lost their lives on the job—most due to car accidents, but some by medical emergency and even murder.

But rural mail carriers are far more often heroes than they are victims.

At a small demonstration in support of the postal service last August in Lawrence, Kansas, Lisa Grossman told me that her father, who was a mail carrier in the small township of Slippery Rock, Pennsylvania, heard a woman screaming from her house on his delivery route in the early 1990s. The woman's husband, unconscious on the floor, had no pulse. Grossman's father called 911, helped the wife administer CPR, and was credited with saving the husband's life.

When I posted to social media about the demonstration, Ann Vigola Anderson, also of Lawrence, recalled the postman who delivered mail—including the all-important seed catalogue in winter—to her grandparents' farm at the southern edge of Topeka when she was a child in the 1950s and '60s. During the Korean War, her grandmother awaited airmail letters from her son, who was a combat soldier. The mailman did more than deliver such important items, though.

"Many times, he would get out of his vehicle and help push Grandpa's old pickup out of a snowdrift, or he would bring orange circus candy that my grandma adored and leave it in her mailbox," Anderson said.

Pumping a dying man's chest, pushing trucks out of snow, delighting a worried mother with treats—these actions should not be expected of mail carriers anywhere or anytime, let alone today's increasingly overworked, underpaid postal workers in rural areas.

But such feats, and the bonds of trust developed on rural

routes, are the most rewarding aspect of the job, according to NRLCA president Ronnie Stutts.

"The rural letter carriers—we connect the world, the country, to a lot of the people out in rural communities," Stutts said by phone from Louisiana, where he lives and is working through the pandemic. Many rural people have limited or no internet access, still pay their bills via stamped envelopes, and encounter few people in their day-to-day lives. Their mailboxes thus are not just points of delivery but points of survival and civic belonging. Medications, mortgage statements, advance voting ballots, goods no longer available nearby due to dwindling rural economies—all come by mail.

Stutts, who has worked for the postal service for forty-five years, noted that the aging demographics of rural communities mean that mail carriers often keep an eye on seniors, sometimes in communication with adult children who have moved away. Rural carriers consider themselves first responders, he said, adding that they might be tasked with delivering coronavirus-related medications in the near future.

Letters come across his desk every day, Stutts said, about a rural carrier who noticed mail accumulating in a box, found someone fallen and lying on the floor inside their home, and saved their life by getting help.

"We're almost like their family," he said.

That is precisely how Vigola Anderson referred to the mailman at her childhood home in Topeka.

"Our mailman, when I was a kid, was like part of our family," Anderson said. "My mom made dill pickles every summer and she always said, 'Just help yourself.' We'd hear the garage door raise, and he'd take one out of the stone crock where they were pickling."

Anderson's cousin was the postmistress of tiny Maple Hill, Kansas, for decades—"the most important job in town," she said—and her great-uncle ran the Taos, New Mexico, post office in the town's more rugged days, from the 1930s to the 1950s.

The much-discussed financial crisis surrounding the USPS today has unique significance for rural delivery. The essential democratic backbone of the agency—guaranteeing the same postage rate for all Americans, regardless of their location—is not profitable. To maintain their own bottom lines, Amazon, UPS, FedEx, and other private delivery companies contract the service for "last mile" delivery to far-flung customers.

In 1970, President Richard Nixon signed the Postal Reorganization Act, abolishing the cabinet-level Post Office Department and weaning the postal service off federal funding; today, the agency relies on postage sales for revenue. In 2006, a Republican Congress passed the Postal Accountability and Enhancement Act, forcing the USPS to pre-allocate up to seventy-five years of postretirement costs—tens of billions of dollars—for its employees. No other agency is required to do so, and many see the rule as an intentional blow to a public function that some corporate lobbyists aim to privatize.

Stutts said that while some rural post offices have been consolidated, efforts to close them altogether have been largely unsuccessful due to public outcry from communities who depend on them.

"A lot of people will say, 'Look, these post offices in these small, rural communities really are not profitable,'" said Stutts, whose fiancée is a rural mail carrier in Farmerville, Louisiana.

"Well, the postal service is not supposed to be profitable. The postal service was created to give service to the American people—universal service."

That service is in jeopardy. The agency's burdensome financial structure has led to higher workloads and turnover rates, especially for part-time carriers whose position was created in 2015 and who receive fewer benefits. From 1999 to 2019, the number of USPS employees plummeted by almost 30 percent, from nearly 900,000 to around 630,000, according to recent analysis by the Pew Research Center.

The coronavirus pandemic increased package delivery this year, giving the USPS a revenue boost. But it also exacerbated the existing employee shortage, as frontline postal workers exposed to Covid-19 fell ill or were forced to quarantine.

Stutts said that the USPS can't continue to function without help from Congress—help that it's not getting.

"President Trump does not like the postal service," Stutts told me, referring to Trump's unfounded allegation that the agency mishandles contracts with Amazon and others. "He said we were a joke, and we got no stimulus money."

According to Stutts, without major reform and funding increases, the USPS will be out of money by September 2021.*

It's an alarming thought not just for rural people who count on mail carriers but for the carriers themselves. The postal service has long provided good jobs for women, people of color, and those without college degrees. The National Rural Letter Carriers' Association does not track racial demographics, but

---

* In 2022, President Joe Biden signed into law the Postal Service Reform Act, which passed Congress with ample bipartisan support. The law eliminated requirements that the USPS pre-fund retiree benefits, which the agency projected would save $27 billion over ten years, and required the USPS to maintain mail delivery six days per week.

57 percent of rural mail carriers are female, compared with 40 percent of the agency's national workforce.

What really stirred my admiration for mail carriers when I was a kid, I see now, is that on some deep level I sensed that our missions were similar.

As a girl on a struggling family farm, I already knew I wanted to be a journalist someday, for the civic purpose of disseminating information and creating connections among people and places. Mail carriers, of course, accomplish those same goals by different means.

During the 1990s, when I was in my teens, our farm's mailing address changed from Rural Route 1 to a more specific description. While that national reconfiguration of rural addresses was necessary to improve emergency response and other systems, I was vaguely annoyed by the assignment of a house number to our farm and a numerical street name to our dirt road, whose location had been described in more interesting terms for my entire life: "When you see the church west of the blacktop, make a right," or "Follow the arrow on our eggs sign next to the highway."

Soon after that street address was assigned, we had to sell the farm.

Happily, it's still a working farm owned by another family. For them, the closest hospital is twenty miles away; the nearby two-room schoolhouse closed when I was in middle school, forcing a long bus ride for their children; and small grocery stores within easy proximity shuttered long ago. But the rural mail carrier abides, and so too does the rural post office, the rural mailbox of my youth.

When we spoke, Stutts had just returned from the Lake

Charles, Louisiana, area where Hurricane Laura had struck a few weeks prior. He'd gone to check on mail carriers and bring them work essentials such as mosquito spray as they delivered mail through disaster zones. Some carriers lost their homes or left the state, Stutts said, and he had carriers in other areas volunteering to help in their absence.

In some places, though, there was no longer need for a mail carrier, because everything had been destroyed. Stutts recalled the devastation he'd just observed in Cameron, Louisiana, a rural area on the Gulf of Mexico thirty miles east of the Texas border.

"There's absolutely no mailboxes up," Stutts said. "Big, huge utility poles were snapped like toothpicks—I mean hundreds, hundreds if not thousands of them, within a twenty-mile radius."

The Cameron post office had operated out of a small metal trailer, which was completely swept away by the storm. The only way you know it was there, Stutts said, is by its blue metal collection box, still standing amid the debris. *

---

* In May 2023, despite objections by Democratic senators, under Trump-appointed postmaster general Louis DeJoy the USPS implemented a new pay system that led to significant pay cuts for rural mail carriers. This threat to rural mail service, and the NRLCA's failure to prevent it, prompted a petition by some rural carriers to decertify the NRLCA and join a new union.

REVISION

The New Territory, 2021

[1]O Earth, we have used you to compliment ourselves.

[2]We are mighty, wild, and free as oaks, rivers, and eagles, we have claimed. You are our favored object of comparison for the subject of ourselves.

[3]Long ago, the simile was reversed. You were primary and we secondary, you the tenor and we the vehicle.

[4]It was night, and you were a fire around which we swirled and howled—not like animals, but as animals.

[5]Then we planted rows of words, breaking circles in order to make lines. We broke the lines to construct a ladder and climbed the rungs. From the top we looked down on you. Dominion, we called it. We wrote a religion and said God created us in His image, which is to say we constructed God in our image.

[6]The problem was not that we believed in God but rather that we forgot what God is.

[7]On Earth, evolution does not select for perfection, enjoyment, or ease but rather for propagation. Our minds have been exquisite tools to that end, selective memory our sharpest weapon. To colonize your surface, we had to forget. We had to call you property and ourselves owners.

[8]If we remembered the truth, our descriptions would change.

[9]The fracking, mining, dumping, and clearing were wrought by the hand of God, because we are God, just like you are God, which is another way of saying there is no God, which is another way of saying everything is God, which is another way of saying we have degraded ourselves by degrading you.

[10]Let our linear prose become an expansive poem. Let the ode be to you, not to us.

[11]O Earth, if our only mirrors were rivers, we would stop seeing ourselves in you. We would instead see you in ourselves. The river would cease to divide nations. You would be sacred as a baby, revered as a priestess, beloved as a dying mother in our arms.

EXTRACTION

The Atlantic, 2021

In January, President Joe Biden canceled the Keystone XL pipeline and ordered a drilling moratorium on federal land. The following month, a historic cold snap and a failed power grid turned Texas into a disaster zone. Even as policy debates about events like these unfold, each one serves as a wake-up call. Our reliance on the fossil-fuel industry is by now so old and deep that overdue regulations, while crucial, will not stop consequences already set in motion. The man-made, carbon-wrought transformation of our climate is here.

As we grapple with this reality, rather than fixating on abstract concepts and quantitative measures—energy prices, geopolitics, emissions rates, climate-science projections—we would do well to zoom in, way in, on those doing and allowing the drilling. Their stories contain a common promise: *You'll make a lot of money.* Yet many lose, as do we all, in other ways before the bargain is closed. We can learn a lot from their ground-level wisdom about the human motives and exploitative economies that got us into this mess, as well as about the dangerous and toxic business of siphoning oil and gas from the earth below.

Two new books take us there. In *The Good Hand: A Memoir of Work, Brotherhood, and Transformation in an American Boomtown*, Michael Patrick F. Smith finds his checking account and personal demons intertwined with the oil industry. At the height of the Bakken Formation oil boom, in 2013, Smith left Brooklyn seeking what he imagined would be challenging but lucrative work in the oil fields. A playwright and musician raised amid poverty and domestic abuse in rural Maryland, he never quite felt at home in gentrified Brooklyn or at his Midtown Manhattan office job that paid the bills. This identity crisis, combined with a penchant for self-punishment previously pursued through drugs and sex, sent him west to see whether he might finally make a man of himself at thirty-six.

What he found in the now-infamous boomtown of Williston, North Dakota, was a cast of characters with even rougher pasts than his own. Smith's memoir is about these men, who showed up from across the country and beyond to risk their lives on a windswept plain where the temperature might be thirty-eight degrees below zero and the pay might be twenty dollars an hour.

During his tenure in the oil patch, Smith worked as a truck driver's assistant, or swamper, for a rig-moving company. His face grew chapped and his body toughened as he threw chains beneath the immense North Dakota sky, but the question that looms over the narrative is whether his sense of self would be transformed. He was smaller and older than most of the men doing his low-ranking job; could he earn the respect of his supervisors—grizzled bastards who pegged him for a wuss and tried to run him off? Would he, in the parlance of those workers, make a good hand?

Smith stayed on for nine months, a fair bit longer than the proverbial journalistic parachute jump, and his pre-Trump-era mission was more personal than anthropological. Still, his most important contributions are not musings about what the experience meant to him but vivid descriptions of the experience itself. *The Good Hand*'s scenes in "the patch" are beautiful, funny, and harrowing, constructed with metal hooks, workplace lingo, poetic profanity, and the author's palpable fear. (From 2008 through 2017, more than fifteen hundred oil-and-gas workers died from injuries sustained on the job, according to a report by the Center for Public Integrity. That amounts to, roughly, a death every other day.) As someone whose immediate family bears the scars of physical labor in another Great Plains state, and who rarely sees her native class convincingly portrayed, I relished these anecdotes and the validation they provide.

Smith's dangerous toil on the job mirrored a dangerous life after work among the same hard men, some of whom were attracted to the area by the possibility of good pay with no background checks. (When Smith arrived at a flophouse, his highly common name—Mike Smith—alarmed the slumlord, who worried that he was another fugitive with an alias looking for a room.) Smith weaves in heartbreaking stories from his upbringing, and from the pasts of the men he came to know, implicitly making a compelling argument that busted men are tasked with busting the earth.

They all looked the same to Smith when he arrived, and trading stories of violent fathers was a standard icebreaker. "The conversation," Smith writes, "can be boiled down to two short sentences: 'What kind of work you do? Man, my dad whipped my ass!' I come to think of it as The Williston Hello." But soon he found the workers he met there to be as distinct as his artsy friends back in Williamsburg. One stood in a "perpetual wrestling stance," feet planted wide and muscles on alert. Another recalled being struck by a heavy object with such force that his intestines were forced out of his anus. These workers—mostly White men, like Smith, but some Indigenous men and men of color as well—were at once deeply exhausted and wired on chewing tobacco and energy drinks. They had a brother in prison, or a brother who'd died in Iraq. They went by handles like "Smash" and "Big Country."

In such an environment, bravado is a survival tool, and Smith played the part while quietly detecting fellow sensitives, including a big twenty-one-year-old named Huck with whom he formed a bond. Such glimpses of male intimacy flowering in harsh conditions are moving. Not every tough guy has a soft side, though, and Williston was rife with bad actors. Smith was troubled by the long rap sheets of some of his new friends—but not troubled enough to skip bar and strip-club outings with them.

Women flit in and out of the story mostly as objects of fantasy or passing references—the young bartender at a local dive, his landlord's girlfriend in another state, sex workers, strangers at the coffee shop where Smith wrote his experiences in real time. He admits that he knew little about these women, and their flatness in a book about a male world perhaps should not be faulted. A lack of context is sometimes problematic, though. The crisis of missing and murdered Indigenous women—an old problem receiving new attention, thanks to Interior Secretary Deb Haaland and others—has been linked to "man camps" populated by transient workers in the fossil-fuel industry. Reports of rape around Williston multiplied during the boom, Smith learned later, yet his few mentions of the term mostly concern fear of man-on-man rape. *The Good Hand*, as the subtitle suggests, is not just about labor but about masculinity—and it is often the toxic sort.

In one instance, Smith's former landlord described a line of men on the stairs of his house "running a train on" a severely intoxicated woman within. In another, an erstwhile coworker told Smith, over whiskey and Cokes, about trying to persuade a sexual partner to let him prostitute her; she was, he said before offering Smith a cell phone recording of her giving him fellatio, "this close to letting me sell her ass." Smith laughed that his friend was "always saying some funny crazy shit," and declined to watch the video. With the age and consent of the female in this anecdote unknown, and in a book about a place brimming with sex traffickers, I did not laugh with him.*

Apparently knowing that the exchange was foul, Smith got a sick feeling, but soon he and the friend were goofing around taking pictures in the bar parking lot with Huck. By contrast, on the occasions when Smith witnessed racism, he named it, agonized over his closeness to it, phoned his brother to talk about how to handle it. Calling out damaging male behavior toward women was clearly a source of greater discomfort. Smith is in rare company, though, for daring to describe the behavior at all. One wishes for similar testimonies from other socioeconomic strata. The soft-handed men, say, who acquire the oil-drilling leases and decide in boardrooms that the pipeline will be laid alongside the reservation—where are

---

* Following this review's publication, Smith sent me a gracious response in which he addressed my pointed criticism on gender: "I don't fully agree with it, but I'm not going to say you're far off either. It was certainly tempting to temper a couple of those scenes to make myself look better, and I left out things that would have put me in a better light. But showing myself surrendering to my fucked-up-ness by the end of the book felt more important than positioning myself as a good guy."

their memoirs describing the sins of their sex, their race? The
worker at the bottom is the most honest because he has the
least to lose.

The landowners who happen to live atop fossil-fuel deposits
occupy a world quite apart from that of transient laborers. It
is, however, similarly fraught. To get to know that world, Colin
Jerolmack, a professor of sociology and environmental studies
at NYU, spent eight months in 2013 living in the fracking epi-
center of Williamsport, Pennsylvania, population about twenty-
eight thousand. In *Up to Heaven and Down to Hell: Fracking,
Freedom, and Community in an American Town*, which also
reflects six years of follow-up research, he investigates individual
and community values among those who have seen the United
States' quest for energy independence play out in their own
backyard. Jerolmack wanted to understand how people weigh
personal decisions—in this case, whether to permit drilling by
gas companies—that ultimately affect neighbors, ecosystems,
and even future generations.

In the US, real-estate ownership historically includes not
just the surface of the land but its subsurface, as well as the air
above it. (The book's title refers to the medieval Roman dictum
said to mark the idea's legal origins.) Governments elsewhere
around the world wield much greater sway over mineral rights
and other matters of public consequence on private land. Jerolmack's many kitchen-table conversations with inhabitants of the
formerly idyllic area of greater Williamsport—or "Billtown," as
it is called, best known as the host of the Little League World
Series—reveal the tensions and trade-offs that follow from
America's liberty-loving ways.

In deciding whether to lease their land to natural-gas

companies, Jerolmack learned, area residents heard front-door sales pitches from landmen brokering mineral rights, attended contentious local-government meetings, and organized collective-bargaining efforts with their neighbors. Ultimately, most of them leaned on a conservative worldview: the two acres, or two hundred acres, belonged to them, and they'd do as they damn well pleased. But for a true understanding of their hearts and minds, political frameworks prove inadequate.

Economic considerations were paramount, of course. For financially strapped homeowners, monthly royalty checks enabled a modest nest egg, a nice pickup, a new roof, their first dishwasher. Leasing allowed some to hold on to the family farm. One man poignantly described his wish to fund a college education for his granddaughter.

Those dreams came with a price, though, often concurrent with the royalty checks. Even adamant supporters of drilling admitted that it had wreaked havoc on their lives. The very things that had attracted them to the area—natural beauty, peace and quiet, dark skies full of stars—were stripped away once fracking moved in. For some, their immediate shelter suffered too. Big rigs and earthmovers rattled one house until the chimney collapsed. In others, tap water turned cloudy. "Fracking is intimate," Jerolmack writes. Some of the transgressed ended up silenced by nondisclosure agreements after reaching settlement deals. "They have us by the balls," one such resident told Jerolmack.

Yet the "fractivism" of outsiders—Yoko Ono is among the many who have traveled from New York City to advocate for fracking bans in rural Pennsylvania—provoked understandable resentment. Natural gas, Jerolmack notes, powers more New York homes than any other energy source, and much of it comes from places like Billtown.

Jerolmack met just one person, he writes with admiration, "who regularly traversed the political, economic, and cultural divides" of Williamsport: Ralph Kisberg, who cofounded a local organization called the Responsible Drilling Alliance. He was the quintessential centrist, critical of fracking but more interested in efforts to mitigate its ill effects than in the far-off goal of ending it. Kisberg went to nearly every permit meeting, drove back roads to chat up landowners, compiled his findings in the group's newsletter. This approach, an information blitz devoid of judgment, was the opposite of a bumper sticker and fostered constructive discussion where many an argument along national party lines breaks down.

Those party lines did not always predict gas-drilling decisions in Billtown. One area resident, Cindy Bower—a former schoolteacher who belonged to Kisberg's advocacy group, held signs on the first Earth Day, in 1970; drove a Prius; and was married to a wealthy hotelier—shook Jerolmack's assumptions. She and her husband, who lived on 150 acres of hilly woods and fields with a big pond, had refused leasing pitches for three years. But as everyone around them leased, often for financial reasons that Bower did not begrudge, industry moved in and their quality of life deteriorated. In the end, Bower and her husband leased their land. She told Jerolmack with some sorrow that holding out had accomplished nothing, and the money was at least some compensation for what they had lost.

Jerolmack warns eco-conscious readers against feeling superior to either liberal Bower or her conservative neighbors. "To the extent that most of us continue to uncritically organize our lives around carbon-intensive energy sources," he writes, "we are coconspirators." To be spared the dire environmental impacts of our species is a privilege.

Environmental hazards of extractive industry impose a

disproportionate burden on Indigenous people, people of color, and the poor: the radiation of a uranium mine, the smells of a refinery, the sometimes predatory men whom oil-drilling companies hire because a felon with no other job prospects is a loyal employee. Jerolmack's own excrement, as he points out, might have moved from New York City on "poop trains" that traveled to Alabama landfills, fouling the air for small towns along its route.

One of the most memorable passages of *The Good Hand* offers a related insight. On a visit to New York, carousing with friends and "holding court, dazzling them with my oil field talk," Smith suddenly saw anew the cabs, the streetlights, the petroleum-derived subway seats, the laminated menus:

> *New York benefits from the oil boom far more than Williston ever will. No one here realizes that. Nobody even considers it. Here in this West Village gastropub. Look at them. Everything they enjoy. Every. Single. Thing. They get it from me. They get it from me and a group of the toughest, meanest motherfuckers I have met in my life. Men they wouldn't like, men they look down on, invisible men they will never see in a state they dismiss as flyover. They owe it all to the hands. All of it.*

This is one age-old problem of hierarchy: toward the top, even those who might want to solve the problems of our society—in this case, the destructive and unsustainable fossil-fuel industry— know very little about the toll they take at ground level.

WHAT TO DO WITH OUR COVID RAGE

The New York Times, 2021

In the spring, I received my Covid-19 vaccination shots from county health workers in an old building on the main street of a tiny Kansas town. My first dose came from a quiet nurse wearing a plastic visor over his N95 mask and a leather cowboy belt with ornate metal inlays. My second dose came from a smiling older woman who, when I reported that I had experienced strong side effects from the first shot, patted me on the shoulder and said, "It's better than a tube down your throat, hon."

Fellow county residents waited their turn in muddy boots and faded work jackets while the April wind stirred their fields of early wheat. There was corn to plant, but they had found time to make long drives to what was then the only vaccination site in five hundred square miles. Our ages, politics, and backgrounds varied, but we were mostly White, rural people who wanted to live.

Today, the wheat has been harvested and the corn is high,

but still roughly one in three people approved for the vaccine across the country has not yet received a single dose, according to the Centers for Disease Control and Prevention (CDC). Indeed, many of those unvaccinated Americans have willfully refused the shot.

Abetted by that slow rollout, Covid-19 has resurged. Following a short, beautiful moment of relaxed precautions while cases were down at the start of summer, we again don masks, change plans, and worry about how to keep ourselves and our loved ones safe. Vaccination rates are on the rise as the hesitant become less so, but the coronavirus will likely be with us indefinitely. How does one process this brutal reality?

Many vaccinated Americans are tired, disgusted, and eager to assign blame. Public health experts and government officials, including some Republicans, have shifted from sensitive prodding to firm condemnation of those forgoing vaccination. Private conversations among the inoculated take an even less diplomatic turn: "We were so close, and these stupid, unvaccinated jerks ruined it for the rest of us."

Fatigue and outrage are appropriate emotions, considering all that has been lost to Covid-19: lives, jobs, experiences, money, physical and mental health. But those feelings, if not properly channeled, can themselves take a heavy toll. What do we do with our anger?

I am a progressive woman who resides in a conservative state. I am on record in this fractured political era as a proponent of maintaining connection across gulfs of understanding, with the caveat that this civic burden falls to people whose social privileges allow them to engage safely with the other side. But seeking to understand dangerous behaviors and beliefs is quite different from permitting them. By many accounts an amiable person, I once yelled at a truck stop full of unmasked people to read the "masks required" sign on the goddamn door.

Fury—collective, generational, political, cultural, individual—is utterly familiar to me, more so than the happy serenity of my current life. I was a child in poverty during the 1980s "farm crisis," when federal policies favoring big corporations devastated rural communities. Everywhere I turned, something was dying: the local grocery store, the family farm, the cancer victims whose water supply contained agricultural runoff. There was joy in my family, but there was also addiction, abuse, and neglect that drew from a deep well of justifiable rage and sorrow.

Anger is a contagious energy that jumps quickly from one person to the next. It will seize your mind and body as its host. If allowed to explode, it will hurt others. If allowed to implode, it will hurt you. I had to learn early how to transmute it for the sake of my own survival. I found that it can be the source of a powerful alchemy. If we are up to the task, it could help us create something good together.

That alchemy begins with awareness. Are we justified in our indignation? Do we have the facts? If we do not understand the problem, our feelings are untethered from reality. Untethered anger tends to be unproductive and selfish, delighting our egos rather than directing us toward necessary action.

So when you are ready—and if you are never ready, whether because you mourn a loved one's death or your altered future, I won't judge—let us hold our rage in our hands and look closely to see what it contains.

Our national conversation has reached the point where many Americans are done with any and all excuses offered by the unvaccinated. Some of the inoculated are not just self-righteous but downright venomous, arguing on social media that hospitals should refuse to admit unvaccinated Covid-19 patients, calling them trash and wishing them a painful death. Residents of blue America have pronounced this a red-America problem. "Our state did a great job fighting the pandemic," one person tweeted. "Our reward? The mouth-breathing knuckle-draggers in adjacent red states flooded their hospitals and spilled over into ours."

Old political resentments have found a new outlet in the fraught vaccine debate. "I've been pissed off since Reagan was elected," another Twitter user quipped in a thread parsing the emotions of the vaccinated. Exhausted, despairing minds find comfort in turning complex realities into simple, opposing categories. The noble, upstanding vaccinated American and the selfish, stupid, unvaccinated one. The good liberal citizen and the far-right anti-vaxxer.

Available images reinforce these notions. A vocal contingent of conservatives appears at meetings holding hypocritical signs about liberty, on the internet sharing memes about liberal sheep, on the nightly news spitting on public health officials. They command attention, and their share of the unvaccinated will increase as more persuadable people get their shots. But, according to research by the Kaiser Family Foundation, those people are not the majority of the vaccine-reluctant. A May study by another nonprofit, Surgo Ventures, showed that 16 percent of eligible Americans refused the vaccine because of skepticism about the pandemic, marked by a belief in at least one conspiracy theory. The same study found that a higher number, some 22 percent, hadn't gotten vaccinated because of concerns about cost, safety, or systems that previously did them wrong. Millions more of the unvaccinated, of course, are children under twelve and those disqualified by underlying health conditions.

My White, working-class extended family contains liberal women and men who have been vaccinated; liberal men who have not for fear of losing a day of work to side effects; conservative men who refuse under the influence of disinformation; liberal women and men who have delayed for fear of the for-profit health care industry; and conservative women who are considering getting their first dose. My grandmother—a former Bernie Sanders voter, a childhood polio survivor, and a strong compulsory vaccination proponent—was the first among us to get a shot.

I cringe when I see the rampant stereotypes on social media painting the unvaccinated as rural White folks, by now a frequent scapegoat for our country's ills. "Spreadnecks," I've seen them newly termed (as in, "rednecks" spreading the virus). Never mind that, per the CDC, the daily case rates in urban and nonmetropolitan areas closely track one another.

This archetypal bumpkin villain of post-Trump America has long received too much credit in a country where Trumpism thrives in affluent, White urban communities bursting with college degrees. In handling the pandemic, such misdirection of attention keeps us from what we should be doing: trying to reach the vast group of people who might choose vaccination if barriers to access and knowledge were removed.

One overlooked barrier, as ever in this country, is socioeconomic class. Polls conducted by the Kaiser Family Foundation earlier this year found that working-class people—White, Black, Hispanic, Democrat, Republican—were less likely to be vaccinated. Vaccination rates for Black and White college graduates, meanwhile, were almost identical. The so-called uneducated of all races and backgrounds are hampered not by a lack of good sense but by a lack of money and power. Their education status keeps their income low, and income predicts insurance status. When the highly contagious Delta variant was taking hold, uninsured Americans had the lowest vaccination rate of twenty-two subgroups examined by Kaiser.

Having gone without health insurance for much of my life, I can attest that the experience does not promote trust in the health care system, better known to the uninsured as a crippling source of debt than a helpful provider of cures. The Center for Economic and Policy Research found that states with higher rates of insured people generally have higher vaccination rates. People of color are disproportionately uninsured, as conditions of class—poverty and lack of education—intersect with systemic racism. Nonetheless, myriad news stories investigating the vaccination divide fail to mention the words "class," "education," or "income" once.

The longer we spend furious at the bad actors among us, the further we move from the truth: that many unvaccinated people are scared just like us, and that with the right help and information, they would sit down next to nurses and pull up their sleeves. We must instead turn our anger into actions that help our cause.

We can demand public-health mandates, political blowback be damned. We can communicate with the cost-anxious and wait-and-see people who remain open-minded despite skepticism wrought by a lifetime of disadvantage. We can do good deeds to negate harmful ones, like donating money to a non-profit health clinic when we see anti-science protesters on the sidewalk or in the news. We can also, in my opinion, occasionally tell those protesters to screw off, if it gets us to our next moment of grace. (I didn't say I was enlightened.)

Most importantly, we can direct our rage not at lost individuals but at systems of power that made our grim national death count the only plausible outcome. Is it so shocking that a caste-based society that exalts individualism and prioritizes profit above wellness—one of the only industrialized nations without universal health care—would fail to rise to the challenges of a collective health crisis?

Despite our failings of national character, Americans were the fortunate few at the front of an eight-billion-person line, saved by stockpiles of quickly developed vaccines that poor countries around the world have struggled to access. We were among the first of our entire species invited to receive a tremendous feat of modern science into our blood—a choice that hundreds of thousands of Covid-19 victims, who died before vaccines were available to them, did not live to make. Those of us who get the vaccines, current data tells us, will almost certainly survive this pandemic and even a lifetime of seasonal, endemic Covid-19 outbreaks.

Maintaining that perspective can be hard when staying healthy requires keeping track of case counts, changing guidelines, the science of booster shots, and the safety rankings of face masks. So when all else fails, if your anger at "the unvaccinated" feels unbearable, focus less on those whose actions are beyond your control.

Remember how you felt last spring, at a city stadium or a suburban pharmacy or a rural community building, when you got a shot. How will you remember its blessing? What will you do with the life that it saved?

IN CELEBRATION OF RARE AND EXQUISITE ACCURACY FROM HOLLYWOOD

The Guardian, 2022

One Saturday last fall, my husband and I bought an antique clawfoot bathtub in Manhattan, Kansas. After loading it from a stranger's backyard into the bed of our truck, we walked to the Chef, a downtown diner, figuring we might be seated quickly with half the town tailgating at the Kansas State University football game.

We drank Bloody Marys on the patio among White, Black, and Brown diners while purple school flags waved in the autumn breeze. Our server pointed to a pile of blankets in case I got chilly.

When we left, I handed my blanket to a trio of men eating bacon and wearing hunting gear. "In case you get chilly," I said. They laughed. Then the server, who was wearing facial hair, makeup, men's shoes, pearls, and a crop top, refilled their coffee cups.

Unfashionable places such as Kansas—"one of the square ones in the middle," coastal acquaintances have said to me with a smile and a shrug—are often portrayed by Hollywood as a homogeneous expanse of "uneducated," White, straight, cisgender conservatives who are cooking meth or terrorizing outsiders.

Perhaps that is because most of those employed as storytellers or gatekeepers in film and television have led urban lives geographically removed from regions condescendingly known as "flyover country." Similarly, many of the people I've worked with at coastal media outlets have never set foot in my region. Their assumptions formed in lieu of direct experience often rely on clichés.

Yet there we were, that sunny Saturday, living amid a richness omitted by dominant narratives: the Hispanic-named woman whom I paid for the tub, the server who refuted gender norms while working for tuition money, hunters with deer blood on their pants, my leftist-carpenter husband, and this farm girl who had returned home following professional stints in major cities.

A few months later, I watched the HBO show *Somebody Somewhere*, improbably set in Manhattan, Kansas. The second episode includes a brunch scene at the Chef involving a biracial gay couple, a transgender agriculture professor wearing purple, and a farm girl who returned home. Any one of them seemed apt to refinish an old clawfoot tub.

The exquisite accuracy of the show—shocking and even moving to a resident of a region more often misrepresented, lampooned, or altogether ignored in popular culture—is not just in its unceremonious diversity. It is in its authentic set design, over which Kansans I know have pointed and exclaimed with glee. There's a candle poured by that company in Ellinwood! A bag of chips from the Kansas City snack factory! The local craft beer, the local-dive T-shirt, the real-life storefronts—on the same TV screen at which we have spent a lifetime groaning when "Kansas" has mountains on the horizon.

As it happens, *Somebody Somewhere*, the first season finale of which aired last Sunday, was filmed outside Chicago. Landscape shots thus feature cornfields rather than Kansas's more common export, wheat. But those steering the show know firsthand the town and region they depict. Star and executive producer Bridget Everett is from Manhattan, Kansas, while creators Hannah Bos and Paul Thureen are both from the Midwest.

Together they give us not just uber-cred detail but regional and rural ubiquities: the Ford Ranger pickup, the small gift shop selling potpourri, the amiable neighbor dealing fentanyl, the antique milk churn on a patio, the dangerous grain bin. The braless, heavy-set grocery shopper in Walmart sweats is there too—not as the butt of a joke but as the talented, compelling star of the show.

Forgoing the caricature of rurality as frighteningly remote and disconnected, *Somebody Somewhere* also nails the liminality of town and country, for many. The main character, Sam, works, eats, shops, and sleeps in Manhattan—which, with a population of fifty thousand, is not small by Kansas standards—and makes a short drive to visit her folks' struggling farm. The show even manages to handle my state's love-hate relationship with *The Wizard of Oz*, referenced both in overarching theme and tongue-in-cheek plot points, without offense.

To get a place wrong, over and over again, is at once an insult to and an invalidation of its people. To get a place right, then, is a healing of sorts.

When my 2018 book *Heartland* was published, I heard from thousands of readers who were relieved and delighted to recognize in its pages their unsexy place, or a place much like it. The book is an intersectional critique of our ill-addressed socioeconomic class structure, my family's rural poverty serving as a springboard to analyzing US history, policy, and culture. But many readers just wanted to tell me where they were from. Across lines of race, religion, class, and political ideology, from the rural South to small-town Idaho to upstate New York, they essentially said, "You captured a place like mine, and now I feel seen and understood."

National headlines often reduce such places to strictly political frameworks: How do they vote, and why? The esteemed panel confidently answering these questions rarely includes someone from the place being discussed. The resulting blind spots lead to false estimations, as a roundly stunned national media proved during the 2016 presidential election.

At a moment when our social fabric is tearing, we would do well to look at the true threads of every unseen and misunderstood place. Efforts to diversify the powerful spaces that tell stories and create culture—newsrooms, publishers, Hollywood writers' rooms—must address place, geography, and class as identity markers.

Somebody Somewhere proves that doing so is not at odds with other forms of inclusion but, rather, elevates accuracy in intersectional ways.

Jeff Hiller, who plays the sweet White dork Joel, recently reflected on finding a script about not just the hardship of fitting into a small town as a queer person but the beautiful ways people do so. Hiller, whose character introduces Sam to an upbeat group of misfits and queers who gather in a church space, had a parallel experience in real life.

"I went to Texas Lutheran College in a small farming town, and there was this one female pastor who held church services on Saturday evenings where we'd have champagne and it was all queer folks," Hiller told the website *Them*. "[There] we could be authentic, genuine people, and we were accepted. So when I read the pilot and saw this character who was gay—for the most part openly gay—and also a member of a faith community, I was shocked . . . I can't think of any other examples of a faith community on TV with queer people in it who aren't being persecuted."

In the show's resoundingly positive reviews, much has been made of Sam's struggle to fit in after moving home to care for her dying sister. She's a White farmer's daughter but also progressive and offbeat—how will she ever be content there, where women collect throw pillows and cook casseroles for their husbands? The question, presented by the show overtly, understandably resonates with TV critics choosing to live in hip, sophisticated environments.

Worth equal consideration, though, is the fact that Joel, who is no less progressive and offbeat, is happy in that same place—volunteering for community causes, dreaming of raising children with his brown-skinned boyfriend, and probably collecting throw pillows in a town where bitchy homophobes and thriving homosexuals coexist. Joel is not in Manhattan, Kansas, because he couldn't make it in Manhattan, New York. He is there because, as he defends it to Sam, "This is where I live."

Sam's trajectory, meanwhile, is not the linear American dream—"get out," climb up the ladder, and never look back—but the circular journey of the hero who returns home. She never did much climbing, it turns out, and "getting out"—even for those deemed successful—is always an illusion. We carry our backstories with us, and many who leave are eventually summoned home, whether by familial duties or an abiding affection for the complicated place that shaped them.

One real-life homecomer, Skylar Baker-Jordan, recently wrote for the *Daily Yonder* about returning to his tiny hometown in

Kentucky. Upon moving to Chicago, he found himself defending his home when repeatedly asked what it was like to be gay in the rural South.

"My answer, that actually I didn't have such a bad time of things after high school, always seemed to disappoint folks," Baker-Jordan wrote. "It was as if they wanted to hear I had spent the better part of my life running from rednecks in pickup trucks firing rifles at me. In reality, those rednecks were my family and friends."

Filmmaker Lee Isaac Chung juxtaposed identities of race, ethnicity, and place with his semi-autobiographical, award-winning 2020 film *Minari*, about Korean immigrants in rural Arkansas.

"Everyone always talks about the immigrant stuff. To me, this is an Arkansas story or a farming story," Chung told the *Arkansas Times*. "There were a lot of people on set from Oklahoma, and on set I felt like there was this interesting divide between the Korean people and the local Oklahoma people. I'm kind of in between both."

Many in our society are untethered from home by the forces of capitalism, the disembodiment that the digital age engenders, and the homogenizing cultural effects of globalization. The class that joins Hollywood meetings via Zoom calls from tropical beaches might even fancy itself post-place. What some of them miss, and what *Somebody Somewhere* makes us laugh and cry by revealing, is that in this moment of cultural division, place is a tie that very much still binds.

In another recent hit show, *Ted Lasso*, the title character leaves Kansas to coach British footballers. Lasso, whom creator and star Jason Sudeikis based in part on his real-life high school basketball coach in Kansas, relishes the professional opportunity but longs for his broken family back home. Tig Notaro's acclaimed dark comedy *One Mississippi*, which shares *Somebody Somewhere*'s themes of mortality and homecoming, occasionally leans on regional stereotypes for a laugh but treats Notaro's native small-town Mississippi with fairness and affection. It is possible to write a story or create a show that scorns or diminishes the place you're from, but these shows successfully handle place because of their creators' geographic identities.

In one of *Somebody Somewhere*'s most touching moments, the cheerful agriculture professor, Fred, stands in a field advising Sam's aging father, Ed, to plant cover crops for soil regeneration. Ed, played by Mike Hagerty, sounds like the actor's native Chicago but conjures for me my gentle, suspenders-wearing grandfather all the same.* He laments the challenge of long-term planting strategies when survival of the farm is a short-term concern. Fred, played by the drag king Murray Hill, consoles him, saying, "You're a real good steward of your land."

Their dialogue was the first time I recall seeing a character on-screen offer the highest compliment, where I'm from—to say, in essence, "you do well by this place."

Storytellers, in Hollywood and beyond, should seek to do the same.

---

* Hagerty sent me an approving comment of my review via Twitter just two months before his death, at age sixty-seven, reportedly following an adverse reaction to antibiotic medication. I was heartbroken over the untimely loss of one of our great character actors—and one of relatively few Hollywood stars with blue-collar bona fides. Hagerty, the son of an Irish-Catholic police officer, worked at a filling station and auto repair shop on the South Side of Chicago before finding his artistic calling.

SHELTERBELT

The New York Times, 2022

Lines of Kansas voters, resolute in the August sun and hundred-degree heat, stretched beyond the doors of polling sites and wrapped around buildings on Tuesday to cast ballots in a primary election. A few suffered heat exhaustion. Firefighters passed out bottles of water.

When polls closed at 7 p.m. Central time, many were still in line and legally entitled to get their turn. The *Wichita Eagle* reported that one Wichita woman cast the final vote at her polling site at 9:45 p.m. after waiting in line for nearly three hours. Volunteer workers at the polls, understaffed amid the record primary turnout, worked brutally long hours for democracy.

This inspired showing responded to a clear threat against reproductive rights. In the first state vote on abortion following the Supreme Court's overturning of *Roe v. Wade,* Kansans unequivocally batted down the legislature's proposed amendment to remove the right to an abortion from the state constitution.

These citizens of the Plains put me in mind of the row of century-old cedar trees, planted close together so that their branches interlocked, that shielded my family's small farm from powerful winds. As such shelterbelts prevent soil erosion across the region, Kansas voters—underestimated by shocked liberals across the country—stood against the erosion of personal freedom.

Passage of the amendment would have made way for the conservative legislature to further limit or completely ban abortion, threatening the health, bodily autonomy, and survival of not just pregnant Kansans but pregnant people who travel to the state for otherwise inaccessible care. Neighboring Missouri and Oklahoma, as well as Texas and other nearby states, have banned or severely restricted abortion. A spokesman for Trust Women, an abortion clinic in Wichita, reported a 60 percent increase in out-of-state patients over the past year and a doubling of overall patient volume since last year.

In a state where registered Republicans far outnumber Democrats, the results reveal that conservative politicians bent on controlling women and pregnant people with draconian abortion bans are out of step with their electorates, a majority of whom are capable of nuance often concealed by our two-party system.

This is not news to many moderates and progressives in so-called red states, living with excruciating awareness of the gulf between their decent communities and the far-right extremists gerrymandering, voter-suppressing, and dark-moneying their way into state and local office. Too often, election results say more about the conditions of the franchise—who manages to use it, and what information or misinformation they receive along the way—than they do about the character of a place.

Not so this time, even as anti-abortion lawmakers and their supporters tried every trick. They placed a major voter referendum on a primary election ballot, in order to sneak it through amid expected low voter awareness and turnout. They wanted to favor conservative votes in a state where Democrats often have little to vote on during a midterm primary and therefore stay home. To boot, per figures provided by the secretary of state's office, some 30 percent of Kansas voters are unaffiliated and so unable to vote for candidates in primary elections. Independents could vote on the abortion measure but might not have known.

The anti-choice side used confusing language in the amendment, which suggested a yes vote would ban taxpayer funding of abortions—a ban that already exists—or allow for laws protecting victims of rape and incest, who already have legal access to abortion. They insisted they had no designs on passing a total ban on abortion, but the *Kansas Reflector* obtained audio from a meeting in which a state senator and amendment advocate promised to attempt to pass just such a ban. On top of that, the day before the election, Kansas voters received deceptive texts to vote yes to preserve "choice," confusing untold numbers of voters.

With this atmosphere in mind, alongside polls that were way off target, cynical pundits and hopeful abortion rights supporters alike were stunned by the extent of the amendment's failure—an 18-percentage-point margin—in an initiative some predicted would require days or even weeks of counting and recounting in order to call.

Even more striking, perhaps, is who helped ensure that it failed—say, Osage County, population about 15,700, which has backed the Republican candidate in all presidential elections after 1964. Donald Trump won 71 percent of the 2020 vote there. On Tuesday, 56 percent of its voters rejected the amendment.

Despite red-and-blue maps suggesting that the political fault line of our era runs between urban and rural areas, much of the countryside joined cities like Wichita and Kansas City in voting down the amendment. Fourteen Kansas counties that went for Trump in the 2020 presidential election, as well as all five that went for Joe Biden, saw majority votes against the amendment. Even in counties where most voted yes, sizable numbers voted no.

Kansas's existing abortion regulations will remain unchanged, at least for now. Kansas requires a twenty-four-hour waiting period before an abortion and permission from parents or a judge for minors seeking the procedure. Providers must share language with patients designed to discourage them from getting an abortion. After twenty-two weeks of pregnancy, abortion is legal only to protect the woman's life or when her health is severely compromised.

Republican lawmakers' attempts to ban second-trimester abortions resulted in a 2019 Kansas Supreme Court ruling of six to one that the state constitution guarantees the "right of personal autonomy," including the freedom to decide whether to continue a pregnancy. The decision, in effect, closed the door on new state legislation curbing or ending abortion rights without first altering the constitution.

Had conservative lawmakers succeeded in doing so with the voter initiative on Tuesday, the state's Democratic governor, Laura Kelly, who is up for reelection this fall, no doubt would have vetoed subsequent anti-abortion legislation. But the legislature's conservative supermajority would most likely have overridden a veto.

Instead, Kansas remains a beacon of liberty within the region. The state has been such a beacon before. In 1861, Kansas established itself as a free state—following murderous raids between abolitionist and pro-slavery factions that helped to incite the Civil War. A few years later, in 1867, Kansas held the first voter referendum on women's suffrage in the United States, also seeking to eliminate the word "White" from voter qualifications in the state constitution three years before the Fifteenth Amendment to the US Constitution was ratified. Both ballot measures failed, but Kansas voters would grant women the full right to vote in 1912, well ahead of the Nineteenth Amendment.

Kansas has a history of relative reproductive freedom, too, and related turmoil. The Wichita clinic of George Tiller, one of the nation's few physicians who performed rare third-trimester abortions, was pipe-bombed in 1986. Anti-abortion zealots from across the country descended on Tiller's clinic with disruptive mass protests during the summer of 1991. He survived being shot by an anti-abortion fanatic in 1993. In 2009, he was murdered inside his Wichita church.

The clinic where Tiller worked is now Trust Women, a stalwart in the national movement for reproductive rights. In this latest struggle, the staff of Trust Women spoke out against the amendment alongside other Kansas voices, including doctors, Christian ministers, small businesses across the state, the music star and state native Janelle Monáe, and even two Catholic nuns. Legions of volunteer phone-bankers and door-knockers prompted voter action and made clear what was at stake.

But Kansans didn't do it alone. Support—donations, text messages of solidarity, a letter of encouragement from Gloria Steinem—came from far and wide, boosting the resources and morale of a place often stereotyped as a conservative monolith and presumed a pointless investment for Democratic campaigns.

One dismal aspect of our political climate is the ease with which many liberals and progressives dismiss and disdain whole states and regions—as though every Kentucky flood victim voted for Mitch McConnell, as though ideology should be a litmus test for assistance amid acute suffering, as though such places are undeserving charity cases rather than rural landscapes from which resources are extracted to make possible the lives of urban dwellers who sit in judgment.

Yet, with the defeat of the anti-choice ballot measure in Kansas, not this time. In many ways, across state and even party lines, we did it together.

There is no other way.

All reasonable Americans must plant ourselves in a long row and lock arms against the terrible wind from the far right. As we brace together for this post-*Roe* season,* take heart: in the first battle, Kansas held the line.

---

* The Kansas vote would prove an inspiration and a bellwether, offering a strategic roadmap for abortion rights advocates across the country and justifying ample resource investment in those battles. In the 2022 midterm election, a few months after the Kansas vote, ballot measures in California, Kentucky, Michigan, Montana, and Vermont all resulted in favor of reproductive rights. Across the country during that election, Democratic candidates campaigned on the issue, which likely mitigated their losses; despite a predicted "red wave," Democrats maintained control of the Senate and only narrowly lost the House. In August 2023, in a special election, Ohio voters rejected a Republican-backed measure that would have made it more difficult for voters to enshrine abortion rights in the state constitution in the general election to follow; in November, Ohio voters approved a constitutional amendment guaranteeing the right to abortion access.

IN THE RUNNING

Harper's, 2022

In January 2019, when I found myself sitting across from Mindy Myers in a cramped DC coffee shop, the new resistance was riding high. A diverse lot of Democrats had just taken control of the House of Representatives, positioning themselves to curtail Donald Trump's devastating abuse of the presidency. Trump's chances of reelection looked questionable amid perpetual scandal and calls for impeachment, and even the Senate now seemed within reach.

Myers had recently finished her tenure as the first female executive director of the Democratic Senatorial Campaign Committee (DSCC). Before that, she'd enjoyed a perfect record managing three Senate races, including Elizabeth Warren's 2012 campaign, and she'd served as Warren's chief of staff during her first term.

That afternoon, we were discussing electoral prospects in Kansas, which national Democrats generally consign to the "red state" pile with little if any thought. I had just come from the nearby PBS studio, where I had recorded a segment on the dangers of using pat binaries—urban and rural, red and blue, coastal and middle—to predict the politics of entire groups, states, or regions. Such crude frameworks render invisible millions of Americans, I'd argued, and often become self-fulfilling prophesies when used to determine the distribution of political resources. So it was heartening to hear one of the eminent political strategists of our time agree that Democrats had a reasonable chance of winning a Senate seat in my home state for the first time since 1932.

Some 30 percent of registered Kansas voters are unaffiliated, and the state defies easy categorization. In the decades after its consequential entrance into the union as a free state in 1861, Kansas led the nation in movements such as women's suffrage and Eugene Debs–era socialism. In more recent years it has produced such far-right forces as the Koch brothers and the former governor Sam Brownback. Kansas has sent a lot of Republicans to Washington, but it is also the only state in the nation to have elected three Democratic women as governor.

From my uncommon vantage among national journalists—as a Kansas resident raised by poor wheat farmers with little formal education—I knew that the results of "red-state" elections often say more about our electoral system than about the people of a place. While a plurality of Kansas voters are Republican, the MAGA-hat-wearing White voters of media fascination are a statistical minority with outsize influence. As I saw it, that minority had seized control via targeted disinformation, voter suppression, gerrymandering, and dark money while the National Democratic Party conceded indefinitely.

Myers and I were talking about changing all that. The longtime Kansas senator Pat Roberts had just announced that he would not seek another term. Assessing potential candidates, the Cook Political Report had moved the race from "likely" to "lean" Republican.

Roberts had held his Senate seat since the conservative take-over of Congress in 1996, and he'd played a crucial role in the Republican Party's rightward shift. During his final term, he voted in line with Trump's wishes 94 percent of the time. But back home, his name had begun to fade. In 2014, his claimed Kansas residence—on a country club golf course—was revealed to be owned by campaign donors. That year, an independent candidate trimmed seven points from Roberts's previous victory margin.

By that time, I had already observed among working-class Kansans a progressive parallel to the more widely discussed right-wing anger toward "elites." Pundits in New York routinely conflate populism with conservatism, but populism is not an ideology directed left or right; it's a rage pointed upward, toward those in power. Over the years, this rage has fueled liberal as well as conservative impulses. Populism built the labor movement, the New Deal foundation on which the modern Democratic Party stands. During the 2016 primaries, more Kansas voters—including my own White working-class family—caucused for Bernie Sanders than for Trump. Though long written off by top Democrats as a waste of campaign resources, the state was ripe for political realignment—if only the right candidates would show up and talk to people.

This was the argument I'd been making in my own writing and in public interviews for years. But in that DC coffee shop, I wasn't just commenting on how to reach blue-collar communities and flip a seat. I was considering trying to flip it myself.

Like many working-class Kansans, I was raised with an aversion to both major parties. "They're all crooks," my family would say, an expression of deserved distrust—but also a defense mechanism, I think, for those lacking the time and resources required for civic engagement.

Nonetheless, I demonstrated uncool activist tendencies at the tail end of Generation X. During my nineties adolescence, downtrodden skater types asked me, a cheerleader who haunted the art department and often got detention for talking back to teachers, to speak on their behalf at student protests against the preferential treatment of male athletes. As editor of the school paper, I rankled the administration by invoking Kansas's constitutional expansion of press freedom for high school journalists. In the same spirit, I joined student government and was even elected speaker during an annual model legislature at the statehouse in Topeka. Wielding the gavel, I relished frowning at bills brought by students from monied Kansas City suburbs to beautify their already lovely neighborhoods.

I came of age at an inspiring moment for girls who sought to change the world. I turned twelve in 1992, the "Year of the Woman," during which a record forty-seven women were elected to the House of Representatives, twenty-four newbies among them. That same year, women gained four Senate seats, joining two incumbents for a (sadly) historic 6 percent of the upper chamber. One of those incumbents was Nancy Kassebaum, a pro-choice Kansas Republican who served in the Senate from 1978 to 1997. During Kassebaum's time in office, the Democrat Joan Finney served as the state's first female governor.

It was a good time to be a girl, yes, but I was a poor one. What threatened my potential was not just my gender but my double shift waiting tables the night before an exam. If I had been at a New England prep school rather than a public school surrounded by row crops, I might have taken the advice of teachers who half joked "you'd make a great lawyer, with the way you argue" and set out for a career in lawmaking. Instead,

I eyed local journalism, which had long been a relatively accessible—if largely White and male—vocation for scrappy talent from low places.

As a first-generation college student fresh off the farm, I experienced not only economic hardship but the brutality of American classism. I reported a story for my college paper about low-income students falling through the gaps of class-biased questions on the Free Application for Federal Student Aid. The Associated Press picked it up and distributed it nationally. This would become a pattern throughout my career: middle-class reporters were blind to stories that I was born to see.

During my senior year of college, I received a research grant from a federally funded program for first-generation, low-income, and minority college students. With it, I began work on a book about the vicious ways our country's class structure affected my family and millions like it. In the coming years, I would write many of its passages between jobs while I had neither health insurance nor sufficient food.

I was an unlikely critic of the American up-by-your-bootstraps narrative. I had left home in 1998 as a "fiscal conservative" and cast my first vote as an independent, in the 2000 presidential election, for George W. Bush. Away from my small town and Catholic church, though, my information sources changed dramatically; so did my ideas. Soon after my college graduation, the revelation of lies about weapons of mass destruction in Iraq turned me completely against the Republican Party, with which I had already disagreed on a host of social issues.

Having awoken to oligarchy while working on my book as a graduate student at Columbia, I cast my ballot in 2004 for Ralph Nader. I remained vexed by corporate influence over both parties and did not register as a Democrat until my late twenties, in order to caucus for Barack Obama in 2008.

By then I had finished a draft of my book, which I had begun showing to agents and editors. For a decade, New York publishing professionals told me they liked my voice but weren't sure why my family's story would matter to readers. Then a handful of my essays on class went viral, and in the spring of 2015 my book was sold at auction. The manuscript grew into a researched cultural critique and intersectional social analysis, blending policy and history with generational stories from twentieth-century rural Kansas. Published in 2018, *Heartland: A Memoir of Working Hard and Being Broke in the Richest Country on Earth* became a bestseller and a National Book Award finalist. Liberal and conservative, Black and White, Indigenous and immigrant alike waited in book-signing lines to convey their own experiences of class and place.

When Roberts announced his retirement a few months later, followers of my work surprised me by posting calls of "Smarsh for Senate" on social media. Young activists began to chant "run, Sarah, run" at my lectures.

I had started receiving requests to speak at campaign events, all of which I declined so as to avoid a conflict of interest. Two days before my meeting with Myers, though, I had served as master of ceremonies at the inauguration of Kansas governor Laura Kelly—a Democrat whose victory had been part of the midterm-election "blue wave" and whose invitation, I reasoned, was for service to my state rather than partisan activity. Inside the state capitol that afternoon, the newly elected US representative Sharice Davids, a Democrat, took a selfie with me. I had recently written a *New York Times* opinion piece about the meaning of Kelly's and Davids's wins for the rest of the country. Speaking with Myers now, I was poised to become part of that meaning.

Myers likened my evolution to Warren's transformation from

young Oklahoma Republican to bank-busting legal scholar to progressive political leader. "People asked Senator Warren to run because of the work she had been doing for years outside of politics," Myers said. "It's more common that someone wants to run, and then they try to figure out what they stand for—what's my message? For you it's the other way around."

The message was my life's work; the rumbling political fault line of our century, the "rural-urban divide," was the defining chasm of my life. I was not just an analyst but an embodiment of the prairie populism that would be essential, it seemed to me, to flip a Kansas Senate seat.

But as a general rule, I prefer that people in the upper echelon of government have experience, you know, governing. If seeking office had been my idea, I wouldn't have thought to start with the Senate. Considering such an audacious move, I heard in the back of my head a criticism that had stung the ambitious working-class girl in me more than once: *Who does she think she is?*

When I voiced this concern to Myers, she smiled. "You're asking very different questions than the last person I talked with about this race," she told me. "Women ask whether they're qualified. Men ask how much money they can raise."

Myers had already referenced money at the start of our meeting, saying that I might receive the full support of the DSCC. The viability of my candidacy, she explained, depended less on common political wisdom than on the rare thing that I am: a progressive woman from working-class, rural America with an established body of work on economic inequality.

"Because of your story," she said, "your campaign could get the sort of national attention that Alexandria Ocasio-Cortez or Beto O'Rourke got during the midterms. Your national fundraising potential could be—I hesitate to say it, but—limitless."

———

Recent elections have seen an unprecedented number of onetime outsiders enter the wealthy, White, male island of privilege that is Washington. These include Davids, a Native American lesbian raised by a single mother who served in the US Army, and Ocasio-Cortez, a Puerto Rican American still in her twenties when elected to her New York House seat.

Many of these candidates have been recruited and trained by new and old organizations committed to diversifying the government. These range from Emily's List, which has raised close to half a billion dollars over four decades to boost pro-choice female candidates, to Run For Something, which was founded on the day of Trump's inauguration and, at its two-year mark, reported that it had connected with thirty thousand young, progressive would-be candidates for local races. Thanks in part to these efforts, the 117th Congress is the most racially and ethnically diverse in US history, while also containing a record number of female representatives. Recent years have seen representational gains for the LGBTQ community and disabled people, as well.

But one area of acute underrepresentation remains underdiscussed, if not ignored: socioeconomic class. According to a study by the political scientists Andrew Eggers and Marko Klašnja, the median individual wealth of Congress members has since the eighties consistently been in the 95th percentile of US households. The same study estimated that two-thirds of Congress members were millionaires.

As outlined in Nicholas Carnes's 2018 book, *The Cash Ceiling*, more than half of US citizens work in manual, service, or clerical labor, yet the average congressperson has next to no work experience in these industries. Fewer than 40 percent of Americans aged twenty-five and older have a bachelor's degree, while 100 percent of current senators and 94 percent of representatives do. This is a notable shift from sixty years ago, when about a quarter of each chamber's members didn't have college degrees.

What are the implications of a government whose members have fuller bank accounts, softer hands, and more academic credentials than the average American? For one, Eggers and Klašnja found that greater wealth among Congress members correlates with more conservative voting records on economic policy around tax rates, finance, welfare, and trade. This holds true for both major parties. As working-class and poor Americans suspect, rich folks of all political stripes generally protect their own.

Hateful dismissals of those with low incomes, dirty jobs, or "uneducated" backgrounds leave us unable to recognize that such people not only are capable of governing but possess insights necessary for fixing systemic woes from which they have suffered—problems that our credentialed leaders often have a vested interest in failing to solve. I was raised by intelligent people whose creative problem-solving, honed not by textbook theories but by lifelong fights to survive, might have made them fine policymakers.

Carnes and his fellow political scientist Noam Lupu assessed the efficacy and educational levels of political officials between 1875 and 2004 in more than two hundred countries. They found that college educations did not denote more successful leadership. Indeed, while many working-class voters have shifted right in recent years, our present democratic disaster was largely plotted and enacted by prosperous White people with Ivy League degrees.

Grassroots movements, such as Black Lives Matter, the Poor People's Campaign, the Sunrise Movement, and Native

American efforts to amplify the crisis of missing and murdered Indigenous women, have disrupted class paradigms in activism. But for those without an ample financial cushion, entering politics—especially to seek high office—continues to entail a potentially ruinous level of sacrifice and risk.

Ocasio-Cortez has written on social media about the particular challenges for working-class people elected to office, such as paying out of pocket for residences at home and in Washington, and has spoken about the economic turmoil her family suffered after her father's early death. While Ocasio-Cortez's aspirational parents and Boston University education afforded her glimpses of the middle class, her work in Washington provides regular reminders of her family's economic origins.

In these terms, the mere notion of my candidacy marked a shift in the post-Trump political landscape. I was a youngish female journalist who grew up in single-wide trailers and farmhouses, tending fields and slopping hogs. The seat in question was occupied by a well-to-do, eighty-two-year-old White man first elected to the House in 1980, the year I was born.

After *Heartland* was published, I looked up from two decades of hustle and realized that I had attained all that I had sought: a safe home, a savings account, creative fulfillment. A powerful producer wanted to make *Heartland* into a television series. I'd been named a fellow at the Harvard Kennedy School. I had stopped collecting coupons and started buying organic. I had a pile of student debt and a house with a caving roof, but I felt satisfied, secure, content—and so very tired.

At the same time, I was being asked to set aside my writing and begin at the bottom of yet another mountain. My instinct was to guard the career I had fought to build. Once I had crossed the threshold from the Fourth Estate to the government it monitors, it seemed to me there would be no going back.

Granted, my own state provided plenty of precedent for ink-stained newspapermen moving into politics. My journalism school's namesake, William Allen White, was a small-town Kansas editor and publisher who became a national voice in the Progressive movement and ran for governor in the twenties; during the same period, the Wichita newspaper editor Henry J. Allen held the governorship and, briefly, a US Senate seat. My own hesitation had perhaps less to do with broad journalistic ethics than with my unusual position as a commentator critical of both parties. While cognizant of the problems with feigned objectivity, I am also wary of the untroubled sliding between paid work for news networks and political campaigns so rampant in today's opinion-dominated media. I value being unbeholden to any organization or agenda over the security such affiliation provides, and I have lived my entire professional life accordingly.

What of personal policies, though, when authoritarianism is on the rise? The stakes of my decision were heightened by the increasing presence of far-right ideologues at all levels of government. Federal elections in Kansas have never brimmed with viable Democratic candidates; in local and even state races, Republicans often run uncontested.

For years, I had occasionally harbored thoughts of one day seeking office. My eventual prompt had come from without, though, not from within, and thus said more about my country than it did about me; this was an encouraging sign for our embattled democracy, I thought—that someone from my broke-ass ranks would be nudged toward holding such a position.

I had covered government as a reporter, but I could only make educated guesses about what it would mean to enter the fray. My initial thought was to run as an independent, maybe even to promise that I'd serve only one term if elected. But I knew enough to recognize these impulses as self-defeating, given my lack of personal wealth and need for party support.

So I set out, as one does in politics, to "explore" the options in our two-party system. As I would learn, my exploration differed from that of many in that I didn't conduct polls to gauge electability or hold meetings to secure endorsements. Most people who explore campaigns are already, in effect, campaigning. For me, the project was to discern whether I wanted to run and, if so, how I would go about it.

While speaking about rural issues on Capitol Hill, I had met the staff director of the Senate Democratic Steering and Outreach Committee, Laura Schiller. She pointed out that a journalistic platform allowed me to effect change without the constraints of political life.

"Do you really want to do this?" she asked in a gentle but warning tone.

Her subtle discouragement felt disappointing, which in turn signaled that something in me wanted the Senate seat.

Schiller connected me with Myers. After our coffee date, my questions multiplied, but I found more people ready to help answer them. Perhaps my most pressing concerns were financial: I didn't have the luxury of spending a year on the stump with no income. I had paid lectures on university campuses and at professional conferences booked well into 2020. If event organizers didn't cancel my contracts when I announced—which some might do to avoid angering taxpayers and donors—could I keep those dates?

Yates Baroody, a regional director for Emily's List, assured me that I could. Describing the ecosystem of organizations that might back my campaign, Baroody observed a paradox: the very thing that made me a good candidate—my direct experience of socioeconomic disadvantage—would be my greatest barrier in a race in which many candidates are millionaires at the starting line. Emily's List could potentially help by funding campaign staff, assisting with messaging and press, and connecting me to other organizations.

Baroody suggested that I wait to see how the field shook out. She urged me to "start lean." Maybe launch an exploratory campaign, which had a different set of reporting rules from a formal candidacy. Hire a fee-based consulting firm. I looked at my house's damaged ceiling, the repairing of which would be done by my construction-worker partner when he found the time. A "fee-based consulting firm" sounded like something on a shiny planet where I had landed in a jalopy space rocket missing a muffler.

Rurality and poverty are formative yet often invisible aspects of identity, and I was relieved to discover fellow hayseeds and class-straddlers as I continued my conversations. PaaWee Rivera, who worked on Warren's 2020 presidential campaign, shared during a phone call that he had grown up in rural New Mexico as a Pueblo of Pojoaque tribal member. He was happy to see a rural advocate considering a run. Warren's campaign manager, Roger Lau, the son of Chinese immigrants, had been working in a cardboard factory when he landed an internship in John Kerry's Senate office.

Lau expressed frank precautions: The financial issue was real. He'd seen candidates spend their retirement savings and go into debt. The campaign would exhaust me. A presidential-election year like 2020 might hurt a Democrat's chances in Republican-leaning Kansas, since more people would show up at the polls. But Myers was excited about my potential, Lau told me, and he was too.

"You and Senator Warren have a lot in common," Lau said. "You didn't plan on this. You didn't seek it. You have a mission you can articulate because of your origins."

He urged me to get as many commitments as I could before the start of the campaign: "Donations, endorsements, help on the trail. Get as much as you can. And know that not everyone will make good on their promises."

"Sarah? It's Elizabeth."

During the 2020 election, Warren's phone calls to shocked small donors would go viral. Her calls to Democratic candidates, or potential candidates, up and down the ballot produced fewer memes but were no less significant.

During the 2018 midterms, Warren raised or donated $11 million to and for other candidates, including about a hundred women. But when she dialed my cell that February, four days after announcing her candidacy for president, I was still so ignorant of campaign finance laws that I had no idea candidates with big war chests could disburse that money to other campaigns. A phone call that I might have approached as an audition was instead an earnest conversation.

I was in a hotel room in Hattiesburg the morning after giving a lecture at the University of Southern Mississippi. Before our appointed time, I'd made a list of things to ask or mention. I'd pulled the hotel phone cable out of the jack and double-checked that I had hung the privacy sign on the door. This felt like the most consequential call of my life. As a citizen and a voter, I believed in Warren. If she believed in me, what choice would remain?

I heard sloshing and clanking. Warren was at home, washing dishes. I refused to call her "Elizabeth." She told me she had read some of my work and felt a kinship.

I asked how she felt about her life since entering politics, and she described her day-to-day.

She admitted that she was in her sixties and at a different phase of life when she "got in," and suggested that I speak with someone closer to my age too.

"Sometimes the fight comes to your door," she nonetheless pointed out. "And we don't get to decide what year it is or whether it's a Tuesday."

With those words, I felt burning within me the hellfire of 40 million Americans living in poverty. I had been agonizing over whether this was the right choice for *me*, and Warren was talking about *us*.

"So how do you know when to announce?" I asked.

"When you have the right team," she said. "The right people come before all else. You want people who are good at the things you're not good at." She said she could connect me with such people.

I told Warren about my family's struggles and about the thousands of messages I had received from people of different races and creeds desperate to share their stories.

"I can hear that you're in this for the right reasons," she said.

We had been on the phone for half an hour, but she was not pulling away. She left a silence for whatever else I needed to say or ask. I couldn't bear that someone so decent was giving so much when she could surely use ten minutes of quiet. I thanked her, signaling goodbye.

"Let's stay in touch," she said.

As I hung up, I was all but certain that I would run.

First, I would need to get my footing in this new public life: pay some bills, restore my health amid a long and taxing book tour. I kicked around the idea of waiting for 2022 to challenge the junior—soon to be senior—senator, Jerry Moran.

Moran is a less offensive brand of Republican than Roberts. His votes occasionally defied Trump's wishes and, unlike four of Kansas's six congresspeople, he and Davids would later vote to certify Joe Biden's victory. His cosponsoring of the bipartisan PACT Act, assisting veterans who suffer from toxic exposure, was vital to its passing this year. Nonetheless, he aligns himself with a party I find vile and destructive.

Excited to hear that I was leaning toward going for it, Myers helped me think through the arguments for and against 2020 and 2022. Unseating a popular incumbent is presumed more difficult than pursuing an open seat, and the iron was hot for untraditional Democratic candidates like myself. But a Democrat running in a majority Republican state could also benefit from lower midterm voter turnout. The 2020 presidential outcome would affect 2022 down-ballot races in unforeseen ways. And there was speculation that Secretary of State Mike Pompeo, a former congressman from my district, would enter the 2020 race; analysts deemed him a shoo-in for the Republican nomination.

Pacing my home office in Kansas, I realized that such calculations meant little to me. If I were someone who made decisions based on probabilities, who took risks only when the odds were in my favor, I might still be waiting tables at a Pizza Hut on a windswept highway.

For the first time, Myers said explicitly that she would be honored to be part of my campaign—an enormous boon not just because of her prominence but because she was, I thought, a humane person trying to do good in a system whose rotten parts she knew well. No one else had clearly stated such a commitment, and her vote of confidence moved me. With one major piece in place, I began to envision how my campaign might look.

I could only do it, I decided, if I did it the way I had done everything else in my life: more concerned about the means than the end. We would value openheartedness over assumptions—over data, even—by knocking on doors where one isn't supposed to bother. We would value life experience over "expert" analysis by putting "uneducated" people in leadership roles. We would resist burnout culture by refusing to run ourselves into the ground. We would be told we were naive and doing it wrong. But how had doing it right been working out for Democrats seeking a Senate seat in Kansas for the past ninety years?

I discussed some of these matters with Davids soon after she was sworn in. Born just two months before me, Davids was better suited than anyone to reflect on campaigning and going to Washington from our state in our season of life.

A member of the Ho-Chunk Nation, Davids was, alongside New Mexico's Deb Haaland, one of the first two Native American women elected to Congress. She was also the first openly gay Native American elected and the first openly lesbian person elected from Kansas. Intersecting with these marginalized identities is Davids's less discussed working-class background, which she described to me as her greatest barrier to entering politics.

By law, candidates are permitted to take a salary from campaign funds, but the practice remains frowned upon, an attitude that clearly favors those of independent means. Davids instead worked ten hours a week as a tribal consultant while on the trail, giving up most of her legal work and with it most of her income. To compensate for the loss, she moved in with her mother. She also deferred her student loans, spent her entire retirement savings, maxed out her credit cards, lived without health insurance for more than a year, and forbade herself from buying moisturizer or a new pair of shoes.

While I worried about money, I told Davids, I was more concerned about my health. As a former triathlete who takes up DIY construction projects for fun, I was startled to find myself so run-down by the book tour. The requests to write, speak, comment, help a cause, or hear a story had not slowed. I had missed Thanksgiving while laid flat by a virus, and I underwent a minor surgery a month later. My blood work revealed severe deficiencies. If I didn't decrease the stress in my life, my doctor cautioned, I might face more serious problems down the road. My body didn't need a Senate race; it needed a cabin in the woods.

I had worked demeaning, back-busting, soul-crushing jobs for inadequate pay—the same jobs being worked by millions of people at this minute—and so hesitated to mention the difficulties that came with my new position of privilege. But as a member of a family prone to desperate situations, I had learned the hard way that there is no caring for others without first caring for yourself. I asked Davids—a former professional mixed martial arts fighter known to do push-ups at the Capitol—how she managed life as a US representative.

"We don't talk enough about the emotional and physical wear of it," she said.

She underscored the importance of delegating tasks and trusting the people around you to do their jobs. She also had a support system outside of politics, which she called her grounding force.

She was guided, she told me, by a question posed by Brené Brown in her bestselling book *Daring Greatly*: "What's worth doing even if I fail?"

"Even if I had lost," she said, "I think it would have been worth it. I would've done it the same way."

—

By March, buzz about my potential candidacy was growing.

I had been ignoring a message on Twitter from a former federal attorney, Barry Grissom, a Democrat planning to run for Roberts's seat. When I finally called the number he'd provided, Grissom—an Obama appointee living in a tony suburb of Kansas City—was surprised to learn that I lived in Wichita, more than a rung below his area in economic and political capital. He let me know that he would be announcing his candidacy, and he suggested that I instead run for the House in 2022. I told him that his plans had no bearing on my decision. He invited me to dinner with him and his wife sometime. I wished him the best.

Later that month, as the cherry blossoms bloomed, I flew to Washington to meet with the Senate minority leader Chuck Schumer and the Nevada senator Catherine Cortez Masto, who was serving as chair of the DSCC, which raises and distributes about $300 million to boost its preferred candidates in election years.

Before our meeting, I went for a run along the National Mall. I petered out by the time I reached the reflecting pool, its concrete and right angles so unlike the catfish pond where I used to sit and think.

It happened to be my mother's birthday. She had died of breast cancer four years prior at the age of fifty-three. I had permanently moved out of her apartment and into my grandparents' farmhouse when I was eleven years old. Still, we had developed a profound friendship later in life. In her last days, I had been one of her primary caregivers, and I'd held her hand when she passed. I thought of her hard early life: abusive stepfathers, destabilizing poverty and transience, accidentally conceiving me with a farm boy in a Kansas basement when she was seventeen. I wondered what she would think of all this.

Brilliant and well-read, my mother was unimpressed by celebrity and carried herself with regal self-assurance despite society's relentless attempts to shame young mothers living in poverty. Throughout my tumultuous childhood of verbal abuse and emotional neglect, much of it perpetuated by her traumatized young self, she still somehow conveyed the idea that I was exceptional and destined for greatness. I could hear her saying, with a shrug and an exhale of Marlboro Light smoke, that my being in Washington to discuss a Senate run was the least surprising thing she'd ever heard.

I made my way past a high school band performing on the steps of the Lincoln Memorial, and I remembered climbing those steps at their age after qualifying for a national communications contest. Now, as I stood in my running tights at Lincoln's marble feet, a male tourist asked me to take his photo. After I returned his camera, he said that maybe we could hang out later. I walked away.

As I attempted to read the inscribed Gettysburg Address and contemplate the meaning of our republic, the man followed and lurked. I was weighing an attempt to become the second woman elected to the Senate from Kansas in its 160-year history. Being sexually harassed at the Lincoln Memorial seemed about right.

At the congested DSCC building, the senior adviser Christie Roberts waited with me for an office to clear. Roberts had managed Jon Tester's successful 2018 reelection campaign, and I told her that the Montana senator had cohosted a conversation about *Heartland* at a summit on rural issues the previous fall. When commenting on the manual labor described in my book, Tester had raised his left hand, three fingers of which had been lost to a meat grinder.

Senator Kyrsten Sinema of Arizona emerged with someone

who apologized for taking more than their allotted time. Schumer arrived, ushered another person into the office, and gave us a "just a minute" gesture. It was 6 p.m. One thing my current profession had in common with government work was that evenings, weekends, and holidays were irrelevant.

"Do you mind if I take my shoes off?" Schumer asked as Roberts and I sat down. I didn't mind, of course, but they were already off. He stretched his feet across the top of the desk and leaned back as though it had been a long day. He looked over a few notes someone had prepared and started grilling me: Where was I from? Why was I here now? If a small-business owner said he couldn't afford to pay his employee's health insurance premiums, what would I tell him? What did I think about the Green New Deal? How would I rank these five adjectives, beginning with the one that described me best?

I lobbed back answers. He turned to my career.

"How many books have you sold?"

No one had ever asked me that, and I didn't have an answer.

"I don't know," I said honestly. "I asked my publisher not to tell me."

Schumer looked as though he didn't believe me.

"Okay, okay," he said. "Was it a bestseller? And I mean a *New York Times* bestseller."

"Yes," I replied.

"Ah, she's modest," he said. "How many weeks?"

"Just one."

"So just a ballpark: you haven't sold a million copies or anything like that."

"No."

Aiming to explain what had brought me here, I told him that my journalism had addressed working-class issues years before doing so was in vogue. He replied that he too had long been talking about these issues, as evidenced by his 2007 book, *Positively American: Winning Back the Middle-Class Majority One Family at a Time,* whose low sales he lamented.

That the leading Senate Democrat would so casually gloss over the vast difference between the working poor and the middle class so beloved by speechwriters dismayed me.

"You do a lot of public speaking," he said, looking over the printouts in his hand.

"Are you going to ask how much I get paid for a speech?" I had taken a tone, and Schumer raised his brow.

"I'm asking you these things to gauge your prominence, your clout," he said. "You get out there and people will come at you, and it doesn't matter how good you look."

I drew a breath and steered the conversation to Schumer's own journey into politics. He lit up at my questions and paused to look at Roberts.

"Now see, *you* don't even know this because you never ask me questions like this."

We went on to discuss the climate in Kansas. Schumer brought up "that fucking Trump." At this, he gazed into the distance with true loathing—the first moment that confirmed we were on the same side.

As he gave his assessment of various Kansas Republicans, including Moran (an all right guy on the wrong team) and former secretary of state Kris Kobach, who would go on to run for the Senate seat (even worse than Trump), it struck me that Schumer was a good judge of character.

He turned back to numbers. Had I done any polls? I should go on a trip across the state and gather that sort of data, he said.

I thanked him for his time and moved toward the door.

"Wait," Schumer said.

I stopped.

"What's your middle name?"

I smiled. "Jean."

"Sarah Jean!" he exclaimed, delighted. "That is what we'll call you from now on. It doesn't get any more down-home than that."

On the plane back to Kansas, I listened to the last voicemail my mother had left me. Her body was so weak by that time that she strained to speak above a whisper. I turned my face toward the window and cried quietly.

The combination of her birthday and a stressful trip dislodged something deep. I had just ended talks with the television network because the offer didn't feel right. I was relieved to be flying away from the center of global power. What the hell was wrong with me?

I thought about my last brush with government work, in my twenties, when I'd struggled to pay the bills while doing freelance reporting for national publications from a region where newspapers were collapsing. The state secretary of corrections had recommended me for a communications job at one of the most visible state agencies in Governor Kathleen Sebelius's administration. The position came with a higher salary and better benefits than I had ever received, and I knew that former colleagues were taking jobs in public relations. I interviewed with enthusiasm and received an offer. But when I thought about why I had become a journalist—to hold government accountable—it felt wrong to write its press releases, even if I happened to agree with them. Instead, I took a position at a nonprofit that came with less money and less prestige.

After I declined the state job, I heard that I had offended more than one person in Topeka. Did I know how many people would love to have that position? Who did I think I was? I recall mailing apologetic thank-you notes.

I thought too of the time that I resigned from a tenured professorship at a small university, a seemingly crazy act for someone with no assets to fall back on. Prompted by a perfect storm of my mom's terminal illness and my employer's savage institutional sexism, the decision had shocked many but also made way for my writing dreams to come true.

One person who had asked no questions and uttered no doubts in either case was my mother, a woman who put little stock in financial stability or job security because she had lived without both—a difficult condition that can contain the magnificent freedom of answering to no one.

When I arrived home from Washington, I told my partner that my mind was made up. I wasn't running.

Well, 99 percent of my mind was made up. The other 1 percent was a real bitch.

Like a test from the universe, a voicemail soon arrived from a *Kansas City Star* reporter, whose online messages I had ignored. More than three months since speculation had begun, I felt I should say something, if only to communicate the care I had put into the decision. In the interest of control, I replied by email with a careful and brief recounting: I was honored to be summoned, I was determining how best to be of service to the marginalized groups I championed in my writing, and yes, I had visited the DSCC.

Eighty-three minutes later, the *Star* published a headline on its website: "Kansas author Sarah Smarsh met with Schumer about possible US Senate run in 2020." The article claimed that a midterms analysis I had written in November for the *New York*

Times hinted at designs on public office—designs I didn't even have at the time. Annoyed and amused, I pointed out on social media that my *Times* piece, which had suggested that moderate Democratic women such as Kelly and Davids might demonstrate how Democrats could reclaim conservative states, was actually an argument against nominating thoroughly progressive me.

That misleading reference had been removed by the time the story reached my doorstep the next morning in the print edition of the *Wichita Eagle*, a sister paper of the *Star*. The front page featured my photo and a teaser: "SMARSH EYES SENATE RUN."

I received an excited text from an old friend who had been a young associate producer for NBC News at 30 Rockefeller Plaza while I was an investigative reporting intern at the network's New York City affiliate a few floors away in 2000. She sent me celebratory emojis and suggested coming to Kansas to make a documentary about my campaign.

Over the previous few months, others who'd seen my name in pre-election chatter had offered to donate their time and skills. This had inspired in me a sense of loyalty and responsibility. In the coming weeks, at lectures across the country, audience members reliably asked whether I was running, told me I should run, and promised they would contribute if I did. What to say, when I didn't want to encourage speculation but wasn't ready to close the door? I said thank you.

At a town hall on rural health in a town not far from the farm where I grew up, a local reporter put a recorder in my face when I walked through the door and was clearly put out when I smiled and said I wouldn't comment on the election. She later filed an open records request to determine how much I had been paid for the appearance. I was a private citizen who had booked the talk for well under my usual rate in order to assist a nonprofit effort, but the reporter wrote a story soliciting outrage.

Event organizers whom the reporter had contacted warned me about what was coming. I rushed to make sure my home address was not included in any of the acquired documents or emails, a precaution that is unfortunately necessary for women in the public eye. My experience was but the tiniest taste of the invasive scrutiny that female leaders endure.

As I wrestled with my diminished but persistent itch to run, I was aware of my vulnerability in a game where most players have thick, expensive walls built between themselves and the world. I was a small woman who was frequently sexualized. I had encountered my first stalker at age fourteen. (He had turned up again, twenty-four years later, at a *Heartland* launch event.) I did not reside in a gated community or a doorman building. I lived down the road from my family in a working-poor neighborhood of cracked sidewalks and condemned houses. My old house had settled in the Kansas silt such that the locks on the windows didn't latch, a defect that hadn't fazed me when I moved in; after growing up in the country with unlocked doors, I thought wedging lengths of two-by-four into the window jambs worked just fine. While the danger faced by candidates and public servants would not keep me from doing any job I felt called to do, my exposed life made the decision that much heavier.

I had been sitting with my potential candidacy since early winter, and now spring was moving toward summer. For months, I'd juggled other professional and personal choices with the possibility that I'd soon be on the campaign trail. Assembling a solid team would require time. I needed to make up my mind.

By June, not long after the *Kansas City Star* headline, I thought I'd finally determined that politics was not the right use of my strengths. Then James Thompson announced that he had stage IV cancer.

An army veteran who had been homeless in his youth, Thompson had altered the political map in Wichita and surrounding areas. Vying in a 2017 special election for the seat vacated when Pompeo joined the Trump administration, Thompson had run as a progressive Democrat against the conservative Republican Ron Estes in the red Fourth District—home to the Koch family. Despite a grassroots campaign that attracted national attention, Thompson received no support from the Democratic Congressional Campaign Committee. During the homestretch of the race, the Kansas Democratic Party declined to pay for a $20,000 mailer while prioritizing other races. Thompson lost by seven points, knocking an incredible twenty-four points off the previous election's Republican victory margin and suggesting that additional party funds may well have altered the outcome.

After interviewing him several times, I had come to know Thompson personally, and I had a deep respect for the civil rights attorney and former bouncer. Thompson ran for the same seat in 2018, losing by a much wider margin, and he told me that his finances had been gutted by two years of campaigning while paying off a mortgage and student debt. He was insured through tax credits in the Affordable Care Act. In effect, Thompson found his cancer treatment options limited by his run for Congress as an anti-corporate fighter for economic justice. He joked on social media that he might finally win an election, since he came with mortality-imposed term limits.

I was devastated for Thompson and enraged at the Democratic Party. In a flash, I resolved to go fight for the goddamn Senate seat. If I ran and won, I told myself, I would add one more vote for structural changes benefiting people in poverty, workers, children, the environment, and public education.

Left-leaning candidates in other conservative-state races might receive more support. If I ran and lost, at least I would have amplified the plight of the poor and marginalized throughout the campaign, possibly elevating class consciousness and inspiring future working-class candidates of all genders and races.

I reached out to Thompson. Over the course of several weeks, he gave me advice and offered to share the impressive data his two campaigns had worked hard to amass. I renewed conversations with Emily's List and with Myers, who would go on to guide Kamala Harris on her path to the vice presidency. I also had discussions with Justice Democrats, Brand New Congress, and Sebelius; these amounted to questions from me rather than encouragement from them, but most doors seemed open enough. I reached out to Kelly, who invited me to the governor's residence in Topeka. I received solid advice from then–presidential candidate Marianne Williamson. I exchanged more texts with Lau.

A rumor emerged that I might run for the House instead, which I never once entertained. I suspected the misdirection had been sown by another Democratic Senate campaign.

"They're scared," Thompson told me. "You are their biggest threat."

It felt, yet again, like everything was falling into place for my candidacy. As Warren had predicted, the fight had shown up at my door, and the knock was not gentle. To refuse to answer felt selfish, careless, a waste of potential influence for a girl born to people who were never given such a chance.

When I was that girl, though, with wheat spikelets caught in my secondhand socks, I already understood what I had to offer the world.

While people I knew lost eyeballs and limbs laboring on farms and in factories, I learned to value the work of my body. I was constantly moving—tending, mowing, clearing, hauling, feeding, cleaning—to avoid being chided for the worst offense in my community: "sitting on your ass." The chiding was born of necessity; there was much to do and no hired help to do it. It was also, though, class maintenance—my elders ensuring that I understood the world's plans for me so that I would fall in line, make a paycheck, and survive.

I did that labor and will be forever grateful for it, but I knew it wasn't the life I was meant for. The books I cherished and the voice inside me demanded a writerly direction that no one applauded. Why would they? In our society, journalism is so devalued as to be expected free of charge, and creative work is often considered to be worth less than just about any other kind.

I long ago climbed over those socioeconomic hurdles and that societal bias to pursue my career. Late in my consideration of the Senate race, though, I realized that my recurring urge to run stemmed in part from an unconscious belief that politics is a more effective means for social change than what I already do. And, perhaps, more worthy of the respect for which a poor farm girl once longed.

The pen is not more powerful than the AR-15, under-regulated carbon emissions, unsustainable consumption, xeno-phobia, unlivable wages, nationalism, the prison industrial complex, the military industrial complex, the medical indus-trial complex, or dark money's political influence. It is, how-ever, antecedent to some future world that will not abide these things. Of all the reasons that I have dedicated my life to wit-nessing intergenerational poverty and trauma—a process that has enriched me professionally but that requires an incessant, unpleasant reconnection with the painful past I overcame—the most fundamental is that I dream of a world in which no child suffers for our country's greed.

In this era of minority rule, the American left has wisely acknowledged the limitations of simply telling people to vote. Some elected bodies are so intractable, in fact, that even holding office may be ineffective. Chloe Maxmin, an environmental activist who in 2018 became the first Democrat to represent her rural district in the Maine state legislature, was a rising political star who wrote, with her campaign manager Canyon Woodward, a well-received book on renewing rural politics. Yet Maxmin herself, now the youngest female state senator in Maine's history, announced earlier this year that she would not seek reelection. For now, she told me, she sees more potential impact in movement building. She and Woodward have founded a nonprofit, Dirtroad Organizing, to empower rural people and combat polarization.

In June 2019, Warren emailed me after receiving my thank-you card, which had expressed with some sadness that running for Senate wasn't right for me—at least not for now.

"Sarah—I got your very generous note," she wrote from the presidential campaign trail, while her candidacy was soaring in the polls. "There are many ways to serve."

I never officially announced that I wasn't running, and my spirit sometimes lingered along the road not taken. Several declared Democratic candidates withdrew from the race, making way for former Republican and pro-choice state senator Barbara Bollier to win the primary. Despite Bollier's impressive fundraising, Representative Roger Marshall defeated her in the general election by eleven points. In one of his first acts as senator, Marshall would join a small handful of colleagues who voted to overturn the presidential election results just hours after the deadly siege on the Capitol by Trump supporters. Alongside my fellow Kansans, I mourned this development in a unique way, and I winced at the many instances to come in which one Senate vote could have changed the world.

I took heart, though, noticing in videos that Ocasio-Cortez had *Heartland* on her bookshelf. More recently, I cheered when, in the country's first vote on reproductive rights following the overturning of *Roe v. Wade*, Kansans across party and urban-rural lines roundly defeated a proposed amendment to the state constitution to eliminate the right to an abortion—lifesaving confirmation of the nuance that my writing had insisted was true.

Throughout, a knowing abided. As society tears, some Americans will emerge, dramatically altered, from a Stars and Stripes cocoon. Some of us, though, will find that the next right thing to be is the thing we have been all along.

In May, before Thompson's diagnosis and my temporary reinvigoration, I'd gone to Iowa to give talks in Des Moines and Iowa City. The latter, a ticketed fundraiser for the public library, paired me with the journalist Connie Schultz. I had long admired Schultz, a first-generation college graduate who grew up in working-class Ohio and won a Pulitzer Prize in 2005 for her columns in the Cleveland's *Plain Dealer*, and she had sent me encouraging messages about my journalism before *Heartland* was published.

When we met in the hotel lobby before the event, Schultz's husband, the Ohio senator Sherrod Brown, was at her side. Earlier in the year, while exploring a bid for the 2020 presidential nomination, Brown had gone on a four-state listening tour with the theme "the dignity of work"—an unfashionable idea among privileged anti-capitalist leftists but one that would resonate for the many proud laborers I know. I had been flattered to learn that he'd given his daughter *Heartland* for Christmas. In March, Brown had announced he would remain in the Senate. This disappointed many but inspired praise for Brown's humility at a time when a dizzying number of Democrats were contending for the White House.

As people streamed toward their seats, Schultz, Brown, and I chatted in the greenroom. I found myself discussing my conundrum with real-life avatars of the vocations I was choosing between: an influential writer concerned with working-class issues and a US senator concerned with working-class issues. As a couple they had taken the two diverging paths before me and wrapped them into a domestic double helix—experiencing together, every day, the line between journalism and politics, between temperaments that carved separate yet kindred pursuits toward the greater good. Schultz had taken a leave from the *Plain Dealer* in 2006 to avoid conflict of interest while on the campaign trail with Brown. He respected her work in kind; when Schultz wrote unsparingly about their campaign experience in the 2008 book *And His Lovely Wife*, Brown didn't ask her to delete or change a single thing. The two seemed sent by the universe to help.

"You have to want it," Brown told me. This sentiment seemed an unhelpful cliché until I unpacked it: proceeding from a sense of duty or sacrifice, or because of other people's expectations, was no good. About the presidency, Brown said, "In the end, I didn't want it bad enough."

The only reason to do something so drastic was raw desire. When people ask how I decided to become a writer, I explain that I never decided. I started narrating the world around me in my head at around age six. Years later, there was no fretting over journalism's low pay, no hesitation about the occupational hazards of being a woman in a man's world. That I had been hemming and hawing over the Senate race for months suggested that it just wasn't my calling—not then, anyway, and maybe not ever. I required no poll, tour, or consulting firm to determine as much.

This conversation with Brown and Schultz was the first clear validation I had received for what, regardless of my internal kicking and screaming, I was about to do—decline attention, power, and opportunity for reasons I had not yet entirely articulated even to myself.

I didn't share my intentions aloud, but Schultz abruptly met my gaze in a way that no one else had throughout my many conversations about the race.

"You're not running, are you." Her inflection voiced a statement, not a question.

I smiled, caught off guard. Everyone else seemed to assume that I would—because, apparently, who wouldn't? I wasn't sure what to say.

Schultz stared at my face for a moment and nodded with a spark of amusement in her eyes.

"You're a writer," she said.

FOR MY LOVER

Oxford American, 2022

Being in love is a state of madness that may compromise decision-making abilities. Sacrifices made for a romantic partner should, therefore, be examined.

In Tracy Chapman's "For My Lover," from her 1988 debut *Tracy Chapman*,* the narrator acknowledges that others think she's nuts and wonders whether the relationship is worth the losses and risks she has incurred: doing time in a Virginia jail, coming up with bail money, lying to authorities to cover for her love.

---

* In 2023, country singer Luke Combs released a cover of the lead single from *Tracy Chapman*, "Fast Car," a top-ten hit for Chapman that won her a 1989 Grammy for best female pop vocal performance. (Chapman also won Grammys for best new artist and best contemporary folk album that year.) Combs's cover of "Fast Car" reached the top of Billboard's Country Airplay chart, making Chapman the first Black woman to be the sole writer of a number-one country song. Previously, four Black women—Donna Summer, Alice Randall, Ester Dean, and Tayla Parx—held cowriting credits for number-one country songs.

The chorus, though, returns to her conclusion: it's the world, not her, that's crazy. I believe her. When Chapman sings "you" over and over with her iconic contralto, it doesn't sound like codependency. It sounds like ardent longing and frustrated adoration, conditions that plenty of good, sane, worthwhile partnerships will endure in hard times.

Those hard times echo in the instrumentation. Chapman's guitar licks are simple and haunting, like something one might strum in a county cell where a small square of light streams from a high window with bars across it. Steel guitarist Ed Black pulls one note down the scale for a full measure, again and again, suggesting the long arc of justice bending down to find the forgotten. The end of the song contains a muffled harmonica, such as that you might hear through a wall.

Is this person for whom the singer burns really worth two weeks behind bars? More privileged listeners of the classic album might say no, assuming such allegiance is wasted on a bad person.

There are places in this country, though—poor places, Black and Brown places—where the criminal justice system is often immoral, and the accused, incarcerated, or fleeing are less the perpetrators of wrongs than the victims of structural inequality.

I come from poor, White, rural Kansas, a place that had in common with communities of color a well-earned aversion to the police. While we did not face the mortal peril of White supremacy, to which Chapman alludes as a Black woman imagining time in a Southern jail, the majority of my close family members have been in handcuffs. Their offenses usually amounted to behaviors that helped them survive working poverty. As a poor teenager and twenty-something, I committed some of those crimes myself—petty theft so that I could eat, falsifying a loan application for my mother, driving without insurance or current tags. While I never got caught for anything worse than speeding, growing up I felt a mix of dread, shame, and guilt when I saw flashing red-and-blue lights.

I am now a law-abiding citizen with relative economic privilege, but I remain critical of a legal system that disproportionately punishes people in poverty and people of color. In some cases, I might lie, like the storyteller in "For My Lover," to protect people I love from the prison industrial complex, which profits from the castigation of mental illness and substance use disorder. As for the $20,000 bail Chapman mentions, you can find a hungry bondsman who will post bond for five percent, which is half the usual rate, so that someone you love can cosign and spring you for a grand; if you show up for your court date, the rest is forgiven. Where I come from, these are not scandals. They are the known surcharge for being poor.

When I met my husband, he had recovered from trauma-induced addictions and propensities for aimless bad behavior. He still has an edge, though; a radical environmentalist, he has told me he fantasizes about taking illicit, disruptive action on behalf of the planet. He wouldn't, he assures me—less because those actions would be felonies than because they are ineffective strategies in a society where massive, underregulated corporations easily rebuild and renew their grip on ecosystems.

I fell in love with him because of that audacity crackling within his gentle spirit. Some of his ideas for change—the kind that Chapman talks about on the album's first track, "Talkin' Bout a Revolution"—are so uncomfortably severe and inconvenient as to affront the law. By my estimation, those are the only sort of ideas that will do for dismantling old systems engineered to maintain inequality and ravage the earth.

After five years, our partnership has never required any major sacrifice from either of us. There is, nonetheless, a sense that we have teamed up against destructive forces and that we have each other's back. Within the electricity of that knowing, the love is steady and the sex is hot.

In the long tradition of songs about how others just don't understand someone's commitment, "For My Lover" stands out by conveying a feeling not of foolish desperation but of courageous passion. Unlike male singers of outlaw country from the same period, the woman of "For My Lover" has abandoned no one for the sake of freedom. Rather, her *loyalty* has made her a rogue who stays. While so many cowboys of song float on a breeze of self-absorption, she revels in the most daring pleasure of all: true devotion.

THE BUTCHERING SHED

The New York Times, 2022

Cold days are better for killing animals. Warmer months demand time in the wheat fields. Plus, heat and sun quickly turn meat rancid.

On my family's farm in rural Kansas, we did our butchering in the fall and winter, when the work drew no flies.

On gray afternoons, I would get home from school—after an hour-long bus ride on muddy roads—to see a large, pink carcass hanging near the cement-block farmhouse where I lived with my grandparents.

Grandpa would have already shot a bullet through the cow's brain, drained her blood, cut off her feet with a handsaw, and begun to peel away her skin. Then, having hooked two of her legs with a steel spreader connected to the long arm of our tractor, he would have used hydraulic controls to lift the heavy creature—who, not two hours prior, grazed in the pasture and huddled against the north wind with her family—and sliced her underbelly from anus to neck.

We would spend the evening in the butchering shed—a small barn next to the house with a garage door, a bloodstained concrete floor, and a rosebush growing up its south wall. Grandpa did the carving. Grandma stood at the grinder making hamburger. My job was to weigh the meat on a metal scale, wrap it in white butcher paper, and label it with a marker. More often than not, friends and family pitched in and left with steaks for their deep freezers. Grandpa saved the heart and liver, which he pickled in a jar in our icebox.

This was an average day for me, growing up. During those formative years, witnessing death did not desensitize me to the plight of our fellow animals. Rather, life on the farm in general strengthened my reverence for the more-than-human world, which so plainly dictated our lives. While we opened and closed the gates that trapped farm animals, we were often at their mercy.

On winter mornings when we would have preferred a warm bed, we crouched in the snow and pulled a breech calf into the world before sunrise. We were aware each day, when we entered the pasture to check the water in the stock tank, that even the smallest of the Charolais cattle could beat us in a fight. We had friends who had been trampled or gored by bulls, and Grandpa told the story of an area farmer who, years before, slipped on a patch of ice while inside one of his pens, hit his head, and was eaten by hogs.

On Sundays at the little Catholic church down the dirt road from our house, we stared up at Jesus's bleeding, hanging body and listened to the sermons about man's dominion over the earth. But in our bones we knew it was the other way around.

Our humility was not just the result of doing hard, undervalued work. It was also the result of being undervalued people.

Even as a child, I understood that families like mine, poor rural farmers, were low in the pecking order. Television shows and movies portrayed us as buffoons and hicks, always the butt of the joke. Our presumed incivility, and even monstrousness, was suggested in conversations, often to laughter, by humming the banjo tune from the 1972 film *Deliverance*, present in many VHS collections during my 1980s childhood. "Squeal like a pig," some jokers continued—a reference to that film's infamous rape scene.

We didn't need those cues to know that society held us in low esteem, though. All we had to do was look at our bank accounts.

We worked the land and killed animals so that others would eat, so that we would afford propane for the winter, and so that the rich, rigged industry to which we supplied grain would become a little richer.

The profound modesty instilled in me by my upbringing left no room in my worldview for exceptionalism of any sort. It also left me troubled by the ways that most humans calculate the value of things—animals, plants, land, water, resources, even other people—according to hierarchies that suit their own interests.

More than once, while wrapping meat, I sliced my finger on the sharp edge of the butcher paper. There was nothing special about my blood. It was red just like the pigs' and the cows'. It was clear to me that there was nothing special about me or my family, either, doing that most essential work of feeding others. Nothing special but also nothing lesser.

From there, near the bottom of the proverbial social ladder—where women drove tractors and people of all races lived in single-wide trailers—I began to see through the many false narratives of supremacy that govern our world. That men are better than women. That White people are better than everyone else. That the rich are better than the poor. Even, yes, that human beings are better than animals.

The experiences of my early life left me forever in mind of the animals that society consumes and the workers who spend their lives among them. It also left me rageful toward industries that devalue both. In some ways, my professional mission to champion the exploited and expose the powerful—as a journalist, an author, and an advocate for social justice—can be traced back to lessons I learned on the farm.

Unfortunately, farms and ranches like ours—and the ancient, intimate tradition of husbandry into which I was born—have been disappearing for decades, forced out of business by policies that favor large industrial operations.

Today an estimated 99 percent of the meat in the United States comes from factory farms, barbaric places that leverage the selfish, amoral paradigm of human supremacy for immense capitalist gain. Industrialized agriculture has made meat, eggs, milk, leather, cheese, wool, and other animal goods readily, cheaply available to the modern consumer but at a terrible cost—both to the animals, who endure savage cruelty, and to the low-wage laborers, many of whom are immigrants of color, who suffer injuries to body and spirit.

This likely isn't news to you. The details of this dark business, while partly obscured by ag-gag laws, are widely documented, yet they remain underdiscussed. The torturous treatment of animals at the hands of multibillion-dollar monopolies is among the greatest horrors being committed on this planet.

In comparison, our small farm was as humane as any enterprise raising animals for slaughter might be. And while we lived in poverty, according to many definitions, it was a fortune and privilege to grow up with a big garden, with cows and pigs and chickens. Subsistence through modest land ownership historically has been refused to people of color, stolen from Indigenous peoples, and made economically unfeasible for poor folks of all stripes, who set off for cities in order to survive.

Whereas most Americans today have no direct contact with the animals they eat, I carried their manure on my boots. Thus, long before I learned about the industry that delivers chicken tenders and bacon strips to the masses, I had an aversion to factory-farmed products. The beef was too gray. The chicken smelled wrong. The egg yolks were too pale.

Ironically, our culture associates eco-consciousness with higher socioeconomic status, as though greater wealth denotes greater character. But in my experience, environmental impacts are most keenly felt and understood by the poor and unheard.

In fact, as I have climbed out of poverty and into a class of highly educated, financially comfortable liberals, I have found that for all their supposed interest in justice and claims of being on the right side of history, most of my peers give little thought to animal suffering in their eating decisions.

Of course, wealth and class play a role in what food and products you can afford. Socioeconomic barriers to values-based eating choices undeniably exist, particularly in urban areas cut off from healthy food options. But one doesn't have to afford expensive grass-finished beef or frozen patties engineered from pea protein to make effective food decisions, and White male chief executives didn't invent plant-based living. Bougie restaurants serving charcuterie boards sure as hell didn't invent local venison salami, which we made from the deer we hunted.

To be certain, many middle-class and affluent consumers

far removed from agricultural work have learned about the problems of factory farming, including its contribution to climate change, and altered their habits. I applaud their important efforts. For some people, though, working near the bottom of the class ladder provides not just knowledge but a knowing, and that knowing deserves respect.

As a young adult who had left the farm, I lived in poverty and faced food insecurity. These conditions limited my choices, but they did not negate my affection for the earth. I grew up driving a farm truck with wheat kernels on the floor of the cab and an "Eat beef" license plate on the front bumper. I knew people maimed by farm machinery and disabled by agricultural chemicals. Regarding the conditions of farm animals and farmworkers, I had no option but to understand.

For me, there is no taste of meat without bodily memory—the heat of a newborn calf in my cold arms, the smell of the mother's cascading excrement, the danger of her heavy hooves. I could see the cows on our farm from my upstairs bedroom window and the pigs and chickens from our front door.

My early proximity to animals did not cause my empathy for them, I suspect, so much as it starkly revealed it. To be sure, similar experiences did not make animal rights activists out of most of the people in my farming community. But in general, I observed more environmentally conscious behaviors among the rural working poor than in other socioeconomic spaces I've inhabited.

Maybe it was because minimizing waste and reusing and repairing old things were economic necessities. Or perhaps it was because carbon-spewing air travel was an unaffordable luxury. Or maybe it was because they had no choice but to look into a cow's eyes before they killed her.

I do not wish to valorize the working class or demonize those who are better off. Both groups vote in droves for politicians who cater to massive agricultural corporations, the fossil fuel lobby, and other powerful entities that destroy our planet.

But guilt for crimes committed against other species and against the earth is not equally shared. Wealthy corporations and the governments beholden to them, choosing profit over sustainability and moral decency, created and fortified the food systems with which the average individual has little choice but to engage.

Navigating those systems today, while living again in rural Kansas after years in cities, I now eat eggs from my neighbor's hens and, about once a month, chicken, beef, or bison raised and slaughtered down the road. At other times, living without access to such food or means to afford it, I went without eating animal products for years at a time. I haven't consumed dairy in more than a decade, but for those who do, the particular devastation of family dairies makes local milk and cheese much harder to come by.

Still, I am part of the problem. I ate fast-food hamburgers well into my twenties, and my home almost certainly contains products that were tested on animals despite my commitment to avoid them. My cat eats canned meat from factory-farm by-products, and I'm wearing mass-produced leather sneakers as I type this.

I am sympathetic to the argument that any consumption of animal products is unethical and unnecessary. Realistically, however, the urgent problem for our time is not whether they will be consumed but how.

While it is important that consumers from all socioeconomic backgrounds care about the earth and its creatures, ultimately only policy has the power to restrain the agriculture industry's worst abuses. I am heartened by long-term legal efforts to extend personhood to other animal species and, more immediately, by the New Jersey senator and famous vegan Cory Booker's proposed legislation to make slaughterhouse practices more humane. In a more perfect world, future farm bills would somehow rebuild the nearly 4 million small farms lost to urbanization and industrialization since the 1930s, allowing future generations the closeness to animals that engenders awareness.

My family, squeezed out like so many others, had to sell our fifth-generation farm more than twenty years ago. I was a first-generation college student by then, working toward a more comfortable life.

No education, however, would surpass the one I received in the butchering shed, where I held a bleeding muscle with my bare hands and placed it on the scale. Today, when I look at that scale—now an antique on display in my kitchen—I give thanks for those who worked and those who died so that I may eat.

UNWANTED GIFTS

2024

On a handful of Christmases and birthdays, my mother gave me a fancy doll with a porcelain head, sausage curls, and a soft body dressed in nineteenth-century garb. These mass-produced dolls were not exactly high-class but cost as much as two or three cartons of Marlboro Lights, no small sacrifice in our parts. Mom presented the frilly effigies as items that I should cherish.

While I never wanted such things and quietly disliked them, I suspect that my mother admired the dolls' rosy cheeks and ruffly Victorian dresses in authentic ways. She genuinely relished and excelled at the tasks associated with traditional domestic femininity—baking, decorating, applying mascara, wearing high heels, being an object of desire. It is not unlikely that she herself once wished for such a porcelain little girl in a household even poorer than ours.

Meanwhile, she openly hated the presence of the living, breathing little girl whose childhood had interrupted hers. While shaming and wild verbal rage were routine, and while spanking and an occasional slap in the face are hardly worth mentioning about a 1980s household, worst was the absence of hugs, kind looks, or loving moments that I imagine soften the sting of other parents' failings. The dolls she gave me were a lot like her, pretty but not inviting touch; I remember her holding me just once during my entire upbringing, after I received the female rite of ear piercing at the mall when I was five.

Occasionally at night, after being tucked into bed by my father—whose own self-absorption engendered negligence but few outbursts and whose affection, while typically blurred by whiskey or stress, I sometimes could feel—I slipped back out of my bedroom, stood anxiously in the hallway until I found my courage, and entered the edge of the living room, where my mother sat, to plainly ask whether she loved me. Embedded in the question was not a manipulation but an honest accusation. I knew that she was supposed to. She would become uncomfortable and say, "Of course I love you," with an eye roll. I would return to my bed in the same emotional agony that propelled me from it, mitigated some by having expressed myself in the situation.

While survivors often recall perceiving abuse and neglect as normal, I took note of the contrast between my domestic situation and that of other children. Once, Dad and I pulled up to a trailer home, and my friend emerged to climb into our work truck. While we were pals in kindergarten class, she drove me nuts staying at our house. After she and I shared a bubble bath in my mother's large tub, she cried as I dried myself off and tied a towel around my body. She didn't know how, she said. Similar situations were common. When adults weren't around, other children were always crying and saying they didn't know how to do what I was doing—prepare food, find their way home, get the mail.

My absence of parental care was revealed again and again until, instead of presuming myself unlovable, I assessed myself to be unloved. While more accurate, I cannot say the latter feels any better. I did not, of course, have the maturity or knowledge to understand that some adults are incapable of feeling or expressing love, such that the rejection still felt entirely personal; I was good and lovable, I felt, but the person who mattered most couldn't see it. A sunny child by nature, I found outlets in school and books, nature and animals. Nonetheless, alone at night in my severe circumstances, I sometimes longed to die.

My most pitiful memory, around age seven, is of taking a steak knife from the kitchen and sitting on my bed with the knife pointed at my chest. I don't think I considered killing myself; the true aim was that my mother would walk in, see, and suddenly awaken to my goodness. I held the knife so long that my small arms ached. It was bedtime, but no one entered, not even my dad. I returned the knife to the drawer and tucked myself in under the gaze of the Victorian dolls.

When my mother did welcome my presence, usually it was for my exploitation: to massage her feet, help clean the house, confirm that she looked beautiful in a photograph. While she might have received a mental health diagnosis, were we of a class and culture with ready access to health care, more important in my view is that her aversion to intimacy surely related to her own profound childhood trauma. More important still, looking back: she was just seventeen when I materialized in her womb. Indeed, her cruelty toward me dissipated with age as a dangerous fog burns off by midday.

Environmental effects go only so far in explaining personality, though. I myself never developed into an abusive or narcissistic person. Nor did my mother's mother, who had the saddest origin story among us. I occasionally heard that my mother's nature showed traces of her biological father, whose violence my grandmother fled to save her life years before I was born. In the end, who knows why cycles of human behavior begin, continue, and end.

The cycle I was born into involved such emotional desperation that I appreciated a collection of Victorian dolls merely because my mother had given them to me, which implied attention—never mind that giving them to a girl who plainly coveted her brother's toys further confirmed that she perceived or validated little about my real self.

That self was beaming through all the while, plain to see now in orange-tinged photographs: On Christmas morning gazing at my little brother's gray trench coat and matching Sherlock Holmes hat with envy. Outside developing a very accurate arm with a baseball, a football. Looking stricken after my brother received another Teenage Mutant Ninja Turtles action figure for his birthday. Dapper in a button-up shirt tucked into navy slacks and a maroon clip-on tie for—hilariously—my first day of Catholic Sunday school. I was a cisgender, heterosexual girl who sought adventure and comfort. These virtues tended to manifest in the boys' section. Perhaps, for all my mother's femininity, I'd also internalized a negative association with being female; both of my parents plainly favored my brother, though I wasn't conscious of it at the time.

While my dad performed some domestic duties that relatively few men did at the time—combing my hair before school, changing my brother's diapers—he was absent in ways that, true to his generation, placed most of the onus on my mother to do the nurturing for which she was so badly equipped. Had *either* parent looked, they would have seen me spending hours sketching on yellow legal pads, their blue lines blurred and puckered where an adult's wet glass of instant iced tea had been set for lack of a coaster, with whatever sorry ballpoint pen or crusty pencil I could find in the junk drawer. I bestowed my objectively impressive drawings upon any adult present, leaving no question about my talent. Surely the welcome gift of art supplies would have been permissible along gender lines.

Yet the doll-giving persisted, indicating not just sexism but one of its many enablers: lazy disregard.

I am not speaking here of the inattention common to parents of previous generations; being left untended suited my independent personality where today's hyper-managed and uber-tracked childhood would have oppressed. Rather, I am talking about being simultaneously unloved and unseen, and the way in which these experiences often intertwine.

Real love requires true attention—seeing another being for what they are, rather than casting upon them projections of our own pain. This love holds the power to remove not just the selfish veils that harm domestic relationships but the ancient, disastrous veils of the world: stereotypes, hateful prejudice, ugly cartoons.

Being female, a child in rural poverty, and the daughter of at least one narcissist, the frustration of being unseen, and by extension misunderstood, haunted me from a young age. What my treatment at home and in society suggested I was—a burden, redneck spawn, even an apt recipient of dolls in lacy dresses— felt to me so plainly incorrect as to cause anguish, for my child self intuitively knew that to love truly is to look closely.

—

Had the early life been less grim, perhaps the dolls I received would have seemed benign. Instead, they came to represent the fracture between my inner reality and an external realm tireless in its refusal to reflect my authentic self back to me. Even my cool grandmother Betty, capable of vast empathy and herself never one for prissy things, got in on the action. One Christmas, she gave me a Victorian doll from Kmart. When I was visibly disappointed despite my best efforts, she declared me spoiled.

That was the fifth and last Victorian doll I received, but the overall imposition of girly affects didn't falter—ruffled dresses in my closet, ruffled pillows in my proverbial pink bedroom. For many birthdays to come, I continued to receive another sort of doll: the Enesco Growing Up Girls.

The Growing Up Girls porcelain figurine set ranged from a newborn in a basket, less than a couple inches high, to a sixteen-year-old perhaps half a foot tall. Each wore a pastel dress and bore the number of the age being celebrated—a gold "1" or "3" adorned a skirt the little girl wore, a "6" marked the cover of a book the little girl held, a "12" rested on a ribboned hat. I handled these hard, fragile shapes carefully, knowing I'd catch hell should one of them break.

The blond figurines, while no more my style than the Victorian dolls, appealed for having a clear function—tracking time and growth—and for the commitment my otherwise unreliable mother maintained in their annual purchase.

I took this small collection of figurines with me when, just after I turned eleven in the summer of 1991, I moved out of my mother's home and into my grandmother's. While Grandma never could bring herself to speak the reason, loving her grown daughter as she did, she surely took me in because I told her about my conditions at home. She acted like she didn't believe me when I said Mom had called me a bitch, but then she went quiet; soon I was packing my things. There was no objection, to my knowledge, from my mother.

The Kmart doll incident notwithstanding, Grandma Betty was unfussy and sympathetic in ways a girl of eleven will notice. Where my mother found confidence in pantyhose, Grandma hated nothing more than senseless discomfort. When my mom gave me one unnecessary "training bra" made completely of itchy lace, Grandma shook her head. Despite Mom's objections, my whole life Grandma had been cutting the tags out of my clothes because they irritated my sensitive skin.

After moving out of her house, I often spent weekends and summers with my mom, who seemed relieved by the lightened responsibility but continued to claim me as a dependent for tax purposes, a point my generous grandmother never raised.

The arrangement lifted a weight from my shoulders too. Largely freed from my mother's dysfunction even as a biological longing for her persisted, I rode my skateboard with glee across the rough Wichita neighborhood where Grandma owned a little house. I climbed the tree next to the driveway, pretending it was my ship, I a captain charting the seas. At a yard sale, when my strange child heart ached at the sight of a yellow manual typewriter from the 1960s, Grandma pulled out her change purse; she later swiped some letterhead from the county courthouse where she worked, and my self-proclaimed career as a writer began.

In early 1992, when I was in sixth grade, Grandma sold the little house. We moved to her and my grandfather's farm, where life only got sweeter. Cats birthed kittens in barns. Vegetables emerged from the garden, and butter went onto the griddle. I qualified for the regional math contest and won medals in track. Grandma and Grandpa threw legendary beer parties. I popped wheelies with our all-terrain vehicle in cow pastures.

In seventh grade, I changed schools and enjoyed a new popularity, a different slumber party every weekend. I collected baseball cards and enraged a male teacher by knowing the answer to an obscure sports trivia question that stumped every boy in class. Besides my long hair, I was androgynous in a forest-green plaid flannel vest over my denim shirt, and Grandma couldn't have cared less.

My halcyon days in the early nineties—the "tween" years, no longer a little girl but not yet a teenager—left such a happy mark on me that through adulthood I would sometimes play a song or wear a fashion from that time to evoke the lightness I felt then. When the year turned to 2011, on New Year's Eve I even had a very specific "early nineties" costume party, to commemorate the twentieth anniversary of my favorite moment. To be eleven again or even twelve!

Social scientists and storytellers have declared this preteen era of childhood the most awkward and unpleasant phase of development. That truism never resonated for me. I didn't start my period until I was just shy of thirteen; this fact, along with the improvement in my home life, meant that I enjoyed the liberations of late childhood without the confusing encroachment of womanhood and its objectifications. As the dolls once signified the pain of being unseen, age eleven came to signify for me the joy of seeing myself.

During my teenage years, as savage irony would have it, the mother incapable of loving me in childhood turned out to be my only family member who could relate to the woman I was becoming. Unlike the rest of my clan, she was a reader, an artist, a woman of words. More fundamentally, we each possessed an organic paganism that my practical, no-nonsense grandmother did not. Mom perceived the world as a matrix of "vibes" and dressed like Stevie Nicks. I communicated directly with the natural world and found emotional satisfaction in funerals, rare events where adults cut the crap and showed their feelings. When I stayed at her house, in the evening we pored over the same astrology books, and in the morning we split the newspaper.

There were, too, as I came of age, remarkable physical similarities between my mother and me. She had brown hair and eyes, and mine are blond and green; she was an inch taller. That's about where the outward differences between us ended. Our looking shockingly alike, combined with our relatively small difference in age, meant that by the time I was a teenager we endured male attention at the same time and in the same way.

Once when I was in high school, as I sat in the passenger seat of her car at a stoplight, I sensed motion to my right. In the lane next to us, a middle-aged man had hoisted his pelvis toward his car's window and was yanking on his penis. It was not clear which one of us he meant to share this with. I turned forward and didn't tell my mom, figuring I'd spare us both the embarrassment.

Another time, she told me that a group of teenage boys had driven up in the lane next to her on a thoroughfare and raised a sign that read, "Show us your titties." Enraged, she had followed them down the next exit ramp, which we both knew probably only thrilled them.

While her self-centered impulses persisted, often to damaging effect for me, as I entered adulthood I found our points of connection worth preserving. Amid her new drinking problem and my new life at college and beyond, I learned to protect myself from her worst tendencies. Over the years—and not without torment and grief—I accepted that, contrary to cultural insistence otherwise, not every mother's love is a precious and unsurpassed thing.

We were more like sisters, maybe, anyway. There was no one with whom I'd rather discuss dark novels, the occult, period fashion, artists of the early twentieth century.

As my experiences with womanhood mounted, our shared knowing about sexism deepened. If at work my intelligence went underestimated or my presence in a meeting full of men was deemed an erotic danger, she required no explanation and extended total solidarity. Once, when I was in my early thirties and she was approaching fifty, I fretted over whether wearing a pair of red heels to work meant I was part of the problem.

"Wear the heels and take whatever it gets you," she said. "They'll call you a slut either way."

I realized cautiously that we were becoming friends.

Soon after her fiftieth birthday, Mom called to tell me she had been diagnosed with a rare, aggressive breast cancer.

Concurrent with my mother's mortal crisis was a series of disintegrations in my own life. I had just ended a fifteen-year relationship (and two-year marriage) with my high school sweetheart. A few months after Mom's diagnosis, I resigned from a recently tenured professorship; soon, the lack of income necessitated selling my house and most of my belongings. I found myself stripped of nearly every identity and security I had built at the precise, destabilizing moment of a parent's terminal illness.

While that life-altering moment hurt, it also cleansed. I experienced no less than what some cultures refer to as a shamanic death. A longtime people pleaser reborn to my inner guide, in that moment I was untamed and honest in ways the civilized world frowns upon.

Before heading west to my mother's place in Denver, to help her husband and my grandmother—still vibrant in her sixties—with caregiving, I held an epic garage sale in Kansas.

The items up for purchase related to not just the "For Sale" sign in the yard but my clear state of mind. Coming from a family with tendencies toward clutter, a comfort for many of those scarred by scarcity, I found freedom in shedding material things big and small. I even got rid of most of my books, trusting the titles would find their way back to me if I needed to hold them again. I kept what was necessary for living. I kept a few things that were particularly meaningful or sentimental. I kept nothing, however, out of obligation, not even to the mother whose love I could now feel.

I will not claim it was easy when I pulled the Growing Up Girls and the Victorian dolls out of storage boxes and marked them with price tags. I will not claim I didn't feel guilt as a blade in my heart, considering the dolls' significance to my cancer-ridden, much-improved-with-age mother. But I was ready to let go of whatever held me down, including the defining discomfort of my childhood that the dolls symbolized.

On her better days during the illness, in her home filled with books about sun signs, moon signs, and reincarnation, my mother loved for me to read her tarot. She was inclined to look for predictions, but I told her that the cards themselves held no power. Rather, they were tools for discerning the truth she herself knew, right then, in the flow of energy currents leading to probable outcomes that she might have the ability to alter. In fact, as she was the seeker of the reading, her presence determined its content—both literally, because I invited her to pull the cards from the deck I spread before her, and in ways that after many years with my deck I can only describe as inexplicable.

"The deck doesn't predict the future," I told her. "The cards are just mass-produced slips of cardboard. We are making space for you and your intuition to have an intentional dialogue."

I explained the meaning of each card and its position and guided her in relating these to her instincts. Sometimes a card's significance would be immediately clear. Even if a card struck her as confusing or wrong, though, her resistance to its meaning was itself instructive. Where she readily connected some current situation to the card's symbolism, she could find her truth mirrored back to her. Where she didn't, she could find her truth in contrast.

Mom seemed slightly disappointed by my self-taught, light-handed approach, which dictated few explicit answers and perhaps thus felt less mystical. She was thrilled to learn, then, when I shuffled the deck and a single card shot out before I asked her to touch the deck, that in the art of tarot such cards are called "jumpers." The jumper was itself part of the reading, all the more significant for whatever force had asserted it—her own astral vibration? The holy spirit? Hell if I knew, but I'd witnessed enough to acknowledge that jumpers were frequently uncanny in their relevance to the seeker.

So it was that, while my bodily memory sometimes buzzed with anxiety in her presence regardless of my spirit's forgiveness, through her three-year illness we enjoyed each other's company—watching home-improvement shows, digging through vintage leather bags at thrift shops, even carousing at the bars together between her treatments.

Once, after last call, we went through a late-night drive-through about ten minutes before closing. We were sensitive to our timing; we had both worked plenty of jobs tending customers until closing time, the approach of which becomes a time of prayer that no one will walk through the door.

When I rolled down my window to place our order, Mom leaned over from the passenger seat.

"We'll take one thousand burritos," she demanded. "And make it snappy."

She then did an impression of the beleaguered teenager in a visor and headset whom we both were picturing. We laughed so hard we shook.

During that period, I spread for my mother the tarot more times than I can recall, cherishing our unique connection in the process. She had no degrees and, prior to her diagnosis, made a living in various sorts of sales, trading heavily on her clever charm; I had several degrees and got paid for my earnest ideas. But there was no doubt we were cut from the same witch's cloak.

After one tarot reading, Mom told me she intended to leave her common-law husband. I gave her a necklace adorned with an image of the Hindu goddess Kali. A Punjabi-American friend had given it to me in recent times, when I was divorcing and ending many things, and declared that Kali's honorable wrath—ruthless, necessary, unapologetic destruction and clearing—was with me.

Now, I told my mother as I handed her the necklace, it's with you.

Mom did move out of the Denver place she shared with her husband, for a time. Eventually, she moved back and stayed in the relationship. I don't know her reasons. I do know that she was fighting for her life, and that such a moment leaves little energy for other conflicts.

———

Throughout her illness, Mom understandably took whatever modern medicine offered. There were radiations and chemotherapy and surgeries, of course, all of which involved side effects and stressful bills. There were well-intentioned doctors and kind nurses. In many ways, though, her body became a source of profit whose nearing death was strategically ignored by the medical industrial complex. Sometimes this meant damaging overtreatment; sometimes, being denied treatment altogether.

Once, Aetna rejected a claim the hospital submitted for a new chemotherapy medication. Her scheduled treatment was thus delayed while we fought insurance to pay for it.

My mother was, as I understood it from her oncologist, the first known patient in the world to be diagnosed with both triple-negative breast cancer, the cells of which are fueled differently than most cancers and are harder to target with available treatment methods, and the then newly discovered PALB2 genetic mutation, which increases breast cancer risk. Leveraging this potentially newsworthy aspect of her treatment, I wrote an email not to the claims department but to Aetna's head of national media relations seeking their perspective on refusal of her time-sensitive care.

The claim was approved three days later.

Despite this small success, bigger problems lay ahead; later that year, the cancer moved to her brain. Before the emergency surgery, I pressed the neurosurgeon to explain the potential side effects.

"Will it affect her words?" I asked him.

He said that it shouldn't, that's a different area of the brain. He suggested that she might die soon without the surgery, which at least created some chance. Of what, I was never sure.

Hours later, when the neurosurgeon finally approached Grandma and me in the waiting room, we stood up. My mom's husband must have been in the recovery room with her, though I don't remember for certain.

"Her brain was just full of cancer," the surgeon said. "Like noodles spilling all over her brain."

I looked at Grandma to make sure she wasn't falling down. The unusual order of death, in generational terms, meant not just supporting my mother as she died but supporting my grandmother—my second mother, really—as she experienced the most dreaded of losses.

After Mom recovered from the surgery, she struggled with brain fog and accomplishing certain tasks. She seemed changed—calmer and more relaxed, which cannot be considered tragic. But she was also the same enough, for a time, her words sufficient.

The broader treatment process—do not, my mother once warned in a Facebook post, call cancer a fucking journey—contained some moments of beauty. Once, a hospital technician pushed in an ultrasound machine; a moment later, I saw my mother's heart on a screen. There it was, contracting, expanding, going on heroically. Mom was not moved, but I watched the screen with tears in my eyes—something like the inverse of a pregnant woman watching her baby's heartbeat in a sonogram.

One might imagine the unsuccessful brain surgery was a turning point toward discussions about mortality. However, the doctors went on with their experiments and proposed treatments. Within months, her pelvis and upper leg bones were riddled with cancer, her skeleton degenerating beneath her flesh. To my amazement, her doctor recommended putting a rod in her femur. *Death?* the doctor seemed to say as she looked past its obvious presence on my mother's face. *What death?*

Before the femur surgery, a hospital orderly showed up to take Mom to an MRI. I followed as he pushed her wheelchair through the hospital's corridors, down to what I recall as a basement imaging area. I waited outside.

Afterward, Mom appeared out of sorts, wide-eyed and disturbed. As I sometimes did, I pushed her wheelchair back to her room myself.

"He watched me," she said quietly.

"What?" I asked.

"That guy who took me down there," she said. "He watched me undress and put on the hospital gown. He didn't leave the room."

With Mom's blessing, I made calls within the hospital; I filed a complaint and raised hell. The hospital assured me that the orderly had been fired. I learned he had tried to reenter the building without his security clearance, which had been removed.

Soon, Mom's husband called my cell phone and yelled at me to stay out of it. I was causing problems that might threaten her treatment, he said, and if her quality of care decreased it would be my fault.

It was unclear whether he believed my mother's story, which she seemed to have told solely to me, but whether the event had transpired might have been irrelevant to him. It was reasonable, I admit, to worry that medical attention to prolong survival might be deprioritized if a patient with grievances were deemed a legal liability. It was reasonable, too, for the spouse who would receive the medical bills to resent the meddling of an adult child.

Nonetheless, I refused to ignore what others might consider trivial. My mother, whose early traumas I had studied thoroughly in order to heal myself, had been devalued throughout her life for inhabiting a female body, at times a female body in economic poverty. It seemed that, for different reasons and in different ways, her treatment in death would be no better.

Soon, they wheeled her off again. This time they pushed a metal shaft into her thigh and sewed her back up.

I spent that week in her hospital room while she winced in pain despite all manner of drugs. Perhaps the femur surgery was worth that misery in ways I do not understand. Two certain beneficiaries, however, were the hospital and the health insurance company.

A violent operation on a dying body is a refusal to see the truth, in order that profitable power structures be maintained. It is in this way the opposite of love. We have created entire systems of deliberate unseeing, to excruciating effect.

One afternoon in early autumn, grief swelled in my chest. My mother had died less than a week prior in Colorado, and Grandma and I were back in Kansas. That last nine-hour trip east along I-70, I had driven the truck with Grandma in the passenger seat and Mom's ashes in the extended cab. All that remained in Denver was a houseful of my mother's belongings to be dealt with later. As when I was eleven, I had moved in with my grandmother.

The grief seemed unbearable. But I was in my mid-thirties and had learned about middle-class pursuits called self-care and emotional regulation. Instead of ignoring or numbing a difficult feeling, as generations of my family had done, I decided to go for a walk.

When the wind came out of the northwest, awful smells from the nearby pet-food plant settled over the working-class neighborhood where Grandma now lived; Grandpa was long dead, the farm long sold. Despite the factory odor, I appreciated her house's location near the city limits, where I could cross the street to a quiet country lane that tapered into overgrown ditches.

That late-September day, I stepped into the sunlight and headed north. I took a deep breath. I noted the spot where I had stopped to watch a baby snapping turtle the previous spring. Another step. Another breath.

Her death was a relief, I admitted to myself—for her because she suffered, and for her husband, Grandma, and me because caregiving can be a devastating exhaustion.

How unlikely that we became great friends in her later years, I thought. Above me, oak leaves brushed each other in the breeze. Another breath, another step.

Guilt turned my stomach as I recalled a moment in the kitchen several months prior. I had become frustrated with her and Grandma and, in a rare moment of assertion among them, raised my voice.

"We don't communicate!" I yelled.

Instead of twisting her face into a look of disgust, as she would have done in her younger days, she replied humbly.

"Teach us how," she said, her wide eyes begging.

Nothing has ever ripped my heart out more completely than this proof of the decent core within the monster of my childhood.

Step, step, step. I heard the pebbles grind into the road beneath my sneakers as my mind returned to just a few nights prior, when I sat next to the medical bed that Hospice had set up in her dining room. She couldn't make it up the stairs in those final days. The Hospice nurse had left, thinking Mom still had a week. Mom's body thought otherwise. There were drugs in her system, but she was coherent. Something led me to hold her bony hand for hours through the night, into the early morning, while her weary husband and mother slept nearby.

Step, step, step. Breath, breath, breath. I was nearing the end of my walk and could see Grandma's house.

Death, I thought, is the most transcendent—

A young man's voice behind me interrupted my reverie.

"LOOK AT THE ASS ON THAT THING!!!"

A car rolled past, turned onto our street, and pulled into the driveway directly across from ours. I realized that the young man hanging out the car window was our neighbor's twenty-something son. I had never met him, but he sometimes leered while I pushed Grandma's lawn mower.

My feet stopped. My breath slowed, and my eyes stopped blinking. I stood in the sun, my cheeks wet from the tears of my cathartic walk. Within me rose a composed rage, prismatic as a rainbow over a grave. As I watched the laughing young men get out of the car, the primal force inside me wished only to destroy them.

I knew, though, that their limited vision for seeing me as a woman related to someone else's limited vision for seeing them as men, probably when they were little boys, possibly wishing for dolls.

On a winter night, in my early forties and contemplating the approaching end of my reproductive years, I realized that I was aging into a freedom that I had not experienced since before puberty. My perceived worth and threat as a sexual object would wane; likely it already had, but I cared so little that I hadn't noticed. I was fortunate, by then, to be valued for my voice, to make a good living with my creativity.

Beyond my gender, as a White woman no other means of erasure remained; society's disregard for its elders would find me, if I lived to old age, but for the moment I had outlasted

familiar means of objectification, diminishment, or discrimination. I was no longer poor, I was able-bodied, and every
intimate who ever refused to acknowledge my value was dead
or divorced from my life.

This new reality evoked memories of age eleven, when I
moved out of an abusive home and came into myself. Now,
though, I was an adult with real agency and means—even better
than those righteous tween years after dolls and before breasts.
Eleven—but better! I thought. Perhaps I'd get out my vests and
Bonnie Raitt tape and party like it was 1991.

That same cold night at midlife, I sat in my home office
sorting through my mother's considerable family photo collection, which I'd finally found time to process more than seven
years since her death. For months, I had been throwing away
bad photos and organizing the ones worth keeping. I discarded
mercilessly, as I once had discarded dolls. In the room with me
were the singed metal rod from Mom's femur surgery, given
alongside her ashes by the crematorium, and the Kali necklace,
which had returned to my stead when I sorted her jewelry box.

As I filed a photo behind an index card labeled with the
appropriate year, from the tub of old pictures yet to be sorted
another photo somehow fell on its own accord—leaped, really,
it seemed. I looked up, startled.

As I picked up this jumper of a photo, my skin raised into
goose bumps. I'd never seen it before, that I could recall.

It was a picture of me, tan and sun-bleached on my eleventh
birthday, cupping in my hands a Growing Up Girl. The small,
porcelain figurine wore a pale blue dress and held a cake topped
with the gold numeral "11." My facial expression conveyed that
I was amused but not elated by the annual gift. *This isn't my
thing,* my eyes said. *This is not me.*

Looking at the photo, my eyes welling, I had to laugh. What

was the doll or any other insult but a tarot card of sorts, a symbol to be embraced or rejected, clarifying the self in either case? What was a mother but the same sort of mirror?

While we long to be understood and loved, and as we seek a just world in which all beings might be so appreciated, our first task is to see ourselves—a process, inevitably, of casting off the false descriptions that a deranged world provides. The dolls I once received were tools for revealing what I am: a defender of those whose sacredness goes unseen.

NOTE ON ORIGINAL PUBLICATIONS

Most of these essays, previously published across a spectrum of magazines and newspapers, have been lightly edited for consistent style and general improvement. Footnotes offering important or interesting updates have been added.

Some titles have been changed: "Highway Construction May Unearth Human Remains" originally appeared under the *Huffington Post* headline "Kansas Highway Construction May Unearth Human Remains." "Lede, Nutgraph, and Body" originally appeared under the *Aeon* headline "Beyond the Churn." "The Winter Wheat I Helped Raise" originally appeared, alongside pieces by other writers, under the *Pacific Standard* headline "Postcards from America." "Writing Assignment" originally appeared under the *Guardian* headline "The Working-Class Kid Who Became a Writer." "Liberal Blind Spots Are Hiding the Truth" originally appeared under the *New York Times* headline "Liberal Blind Spots Are Hiding the Truth About 'Trump

Country.'" "At the Precise Geographic Heart of the Dark-Money Beast" originally appeared under the *Guardian* headline "They Thought This Was Trump Country. Hell No." "Blue Wave in Kansas" originally appeared under the *New York Times* headline "A Blue Wave in Kansas? Don't Be So Surprised." "Brain Gain" originally appeared under the *New York Times* headline "Something Special Is Happening in Rural America." "I Am Burning with Fury and Grief" originally appeared under the *New York Times* headline "I Am Burning with Fury and Grief Over Elizabeth Warren. And I Am Not Alone." "Rural Route" originally appeared under the NationalGeographic.com headline "America's Postal Service Is a Rural Lifeline—and It's in Jeopardy." "Extraction" originally appeared under the *Atlantic* headline "The True Costs and Benefits of Fracking." "In Celebration of Rare and Exquisite Accuracy from Hollywood" originally appeared under the *Guardian* headline "From Kansas, With Love." "Shelterbelt" originally appeared under the *New York Times* headline "Why the Defense of Abortion in Kansas Is So Powerful." "The Butchering Shed" originally appeared under the *New York Times* headline "What Growing Up on a Farm Taught Me About Humility."

ACKNOWLEDGMENTS

Thank you to the magazine and newspaper editors who first published these essays, especially Jessica Reed, with whom I have produced many pieces for the *Guardian*, and Chris Beha, the editor in chief when *Harper's* put this rural, working-class-bred woman's face on the cover.

Thank you to others who have shared and boosted my work and my voice: editors of many essays and news stories not included in these pages, social media followers, public radio hosts, television producers, curators of newsletters and recommendation lists, policymakers, and public figures with followings much larger than my own; my speaking agent, Trinity Ray, and others at the Tuesday Agency, whose efforts put me in direct communion with an array of audiences across the country; especially, the teachers and professors who have included my writings on their syllabi—a full-circle honor for someone who owes her good life to a good education.

Thank you, as ever, to my literary agent, Julie Barer; my

editor, Kathryn Belden; and my publisher, Scribner, led by Nan Graham. These brilliant, daring, powerful women have changed the world with the books they've developed and championed, and I'm fortunate to have their endorsement.

Thank you to Amy Martin, whose close reads of the new essay included here, "Unwanted Gifts," were crucial to its development.

Thank you to Andrew Spackman, a construction worker who was so startled when he saw his name in the acknowledgments for my first book that he cried. I am grateful to be surrounded, through my family and community, by the specific wisdom of those accustomed to going undervalued and unmentioned.